Peter M. Hale

In the Coal and Iron Counties of North Carolina

Peter M. Hale

In the Coal and Iron Counties of North Carolina

ISBN/EAN: 9783743327351

Manufactured in Europe, USA, Canada, Australia, Japa

Cover: Foto ©ninafisch / pixelio.de

Manufactured and distributed by brebook publishing software (www.brebook.com)

Peter M. Hale

In the Coal and Iron Counties of North Carolina

IN THE

COAL AND IRON COUNTIES

OF

NORTH CAROLINA.

By P. M. HALE.

A Compilation from the Geological Reports of Drs. Emmons
and Kerr; Colonel Laidley's and Admiral Wilkes'
Reports to the War and Navy Departments;
the Census Reports. Supplemented by
Accurate Sketches of the Fifty-Six
Counties, and illustrated by a
Map of the State.

RALEIGH:
P. M. HALE, PUBLISHER.
NEW YORK: E. J. HALE & SON.
1883.

PUBLISHER'S PREFACE.

Dr. Emmons, whose Reports form the basis of this volume, was Geologist to the great State of New York, and his work in that State and afterwards in this, and his treatises on the Science of Geology, made him an authority in Europe as in America.

Dr. Kerr, who succeeded Dr. Emmons as State Geologist, and whose later observations are embodied in this volume, is now Geologist in charge of the Southern Division of the United States Geological Survey.

Colonel Laidley, whose report to the War Department follows, is one of the most distinguished and useful officers of the United States Army, his ability for duty only surpassed by the thorough conscientiousness with which it is discharged.

Admiral Wilkes, late of the United States Navy, whose valuable paper accompanies Col. Laidley's, was sent here by the United States Government on account of peculiar fitness for the work of scientific and common-sense exploration.

The contributors of the sketches of the several Counties are well known to North Carolinians as men of sense, information and character; and the Census figures which supplement the sketches of the Counties are of course "authority" outside the State. Plainly, there is here abundance of the raw materials, coal and iron; equal

PUBLISHER'S PREFACE

abundance of both water and steam power for their manufacture; a healthy country, and a soil yielding most generous return for the labors of the agriculturist.

The excellent Map of the State will show the facilities for transportation. Thirty railroads enter or traverse more than sixty Counties, and give their people choice of markets within and without the State. Roads now in course of rapid construction will soon give the same advantages to the few outlying Counties.

It has been for many years a chief object of the compiler and publisher of this volume to make the State thoroughly known to its own people. Prejudices will pass away with knowledge, and a united people will work with vigor to raise still higher a State of which they have learned that there is reason to be proud. The little book published in January last—*The Woods and Timbers of North Carolina*—has contributed materially to the end in view, and has also contributed largely to the pecuniary interests of the State. It is hoped that greater good may come from this second volume of a series of industrial books, in that it will place within reach of home people and people abroad the knowledge that North Carolina contains inexhaustible supplies of coal and iron of superior quality. These are the raw materials which, developed, make large towns, large markets, and great and prosperous States. That they exist in North Carolina in sufficient abundance, that there is abundant power for their manufacture, and that the way to market is cheap and certain, the papers here collected make very plain.

Raleigh, August 15, 1883.

CONTENTS.

PART I.—The Coal and Iron.

		Page.
The Coal Fields,	*Emmons*,	11
Deep River Coal,	"	19
Dan River Coal,	"	45
Coal Deposites,	*Kerr*,	52
The Ores of Iron,	*Emmons*,	55
The Ores of Iron,	*Kerr*,	73
Deep River Timber and Minerals.	*Laidley*,	139
Deep River Region,	*Wilkes*,	147

PART II.—Coal and Iron Counties.

Piedmont and the Mountains.	*New Englander*,	185
From the Sea to the Ridge.	*Kerr*,	216

Transmontane Counties.

Mitchell,	*J. D. Cameron*.	236
Yancey,	"	237
Buncombe,	"	239
Madison,	"	243
Henderson,	"	245
Transylvania,	"	247
Haywood,	"	248
Jackson,	"	250
Macon,	"	251
Macon,	*Wm. Beal*,	252
Clay,	"	253
Cherokee,	"	253

Graham, - - -	*Wm. Beal.*	- -	253
Haywood, - - -	"	- -	253
Jackson, - - -	"	- -	253
Swain, - - -	"	- -	253
Alleghany, - - -	*E. L. Vaughan,*	-	258
Ashe, - - -	*J. W. Todd,*	- -	261
Watauga, - - -	*W. W. Lenoir,*	-	262
Mitchell, - - -	*J. H. Greene,*	-	262
Henderson, - - -	*W. W. Jones,*	-	264
Wilkes County, - - -	*Rev. R. W. Barber,*		265
Caldwell, - - -	*M. V. Moore,*	-	270
Burke, - - -	*S. McD. Tate,*	-	278
Cleveland, - - -	*H. F. Schenck,*	-	282
Lincoln, - - -	"	-	284
Gaston, - - -	*W. A. Graham,*	-	286
Catawba, - - -	*R. K. Bryan,*	-	287
Iredell, - - -	*J. P. Caldwell,*	-	289
Alexander, - - -	"	-	291
Yadkin, - - -	"	-	292
Surry, - - -	"	-	293
Stokes, - - -	*E. T. B. Glenn,*	-	294
Forsyth, - - -	*C. B. Watson.*	-	296
Davidson, - - -	*M. H. Pinnix,*	-	298
Davie, - - -	*L. S. Overman,*	-	301
Rowan, - - -	"	-	302
Cabarrus, - - -	*P. B. Means,*	-	304
Mecklenburg, - - -	*Wm. Johnston,*	-	312
" - - -	*Chas. R. Jones,*	-	317
Anson, - - -	*R. T. Bennett.*	-	326
Montgomery, - - -	*C. C. Wade,*	-	329
Randolph, - - -	*Lyndon Swaim,*	-	333
Guilford, - - -	"	-	338
Rockingham, - - -	*J. D. Glenn,*	-	344
Person, - - -	*J. W. Cuningham,*	-	347
Orange, - - -	*K. P. Battle,*	-	349

CONTENTS. vii

Durham,	- -	W. W. Fuller,	- 351
Chatham,	- - -	M. Q. Waddell,	- 353
Moore,	- - -	Mc Iver & Black,	- 355
Richmond,	- - -	W. L. Steele, -	- 357
Cumberland,	- - -	Jona. Evans, -	- 361
Harnett,	- - -	J. P. Hodges, -	- 364
Johnston,	- - -	M. Q. Waddell,	- 371
Wake,	- - -	R. B. Haywood,	- 374
"	- - -	A. W. Shaffer,	- 375
Granville,	- - -	A. H. A. Williams,	376
Vance,	- - -	J. R. Young, -	- 379
Franklin,	- - -	J. J. Davis, -	- 382
Halifax,	- - -	W. R. Bond, -	- 386
Nash,	- - -	A. W. Bridgers,	- 387
Wilson,	- - -	J. E. Woodard,	- 389

The Census Figures.

Alexander County, - - - - - -	393
Alamance, - - - - - - -	393
Alleghany, - - - - - - -	394
Anson, - - - - - - - -	395
Ashe, - - - - - - - -	395
Buncombe, - - - - - - -	396
Burke, - - - - - - - -	396
Cabarrus, - - - - - - -	397
Caldwell, - - - - - - -	398
Catawba, - - - - - - -	398
Chatham, - - - - - - -	399
Cherokee, - - - - - -	399
Clay, - - - - - - - -	400
Cleveland, - - - - - - -	401
Cumberland, - - - - - - -	401
Davidson, - - - - - . -	402
Davie, - - - - - - -	402
Forsyth, - - - - - - -	403

Franklin,	404
Gaston,	404
Graham,	405
Granville,	405
Guilford,	406
Halifax,	406
Harnett,	407
Haywood,	408
Henderson,	408
Iredell,	409
Jackson,	409
Johnston,	410
Lincoln,	411
McDowell,	411
Macon,	412
Madison,	412
Mecklenburg,	413
Mitchell,	414
Montgomery,	414
Moore,	415
Nash,	415
Orange,	416
Person,	417
Randolph,	417
Richmond,	418
Rockingham,	418
Rowan,	419
Stokes,	420
Surry,	420
Swain,	421
Transylvania,	421
Wake,	422
Watauga,	423
Wilkes,	423
Wilson,	424
Yadkin,	424
Yancey,	425
Map of North Carolina.	

PART I.

THE COAL AND IRON

OF

NORTH CAROLINA.

The Coal Fields.

[Emmons's Preliminary Report, 1852.]

The Deep River coal field is in the form of a trough. The inferior rocks extend further than the superior. They may be regarded as beginning in Granville County, in a wedge-form, or pointed mass. The northwest and west outcrop runs, at first, west of south; and passes through a part of Wake, and sends up a short arm to within three miles of Chapel Hill.

The direction of the outcrop has gradually changed to south, 50° west. This direction is very nearly preserved to the South Carolina line. The outcrop is about six miles west of Carthage.

In this coal-field, the uplift has been made upon the northwest side. Its line of demarkation is distinct;—while, upon the southeast side, there is no outcrop. All that is in view, is the superior rocks, still dipping southwest—their lower edges being concealed beneath a thick mass of soil.

The dip is slightly variable—being, on the south side of Deep River, south 60° east. North of the river, it is south 50° east. At the easterly end, at Farmville, south 10° west. At Horneville, south 45° west. These last were taken from the coal-slates, where a change has taken place, which is due to the position of the outer and easterly edge of the trough, as it is turning westwardly; and where the uplifting forces have acted upon the other side, the angle of dip varies from 10°, in the upper strata of the sandstone, to 25° in the inferior beds; and may, probably, exceed 30° at some points of the outer edge, near the rocks upon which they repose.

The lithological characters of the whole system furnish considerable variety. But they may be classed as conglomerates; sandstones, soft and hard, gray, red, and variegated, or mottled; and green and black slates; with certain subordinate beds.

QUALITY OF THE DEEP RIVER COAL.

The two varieties of coal, the bituminous and semi-bituminous, passing into anthracite, are known in this coal-field. The bituminous is scarcely equaled for fineness and excellency in this country, and it has been said by a gentleman, who is well acquainted with Liverpool coal, that it will burn twice as long. A direct comparison has not been made, to my knowledge, but that the assertion has much truth in it, I have no doubt.

The Deep River coal is, in the first place, quite free from smut; it does not soil the fingers, but in a trifling degree. It burns freely, and forms a cake; or it undergoes a semi-fusion, and agglutinates, and forms a partially impervious hollow cake, within which combustion goes on for a long time. When a small pile of it is made upon the ground, it may be ignited by a match and a few dry leaves or sticks. It may be ignited in the blaze of a lamp or candle. The coal is, therefore, highly combustible, easily ignited, and burns with a bright flame like light wood, for a long time. It may be burnt upon wood fire. It may be burnt in the common fire-place, and it is not a little strange that gentlemen, who have used it for many years, in a blacksmith's forge, should not have used it in their parlors, instead of green black oak.

This coal is adapted to all the purposes for which the bituminous coals are specially employed. Thus, for the manufacture of the carburetted hydrogen, for lighting streets and houses, there is no coal superior to it. It will require less expense for furnishing it; because it contains so little sulphur, from which sulphuretted hydrogen is formed. So, also, in the grate, it will be far less offensive, for the same reason. But, as it is rich in bitumen, it will furnish a large amount of gas, and that which is, comparatively, pure. This advantage is one of great importance. It should also be stated that it furnishes an excellent coke, which may be used for manufacturing purposes, and as it is left very porous, it is in a condition to absorb a large quantity of the solution of cyanide of potassium; and hence, is well adapted to the work of reducing the metals. It is scarcely necessary to add, that it is admirably adapted to steamings, inasmuch as its flame is free and durable. For forge use, it is not surpassed by any coal in market; and for parlor grates, it is both pleasant, economical, and free from dirt. If a chimney has a poor draft, it is liable to the objection common to all coals of this kind—the escape of soot into the room.

The qualities of the Deep River coal are of that character, then, which will give it the highest place in the market. The localities which have been best explored, and where coal of a decided character has been attained, are at Horneville and Farmville, both in the same neighborhood. The Taylor mine, the Gulf or Haughton, and the Murchison mines, all furnish a bituminous coal, which may vary in some minor points, yet is quite similar as a whole. The Haughton mine has been used the longest. It was known in the revolution, and a report made to Congress, respecting it, is still extant. Had the propositions or views been carried out, which were expressed in that report, we can scarcely tell what the results would have been, not only upon the population of Deep River, but also upon the enterprise of the State. It must be noticed that Deep River is central, and in the interior of a country abounding in iron; that it is navigable, by aid of certain improvements; that it communicates with the ocean, and finds a market abroad, for a surplus of the products of manufactures and agriculture; that a use of the natural advantages, to a partial extent only, makes a home market. But the time had not come for improving the resources of this district. They are, therefore, reserved entire for the present, and they cannot be neglected longer, unless a suicidal State policy is pursued.

But however fine and excellent a coal may be, it is necessary that it should form extensive beds, in order to have a commercial value.

THE COAL SUPPLY.

The next question, then, of interest to the community is, (for the community is interested as much as the owners,) will it bear mining, and the expenditure of the necessary capital to take it to market? To answer this question, it is necessary to make some calculations by which we may form a just view of its quantity. In doing this we may venture to assume, on a geological basis, that the coal seams, which outcrop from beneath the sandstones, extend beneath them, and for what appears to the contrary the slates, with their coal beds, are co-extensive with the under and overlying sandstones. This formation is known to form a belt of rocks, from 12 to 14 miles wide. The line of outcrops of the slates, upon which coal has been raised, is about 20 miles. But the line of outcrop of the unexplored slate, which embraces the coal, is at least 60 miles within the State, on a line running south of west. We may assume the following data, viz. : that the coal beds extend from their northern outcrop, three miles beneath the sandstone, which is about one-third their natural extent; and that the line of outcrop upon which coal is and will be found, is thirty miles. If the thickest seam of coal is worked, which has a thickness of 6 feet, exclusive of a thin band of slate, it will give for every square yard of surface, two square yards of coal. A square acre has 4,900 superficial yards; hence, there will be 9,800 square yards of coal in each acre, and as a square yard of coal weighs a ton, there will be for every acre, 9,800 tons of coal. A thousand acres will give 9,800,000 tons of coal, or a square mile, 6,272,000 tons. This coal field is known to extend thirty miles, in the direction of outcrop, and to be workable for a breadth of three miles. We may, from this data, calculate how much accessible coal we may expect to find in this quite limited field. If the field covers only 43 square miles, the lowest estimate to be taken, we may calculate its value by the following mode :

If one hundred tons of coal are taken out daily, thirty thousand tons would be removed annually, reckoning three hundred working days to the year. It would, at this rate, require over three hundred years to remove the coal from a thousand acres, or, over two hundred years to remove that which underlies a square mile, or, eight thousand six hundred years, to remove the coal of forty-three square miles. If in estimating the value of this coal-field, we base our calculations upon time, they should satisfy us, or, if we base them upon quantity, they will warrant the investment of capital. In these calculations we have both time and quantity; and the State, in encouraging improvements, as well as individuals, may look forward with confidence on the permanency and safety in investments in this kind of property. The wants of the world are with the population—indeed, they keep ahead of simple increase of individuals. The quantity to be removed annually may be increased, and leave the time sufficiently long, to satisfy the investment of capital; or the time may be increased by diminishing the quantity, and still the annual profits of the investment should satisfy the capitalist. But while population increases at a rapid rate, the resources of the forest for fuel are diminishing at a greater ratio than the simple increase of population; therefore, there is no way in which capital can be so safely invested as in coal lands.

If the foregoing calculations are correct, they justify the work which has been undertaken to improve the navigation of Deep River. It is prudence to be cautious in schemes of this kind, but in this case the amount of property beneath the surface or in the rocks, upon this river, is enormous—it should be dug out; and what it costs to do this, will be turning materials and labor into money. If the whole enterprise is begun, and carried on in a proper spirit, every nook and corner of the State, from Currituck to Buncombe, will feel an invigorating influence.

But the calculation as to the quantity of coal, will probably far exceed, than fall short of the estimates. In the first place only a part of the area is taken into the calculation, and then, in assuming the thickness of the principal beds as only six feet, it may be regarded as only the minimum thickness. It will rather increase than diminish; this view of the matter is supported by observation. For as the slopes have been carried along the dip, there has been a perceptible increase already. It is also to be considered, that at the outcrop, when vegetable matter forming the coal is only upon the outer vein, it should be twice that at a distance from the outcrop; for we may suppose that in the middle only of a coal basin, do we obtain the maximum thickness. Thus one of the coal seams in the Richmond basin is forty feet thick. The Deep River beds, not having been broken up, or not having suffered an uplift through the middle of its trough or basin, exhibits nowhere near the surface, an outcrop of coal, except *upon the rim*, or outer edge of the basin. As we penetrate into it, we have grounds which justify the view, that the seams will increase steadily in thickness, as the slope penetrates into the basin, towards the center, and then the seams, which now appear only upon the outer rim, will thicken and perhaps unite and form one distinct heavy seam towards the middle of the basin or trough.

The foregoing views as to quantity are founded upon data derived from observation, the phenomena of coalfields, and theory, which is well sustained, respecting the manner in which successive seams of coal have been formed. The calculations as to the quantity of coal in the Deep River coal-field are based upon what is known, and without reference to what we may possibly find by exploration hereafter. These calculations must be regarded as satisfactory, and such as will justify the hopes and expectations of the owners, and those who are interested in the improvements of the day.

THE DAN RIVER COAL FIELD.

In Rockingham and Stokes Counties, a series of rocks have been known for a quarter of a century, as coal-bearing. These rocks are similar to those of Deep River, and consist of the same members. They lie in the same order and have the same relations to each other, as those of Chatham and Moore, or Deep River.

The several parts constituting a complete and perfect system, occupy a synclinal trough, and lie in the primary or stratified pyro-crystalline rocks. Its direction is northeast and southwest. The axis may be defined by uniting Leaksville and Germanton by a line. This line will represent the direction of the coal slates.

The general dip of the system is to the northwest;—the angle of dip lies between 15 and 40°. The dip is usually above 20°. In North Carolina the rocks extend 40 miles. The breadth is between four and seven miles. The system extends into Virginia on the north; but how far, I am uninformed.

This field, it will be observed, covers a smaller area than Deep River. It is similar, in some respects, to the Richmond coal fields, but is disconnected by the intervening primary rocks.

The attention which has been given to the Dan River coal field, has as yet been too inconsiderable to develop its riches. It appears that from Leaksville to Germanton, coal is exposed at several points, besides at the extremes of the formation, leaving out of view its extension into Virginia.

The Deep River Coal Field.

[Emmons's Report, 1856.]

It is evidently important to determine the area over which a coal series extends. Their importance or value rests upon such a determination when their value to the public at large is to be decided and especially when large expenditures are required to convey it to market. It has been maintained that this coal field is of little value to the immediate country in which it is situated. This view is undoubtedly erroneous, though the fact upon which it is founded may be true. For the warming of houses, for example, it may not be necessary, in consequence of the forests which still remain, and the rapidity with which they are renewed when removed for tillage; yet coal is important in the arts, it is important as a fuel everywhere in conducting most branches of manufacturing industry. It is so, because it is cheaper and better adapted to many pursuits than wood or charcoal. The coal, therefore, is important in the immediate neighborhood where it is found, inasmuch as it is the best or cheapest fuel which can be employed in the manufacture of iron. It is taken for granted, that the people require additional means for getting their produce to market. The time has come when the ordinary means of transportation of the produce of the plantation must be superseded by those which are more rapid and certain, and which can be relied upon for quantity; so also, those which cheapen transportation must be constructed, if the country wishes to prosper. The manufacture of iron, therefore, by means of coal, does not presuppose that new and expensive means of transportation to market for its own accommodation. It comes in, however, in aid of those means which the planter and farmer require, whether manufacturing projects are devised and carried into execution or not.

The coal of Deep River will be useful at home, and may be explored for domestic manufacturing with profit, although the country in its immediate neighborhood is well wooded. When this view is taken in connection with the fact that it may also be transported to market with the ordinary profits of this business, the value of the coal field begins to assume its importance.

GEOGRAPHICAL EXTENT OF THE COAL MEASURES.

The first statement respecting the geographical extent of this series with which the coal stands connected, is that relating to the sandstones, which occupy a much larger area than that part of the series which contains the coal, or which has been called the coal measures.

The rocks occupy a deep depression in the oldest sedimentary slates. In whatever direction the series is approached, this fact becomes perceptible; the outer border is always below the surrounding country; and to reach the sandstones, there is a descent both on the north-western and south-eastern sides. This long valley, prior to the deposition of the rocks which now occupy it, must have been very deep. This is evident from the fact that the series is very thick.

This valley is now isolated or cut off from those in which similar formations are known to exist. It is therefore an independent one, so far as the Dan River or the Richmond series are concerned. The long axis of this valley is parallel, approximately at least with both, though it has no connection with either. I have traced this valley, with its sandstones, from a point about six miles from Oxford, in Granville County, across the State in a south-westerly direction. It passes into South Carolina, about six or seven miles, where it terminates. Within the State its length is about one hundred and twenty miles. Its breadth is variable. Where it terminates near Oxford, in Granville County, it is very narrow, or indeed runs to a point. The widest part is between Raleigh and Chapel Hill, on the line of which it is eighteen miles wide. On the Neuse it is twelve. On the Cape Fear, between Jones' Falls and the Buckhorn, it scarcely exceeds six miles. This is one of the narrowest places of the series; it widens rapidly in a north-easterly and south-westerly direction, till, towards Chapel Hill, or rather eastward of that place, it becomes eighteen miles, as stated, from which it soon diminishes in breadth. From Capt. E. Bryan's at Jones' Falls, the direction of the western margin, for about six miles, is about south-west. Soon afterward its course is more westerly, and even sweeps around and takes a northerly course; but afterwards resumes a south-west course into South Carolina, after crossing the corner of Union County. The auriferous slates may be observed at numerous places on the north-western border. The exceptions which have fallen under my notice show the series in a metamorphic condition. At Capt. Bryan's, a belt of chert and porphyry rises from beneath the sandstones, and extends seven or eight miles in a northeasterly direction. A similar belt also rises up from beneath the same series one-and-a-half miles northerly from the Gulf, on the plankroad, and pursues a course parallel with the former. This is probably a repetition of the series at Jones' Falls. But the unchanged slates emerge in an uncomformable position at numerous places in Chatham and Moore Counties, among which I may mention the millstone quarries on the waters of Richland Creek, the tributaries of Indian Creek within one mile of Evans' bridge, and on the road leading to Salem, and again about a mile above the mouth of Line Creek, which enters Deep River not far above the same bridge. An important point which exhibits the junction of the series is about one-and-a-half miles from Farmville, on the Pittsborough road, where a deep ravine divides the lower conglomerate and red sandstone from the slates of the Taconic system. The slates, as usual, dip nearly to the north-west at a high angle, while the sandstones dip from them, or southerly, at a very moderate inclination. An interesting exposure of the inferior beds of these sediments, resting upon the slates, occurs at the quarry of

Mr. Seawell, where the conglomerate or millstone has been entirely removed, by which an intervening stratum of clay which rests upon the edges of the slate is exposed. The conglomerate or millstone grit is about forty feet thick. It dips at an angle of seventeen or eighteen degrees, and to the south-east. On the north-west side it appears, from observation, to repose upon the gold slates, especially all of it south of Orange County; or upon rocks of the same series, and which have been changed, or have been porphyritic. The width of the lower sandstone on the north-west side, beyond its junction with the bituminous slates, varies at different places; it is from three-fourths of a mile to three miles. Small fields are still further removed, but they are usually isolated, and cut off by protecting ridges of the older slates. The largest field which is thus isolated is in Anson county.

The south-east margin is concealed through all that part which lies south-west of Cape Fear River but at several points near the margin where the auriferous slates make their appearance. In Anson County, one mile-and-a-half south-east of Wadesborough, the red sandstones dip gently to the west. But the characters which these rocks exhibit indicate that it is the upper sandstone which is thus prolonged. It resembles that of Brassfields sixteen miles from Raleigh, on the Hillsborough road, where the sandstones become calcareous and somewhat nodular. But neither place furnishes fossils, and hence the criteria by which to judge of their identity are indecisive. I would not make the statement respecting this question without reservation. Yet, those calcareous concretions seem to belong to the **upper** mass at Brassfields, and those near Wadesborough closely resemble them. The south-east side, from its crossing of the Cape Fear to the Pee Dee, is usually covered with the tertiary sands. We are unable, therefore, to learn the character of this margin, whether it is horizontal, or dips away or towards the axis of the formation. There is no exposure by which the position of the coal measures can be determined; this part of the series does not appear on this side; there is no positive fact from which we can judge of its existence at all; and this becomes still more obscure, in consequence of the facts which have been already stated, which have led me to believe that it is the upper sandstone which is prolonged, and forms the extreme points of the formation. Hence, it is not improbable that the upper sandstone extends beyond the coal measures, and conceals them from observation. If so, there are no inducements of sufficient value which would warrant the expenditure of capital in attempting to obtain them upon the south-east side. North of the Cape Fear, as the formation passes onward through Orange into Granville County, the south-east side is equally unpromising for coal; while on the north-west side, about six miles from Chapel Hill, in the neighborhood of Mr. Moring's, in Chatham County, there is an exposure of black slate, containing the common fossils of this part of the coal measures. But this exposure is limited; and from this locality the indications of the presence of coal cannot be discovered, or they are merely lignite beds, which are the products of a single coniferous tree. It is not difficult to distinguish these appearances from those which accompany the coal seams. In the former, its speedy removal from its bed should be sufficient to satisfy every reasonable mind, though many still persist in seeing a coal seam in a flattened stem of an ancient tree, provided it is fully carbonized.

We find the coal measures confined mostly to the central part of the sandstones, where they traverse the counties of Chatham and Moore. The formation pursues a westerly course, parallel with the general direction of Deep River. The outcrop crosses the river between Evander McIver's and the Horneville property, thence by Farmville, it crosses the river obliquely at Egypt, and soon recrosses it again near the fish-trap, and passes into the Taylor plantation. It continues on the north side of the river until it passes the plantation of Mr. Murchison from which it crosses it again for the last time into the plantation of Mr. Fooshee, where the coal series is well developed, three or four seams of good coal having been exposed by several excavations directly over the outcrop of the seams. The direction of the outcrop of the coal seams from Murchison's to Fooshee's is S. 54° W., which may be taken as the direction which the north-western margin pursues for the next eight or ten miles; after which the direction is about S. 45° W. The extent of the coal seams in this direction is not determined. The features of the formation are still favorable for their continuance. The coal seams upon the plantation of Mr. Fooshee are equal in thickness, and possess qualities of the same nature as those of Egypt. There are, therefore, grounds for the expectation of its continuance still further in this direction. But the outcrop of the series is concealed, and requires the expenditure of capital to test the correctness of this expectation.

The whole length of the outcrop, following its windings, is about thirty miles. The extreme point beyond Evander McIver's, where the coal seams have been discovered, is at Martin Dyer's, where a boring cut a seam near the outcrop ten inches thick. The locality still further northeastward in this direction, known as the Rhiney Wicker's property, but owned by Mr. Ellington, does not belong to the same series as the Egypt and other seams, whose value has been tested. The Ellington seam is in connection with the plant bed I have spoken of, and undoubtedly belongs to the upper sandstone. It is less than three inches thick, and therefore of no importance. I have spoken of this locality in former reports, but had not visited it. When, however, I had an opportunity to examine the character of the beds in which it occurs, I was satisfied it was wholly unconnected with the true coal measures of the lower series. The existence of coal seams has, therefore, been determined by the auger, and by excavations from Martin Dyer's to Mr. Fooshee's, on the south side of the Deep River, in Moore County. The coal slates are known to be prolonged in each direction from these points; and though the existence of the coal seams in the prolonged slate may be questioned, still, there are no reasons for their immediate discontinuance. It should, however, be stated here, that the slates beyond Martin Dyer's are known only for about two miles, where they are accompanied with fine beds of argillaceous oxide of iron. But they extend much further to the southwest, and nearly to the Great Pee Dee. But their thickness is diminished at Drowning Creek, and there are no exposures of iron ore. Beyond the Great Pee Dee, in Anson county, the black slates, if they occur at all, are feeble or thin; though this plat of the formation may be concealed by the deep soil of the valley, still the prospects for finding coal are not encouraging. My opinion with respect to the extent of the coal is, that it will be prolonged about ten miles; that it will turn out that the continuous outcrop will be, ultimately, about forty miles; that it will be extended further in a south-west than in a north-east direction is rendered probable, from the fact, that in the latter direction I am unable to perceive that the seams show any signs of giving out; and it is in this direction that the black slate is extended much further than in the others I have referred to.

QUALITY OF THE DEEP RIVER COAL.

The quality of the coal is of a high order; it is true it is not equal to the Breckinridge coal for its volatile matters, but it equals it in its combustible products. For the purpose of giving a greater publicity to the excellent character of this coal, I shall make use of the analyses which have been made of it, together with others which are well known, and which will serve as standards for comparison. No one had pursued a plan so thorough as the late Prof. Johnson, whose experience in this line of investigation was equal, if not greater, than any of whom we could boast. They are characterized by thoroughness, which gives confidence in their accuracy.

The first analysis of this order was made of the coal of the lower seam, at Farmville, and recently mined. The composition was found to be as follows:

Volatile matter	30.91
Fixed carbon	50.70
Earthy matter	18.32
	99.93

The specific gravity of the specimen 1.416. The coke of this coal is light and puffy, ashes purplish gray.

A second specimen gave—

Volatile matter	28.47
Fixed carbon	64.70
Earthy matter	6.83
	100.00

Specific gravity 1.497. Coked very slowly. Ashes brownish red.

A third specimen from the lower seam, gave—

Volatile matter	30.85
Fixed carbon	63.90
Earthy matter	5.25
	100.00

Specific gravity 1.415. Ashes white and very light.

The fourth specimen gave—

Volatile matter	31.30
Fixed carbon	64.40
Earthy matter	4.30
	100.00

Specific gravity 1.308. Coked slowly. Ashes nearly white.

The foregoing analyses were made of coal taken only a few feet from the surface. They are designed to show, in part, the effect of meteoric influences which had necessarily diminished the amount of volatile, and increased relatively the earthy matters, as well as to increase also the quantity of hygrometric water. This coal at greater depths is found to sustain this view, as will be seen by analyses of coal taken from greater depths, and further removed from atmospheric influence.

Coal taken from the deep pit at Egypt, and analyzed for me by Dr. Jackson, gave—

Fixed carbon	63.6
Carb. Hydrogen gas	34.8
Ashes	1.6
	99.0

Color of the ashes reddish brown.

This coal, it is true, was not taken from the same place as those whose analyses have been given in the preceding paragraphs; but the Egypt and the Farmville coal cannot be distinguished from each other, when taken from about the same depth. The analysis of the Egypt coal shows a better quality and an increase of volatile matter, and less earth or ash; probably no analysis shows a better composition for all the purposes for which coal is employed. Another mode of testing the value of coals, is to determine the amount of steam which a given quantity of coal will generate. Thus Johnson found, by experiment, that the steam producing or evaporating power of this coal, was equivalent to 8.1; or that one pound of coal would convert 8.1 pounds of water into steam; and also, that one part, by weight, of dried coal, will reduce twenty-six and ninety-seven hundredths times its weight of lead.

The following table of comparison is quoted from Prof. Johnson's report, showing the evaporative and lead producing power of coals taken from the different pits of the Richmond basin, and certain foreign bituminous coals, which hold about the same rank as to reducing and steam producing power. In an economical point of view, this comparison is interesting; showing that the coals of the Richmond and Deep River basins do not differ materially from each other, or from those of the carboniferous period:

	Names of Coal.	Lead reduced by one part of Coal.	Steam generated by one part of Coal.
1	Chesterfield Mining Co. Va..	25.78	8.09
2	New Castle, Eng,...........	26.78	8.65
3	Clover Hill, Va............	26.96	7.67
4	Liverpool, Va..............	27.07	7.84
5	Pictou, Nova Scotia.	27.24	8.41
6	Midlothian, Va. (screened)..	27.28	8.94
7	Midlothian (average)........	27.34	8.29
8	Pittsburg, Pa...............	27.54	8.20
9	Farmville, N. C............	26.97	8.10

Other foreign, and particularly British coals, produce similar results; the reductive and evaporative powers do not exceed those of Deep River. Thus, according to the results obtained by the British Commissioners on coals, the following kinds yield the following numbers, expressive of their power, as in the foregoing table:

	Names of Coal.	Lead reduced.	Steam generated.
1	Broomhill coal..............	25.32	8.85
2	Coleshill........	26.14	8.00
3	Dalkeith Jewel seam	27.42	7.08
4	Three quarter rock vein	26.62	8.84
5	Ponty-Pool..................	27.46	7.47
6	Bedwas	28.20	9.97
7	Cwm Frood rock vein......	28.30	8.70
8	Grangemouth..............	28.45	7.40
	Averages...............	27.11	8.09

The composition of the Farmville coal, in a raw state, as determined by organic analysis, is as follows, the water being determined by a separate process, and, as equal to 1.71 per cent.:

Sulphur	3.30
Carbon	68.41
Hydrogen	4.64
Oxygen	8.37
Earthy matter	13.60
Water	1.71
	100.00

The excess of hydrogen which the foregoing analysis exhibits, over and above that which is necessary to form water, is equivalent to 3.57 per cent.

The earthy matter in the better specimens of the Farmville coal, though taken near the surface, where it is less exposed to meteoric influences, is only 3.81 per cent., instead of 13.60, where it is still more exposed; and an analysis of this coal gave Johnson:

Moisture	2.35	per cent.
Sulphur	0.22	"
Carbon	80.20	"
Hydrogen	5.45	"
Oxygen and other vol. matter	7.97	"
Earthy matter	3.81	"
	100.00	
Hydrogen in excess	4.46	

The fixed carbon of this variety, when coked slowly, is 64.57 per cent. The volatile carbon of the 80.20 per cent. is 15.63 per cent.; which leaves the 64.57 as the fixed carbon of the specimen. Three thirty-seven hundredths per cent. more passes off in vapor when the coal is coked rapidly.

The question respecting the presence of injurious matter in this coal, is also determined by the foregoing analyses. Thus, sulphur is injurious in various ways. If present in a large quantity when burnt in grates, its odor is extremely offensive, and it blackens the several articles of furniture which are often used. Twenty-five grains triated for sulphur gave 3.3 per cent. Another analysis gave 3.20 sulphur. It is evident, both from experiment and observation, that the sulphur diminishes as the depth increases; or as other foreign matter diminishes, the sulphur also becomes less. The sulphur in all the pits appears disseminated, and sometimes in lumps, in the slate, while I have observed it in the coal seam, only in one or two instances, in a visible mass in the coal. The impure coals, those which contain slate, contain the most sulphur. When the coal is therefore pure and free from the foreign intermixture of slate, coprolites, animal and vegetable matter only partially changed, then the sulphur is in excess.

The combustion of this coal, and the ease with which it can be ignited, are important qualities. It burns briskly with a brilliant and free combustion. It therefore gives a pleasant and agreeable fire in parlor grates. In this respect, I believe it is not excelled by any coal now in market. This brilliant combustion is attended with a swelling of the whole mass, by which a good hollow fire is maintained, agglutinating as the combustion proceeds, and ending in the production of a light porous coke. It is for these qualities, that it is so well adapted to the use of smiths; and it is invariably remarked by them, that they wish for no better coal. In market it sells to blacksmiths for forty cents per bushel. The amount of sulphur in the iron of the coal produces injurious effects in iron which is heated and welded by it. It is stated by Johnson, that the sulphur will not injure it on shipboard or on shore.

Sometimes in a rapid combustion of the coal in a grate, it melts partially, and exhibits a tendency to flow. This fact shows that its volatile matter or bitumen is in large proportions. This tendency, however, does not exhibit itself in slow combustion.

The Breckinridge coal melts and flows when ignited. This, however, contains nearly twice as much bitumen or volatile matter as the Farmville coal. The Breckinridge has about 61 per cent. of volatile matter, while that from the Egypt pit has only 34.8, or nearly 35 per cent. Whether the Deep River coal can be profitably employed for the production of *coal oil* and other matters for light, has yet to be determined by a series of well conducted experiments. It is desirable that its value for light should be determined, but it is probable that it cannot compete with several richer coals now in market.

The value of the bituminous coal for the common furnaces, seems to be well established; there can be no doubt of its value for warming parlors, or for grates, for smith's work of all kinds, being both cheaper and more economical than charcoal; that is, at forty cents per bushel, it is more economical than charcoal at five cents. The value of the semi-bituminous coals is not so well determined. From several analyses by Johnson, its composition near the outcrop has been determined. Thus the percentage of volatile and fixed matters gave, in

No. 1, Fixed carbon 83.12
Volatile matter.............. 8.28
Earthy..................... 8.60
_____
100.00

The ash is purplish gray. This specimen had been long exposed to atmospheric influences; its specific gravity 1.45.

No. 2, Fixed carbon............... 83.76
Volatile matter 6.64
Earthy 9.60
_____
100.00

Ashes reddish gray. Specific gravity 1.54.

No. 3, Fixed carbon............... 87.18
Volatile matter.............. 7.35
Earthy matter 5.47
_____
100.00

Specific gravity 1.47. Ash reddish gray. Obtained from a fresh opening, and taken from the 2½ foot seam.

In this semi-bituminous coal of George Wilcox's seams, it appears that the volatile matter is less than one-fourth of that which belongs to the Farmville or Egypt coal. The value of this variety has not yet been determined; it is doubtful whether the semi-bituminous coals can be carried to market, where they will have to compete with the Anthracite of Pennsylvania. They have their place, however, and will be employed for warming apartments in the large villages and cities of the State, both in grates and coal stoves. These coals would be well adapted for the Raleigh and Wilmington markets, or for home consumption; and it is probable, may be employed economically in the manufacture of iron. But the question is not yet settled whether these semi-bituminous seams are permanent, or may not prove to be locally anthracite or nearly so; but which may become bituminous at greater depths upon the dip of the seams, and perhaps even at comparatively small depths, the semi-bituminous seam may become a bituminous one. As the value of the latter is greater, such a result is to be hoped for.

ECONOMICAL PRODUCTS OF THE COAL FIELDS.

Industry never lacks materials upon which to expend its energy. It is not cupidity which always seeks the useful, in the rough quarries of nature. The occurrence of one valuable product is but a step towards the discovery of another; and we are frequently surprised at the numerous wants which are supplied in a single series of sediments. In addition to the coal, which is the first object of pursuit, and the discovery of which has opened the way for others, and which probably would be useless were there no coal, iron ore, free stones, grindstone grits, and fire-clays, may be enumerated.

The iron ores belong to two or three distinct kinds:

1. The ordinary hydrous peroxides, with argillaceous matter, which are undoubtedly the altered products derived from the argillaceous carbonate.

2. The same kind in appearance, but which is magnetic.

3. The black band of the Scotch miners, and which is regarded by a gentleman well acquainted with this ore as the *Blackbest* of the Scottish miners.

All these kinds appear to be abundant, or to be co-extensive with the coal slates. I am not able to speak of the extent of the brown magnetic ore which occurs upon the plantation of Mr. Tyson. It is an interesting anomaly in the way of iron ores to find the brown ores, with their ordinary aspect, strongly magnetic. I suspect this kind may be confined to the surface, inasmuch as, under the action of light, and perhaps certain atmospheric influences, the black ores of the older rocks become very strong magnets.

The argillaceous carbonate, when exposed to meteoric influence, the hydrous peroxide, with argillaceous matter, occurs at the depth of about two hundred and thirty feet in the shaft at Egypt. It is frequently found outcropping above the coal seams, in nodular masses of different forms and sizes, and may be employed as a clue to the position of the coal seams; inasmuch, as there are no known bituminous seams above the iron ore beds. The principal seams are below; but inasmuch as there is another outcropping of iron below the seams, about thirty-four yards distant, it is necessary to be on guard, so as not to be led astray by the inferior beds of iron. These outcropping beds of iron ore at the Gulf are undoubtedly the seams of black band, belonging to the next seam of coal below the main seam, which at Egypt is thirty feet below in the shaft. But this ore, though traces of its outcropping may be seen at several places, is not always to be found upon the surface. It is rarely as strong at any place as at the Gulf.

The argillaceous carbonate occurs in balls, and in continuous beds. They are adjacent to each other. The color of the ore is gray or drab: it effervesces with acids, and is somewhat silicious: and certain parts of the seams of ore are tough. It differs in no respect from the argillaceous carbonate of the carboniferous series. It contains about thirty-three per cent. of metallic iron. The surface ores being altered, the carbonates contain fifty per cent. of metallic iron. This is not too large a percentage to be estimated for the magnetic ores of the Tyson plantation. Of the quantity of these carbonates there can be no doubt; since they occur along the entire outcrop of the slates of the coal series. A very beautiful and rich kind is found at Benjamin Wicker's, beyond the known limits of the coal seam; so, at the other extreme, at Murchison's, it is still in place, and holding the same relations as at the Gulf, at Egypt, or McIver's.

I am unable to distinguish the black band from the argillaceous carbonate, where it has been subjected to meteoric influences. I have, heretofore, maintained and expressed the opinion, that there were two bands of the ore under consideration; one above and the other below the main coal seam; but the shaft at Egypt proves the existence of the black band accompanying the little coal seam; and hence, it is probable that what appears to be argillaceous carbonate is the black band, changed by exposure to the air. There is, probably, only two bands of the argillaceous carbonate —the continuous band or seam, and the band of iron balls in proximity with each other.

This is mined with great ease and facility. Although hard and difficult to penetrate with the auger, yet, when the slate beneath the band is taken out tons of it fall into the pit at once. The expense, therefore, of mining is trifling, under the circumstances; and hence there is no reason for doubting the feasibility of making iron from it at a profit.

The black band invariably accompanies the coal seams. There are now known three seams of it; one between the main coal seams, another immediately below, and a third, equally important, accompanying the little coal seam thirty feet below the former, and from which it is separated by slates and gritty fire-clay, fifteen feet thick.

The black band owes its high value as an ore to the facility with which it is converted into pig, and the quality of the pig produced from it. The ore itself is black and somewhat massive, as a slate; fracture compact and even, or only slightly conchoidal. It would be mistaken for a heavy massive slate.

This ore was first discovered at Farmville; but it was not suspected to be the *Scotch black band;* but that it would prove available ore there could be no doubt. Mr. Paton, a gentleman of great experience in iron-making, first suggested to Mr. McLane the character of the ore. Examination proved the correctness of the gentleman's opinion already referred to. When roasted it is strongly magnetic, and probably the brown magnetic ore of Tyson's is only an altered black band, as it occurs also in layers, or in the form of a fissile ferruginous slate.

The composition of the black band was determined for me by my friend Dr. Jackson. It is composed of,

Carbon	31.30
Peroxide of iron	47.50
Silex	9.00
Bitumen and water	8.81
Sulphur	3.39
	100.00

The roasted ore yields only 0.89 per cent. of

sulphur. Sulphur, as in the case of the slate, seems to attach itself to the slaty parts of the mass; but I should have expected also a small percentage of phosphoric acid, seeing that coprolites are very common in the black band. The fossils of the black band, too, are more abundant than in the slate; it is at the junction of this ore with the coal that the saurian teeth occur in the greatest abundance, especially in that stratum which intervenes between the coal seams.

This ore becomes important, in consequence of the facility of its conversion into pig. I am not able to say whether the 89 hundredths per cent. of sulphur in the roasted ore is sufficient to exert much influence in the furnace product; probably not. In the progress of mining the black band is so closely connected with the coal, that it will necessarily be raised; and hence a valuable ore will be obtained at the surface, with only a trifling additional cost over that which attends the mining and raising of the coal only.

From the occurrence of this ore, the mineral resources or the wealth of the coalfield is very much increased. We may, therefore, congratulate the friends of the Deep River improvement, and those of the mining interest of the country, of this accession of valuable products, which must secure for this region important establishments for the manufacture of iron.

In connection with the subject of iron ores, I may very properly introduce those which are denominated materials for construction, such as freestones and fire-clays. The red and purple sandstones abound, in the lower red sandstone, with beds suitable for building stone. The color of these beds, whatever it may be, is lively and inviting. Indeed no difference can be discovered between those of Deep River and those of the Hudson River or the Connecticut River sandstone. As these beds are extensive, they furnish, at many points, stone of a suitable quality for any purpose which may be required.

The *fire-clays*, though they are not found beneath every coal seam, still are common in connection with the coal, and between the main and little seams. It is well known that they are important for fire-brick and other kindred purposes where a refractory article is required. We find not only coal, but also fire-clay, bands of iron both nodular and in continuous beds, but even the rarer ore, the *black band*, which is found only in the coal measures of Europe.

Millstones.—Beneath the red sandstone the conglomerate is so perfectly consolidated that it forms a valuable millstone. This is made up almost entirely of compacted quartz pebbles, which are so firmly imbedded that their fracture is often directly across the axis of the pebble, where it would be expected to break out. These pebbles are derived from the quartz veins of the Taconic system, and hence, consist of milky quartz.

The beds vary in thickness from six inches to eighteen, or even two feet.

The stone is adapted to the grinding of indian corn. They are said to be better cornstones than the French Buhrstone; for grinding wheat, the latter have been always preferred, as they are far less liable to heat the flour. Several quarries are opened in Moore County, and from them the country is principally supplied. The conglomerate at or near the base of the upper sandstone is less consolidated, and is not so well adapted to the formation of millstones. The thickness of the beds is from forty to sixty feet; but it is a mass which thins out, and hence its thickness at several points is extremely variable. The lower sandstone, with its conglomerates, is better developed in the south-west part of Moore County than elsewhere. We find, even at the Gulf, the conglomerate ceases to be an important stratum.

As a whole, the mass is made up of rounded pebbles in beds of variable thickness, which are separated from each other by finer and softer varieties. The conglomerates rest almost immediately and unconformably upon the slates of the Taconic system. A circumstance worthy of note, is the fact that the pebbles are auriferous; hence, the opinion expressed by distinguished geologists, that gold is a recent product, probably of the Tertiary period, is erroneous. It must have existed at the time of the laying down of the bottom rocks of this coalfield; indeed, long before. So that instead of its being a recent metal, it is one of the oldest, being certainly coeval with copper and iron pyrites.

Grindstone Grits.—In the midst of the gray stone beds, more particularly those which occupy a place between the two red sandstones, I have frequently observed valuable grits, which are suitable both for coarse and fine grindstones. Grindstones have, however, been frequently made from the reddish bed as well as the drab and gray grits. These stones have been made to supply the wants of the citizens in a neighborhood far removed from the means of transporting heavy materials. No systematic efforts have been directed steadily towards the business of preparing these stones for market. It is only when manufactures are established, that a demand will arise out of the interests and wants of the community, that these lesser products of industry will take their place in the regular trade of the country.

Bituminous Slate.—The slates of the coal series, especially where they are very near the coal seams, are highly bituminous. They are known to contain 28.6 per cent. of volatile matter, and 19.55 per cent. of fixed carbon. Slates are employed for illumination in Europe, when they are near a large population. It would seem, therefore, that the slates of Deep River may, under favorable circumstances, be employed for this purpose. It is evident that they cannot be transported far for any purpose. They ignite readily in the fire and in a candle, blaze and burn with a good flame, emitting a white light. The question may be entertained, whether it is not possible to obtain the bitumen or volatile matter in a portable slate. The importance of light and fuel certainly warrants trials for this purpose. Even the slate far removed from the coal seams is combustible, and highly so. It is doubtful whether such a mass of bituminous slates exists even in the carboniferous series. It is impossible to estimate the amount of combustible matter locked up in them, and which it is possible may be turned to some account.

ADVANTAGES OF DEEP RIVER FOR MANUFACTURE OF IRON.

It is the centralization of materials which creates an important manufacturing locality when combined especially with a power to move machinery, and an agricultural capacity to sustain a large population. These give importance to any location for establishing a manufacturing interest upon a large scale.

Assuming the doctrine as true, we may proceed to ascertain whether there is such a centralization of means upon Deep River, sufficient to build up the interests alluded to. First, it has already been proved that the products of the coalfield make good the assumption. The hydrous peroxide of iron, the black band and coal, need not be spoken of again. The fuel and the material productions are abundant for any projects in this line of operations.

But the additional means in other ores in striking distance, add to and greatly increase the means for the purposes in view. Thus, the inexhaustible specular ore, four miles from the Gulf, the magnetic ore a few miles further, the hematite ore, will make an addition of three kinds of ore to those already known in so much abundance in the coalfield. There is, then, the water-power, if it is wished to employ it for moving machinery; or what is better, the employment of steam may be substituted for it; and still this power should not be lost.

The next important material is timber. The timber of Deep River and vicinity furnishes a variety not excelled in the State, or any State. First and foremost is the long leaf pine, of which forests line its banks. The growth is large, the wood mature, and is unimpaired by age or by the woodman's ax. The next most important timbers are the oaks and hickories. The manufacturing interests have been scarcely encouraged hitherto; all the materials in the line of woodwork remain as in a new country.

The next article of importance is stone for construction. These have been spoken of already. The free stone is not only well adapted to the construction of durable or imperishable buildings, but it is adapted to the construction of elegant ones. Whether strength, durability or beauty, or all of these characteristics are combined, there is ample room for obtaining all that can be wished.

The last essential qualification for manufactures, is an agricultural country; one whose soil is adapted to the production of the cereals; for if these can be grown, every other necessary is provided for. The adaptation of Chatham County to the growth of the cereals cannot be doubted; past experience may be cited in proof, or rather the testimony of the whole community confirms the position.

But climate should not be overlooked. There is a temperature suited to the constitution, which, while it favors longevity, favors also the sustenance of life at the lowest expense; while it preserves the strength, and does not weaken the body by a high summer range. Such, I believe, is the favorable climate of North Carolina. The moderate range of the thermometer, the freedom from long and excessive heats, or long continued cold, favors the cheap sustenance of laborers, both as to food and clothing, and adds several numbers to the percentage of advantages over a climate which is subjected to either extreme of temperature. But an accessible market is indispensable to prosperity. We do not, and cannot rely upon what has hitherto been done, it is what may be, or what improvements the country admits of. The outlet for trade is not restricted to one direction. It is not Raleigh, nor Norfolk, Fayetteville or Wilmington, but it is in all these directions; and so also a route may be opened to Charleston and the West. The position of Deep River is central. If the manufacturing interest is fostered, intercommunication with distant towns follows of necessity. A town will grow up with greater rapidity on Deep River than at Beaufort. Here are the elements which always draw together an active and intelligent community. These elements have ever created wealthy and flourishing towns. If, then, we require a concentration of means and interests to build up large towns, I do not know where a greater number of the requisite elements can be found in the interior of any State.

The Dan River Coalfield.

[Emmons's Report, 1856.]

The counties of Rockingham and Stokes contain within their respective areas a series of deposits, which do not differ materially from those of Deep River. They contain coal, but the seams are less known; and, judging from the depths of the works which have exposed them, they seem to be less promising than those of Deep River. While all the beds which are connected in this formation, or which stand together, are much the same as those of Chatham and Moore, the coal seam is mostly semi-bituminous, or similar to the George Wilcox seam which has been described.

There are certain peculiarities, however, worthy of notice, which do not exist in the Deep River formation. Those peculiarities will be recognized in the following division of the Dan River series:

1. And at the bottom, conglomerates and breccias.
2. Lower sandstones, including the soft and hard.
3. Gray sandstones, with bituminous shales, fire-clays, etc.
4. Upper sandstones and marls.
5. Brecciated conglomerates.

These parts are all distinct and separate at Leaksville, where the system is probably more perfect than elsewhere. They lie in a trough in the primary series, or in the laminated pyrocrystalline rocks, whose direction is about north-east and south-west. The axis of the trough runs parallel with a line which connects Leaksville with Germanton. The system dips to the north-west; the angle of dip is variable, and ranges between 15° and 40°, it is usually greater than 20°.

The whole extent or range of the Dan River series is about forty miles, thirty of which is comprised within the bounds of North Carolina. The north-east extremity extends into Virginia about ten miles. The breadth of the series is not less than four, and not greater than seven miles.

It has no connection with the Richmond coalfield, though it is prolonged in that direction; neither is it connected or continuous with another small coalfield in Halifax County, in Virginia. These several troughs are, all of them, isolated depressions in the primary series.

The lowest mass of the Dan River series is conglomerate; but it is badly developed. It is not exposed at Leaksville, the north-east extremity; but at Germanton these beds consist of angular fragments of granite and gneiss, intermixed with a few imperfectly formed pebbles. This mass might be mistaken for granite, were it not that it contains here and there the pebbles referred to; or it may be fragments of silicified wood. In this mass I have also found the roots of the silicified trunks penetrating and branching into it, showing that the trees grew upon the spot where they are now found. Above the conglomerate, or brecciated conglomerate, the silicified trunks of coniferous trees are sufficiently numerous to be regarded as an ancient forest. The roots are sometimes changed into lignite. What appear to be trunks are always silicified. These, sometimes, exceed two feet in diameter; segments of which stand out from the sandstones at an angle of 45°; but they are usually prostrate. It is remarkable that at this locality the trunks and roots only remain. All the tender and leafy parts are destroyed. The beds containing the silicified trunks extend half a mile. In immediate connection with the soft sandstones which contain the vegetable products already referred to, I found a concretionary clay. Large concentric circles mark the boundaries of the concretions, some of which are four feet in diameter. Above the argillaceous concretionary mass, we find the regular bedded red sandstones, consisting of variegated strata in part—but mostly red sandstones, of various degrees of coarseness. These terminate in the black and green shales and slates, which contain the seams of coal.

At Leaksville, where the series is best exposed, they consist of the following strata:—

1. Shale or black bituminous slate below the coal; thickness undetermined.
2. Slaty micaceous sandstones two feet.
3. Shaly coal at the outcrop eighteen inches.
4. Micaceous shale two feet.
5. Semi-bituminous coal from two to three feet at the outcrop.
6. Shale one hundred feet.
7. Strata of a semi-concretionary limestone more or less silicious, from four to six feet. This is probably an equivalent of the argillaceous iron ore.
8. Soft green, bluish and black shales with posidonias, sixty feet.

The shales, however, still continue; but being covered with soil their thickness remains to be determined. The calcareous strata are above the coal seams; as no others are known, and as they extend through the coalfield, they become way boards for the discovery of the seams of coal beneath them. These layers are well preserved at Madison, and contain septaria.

The dip of the slates at Leaksville is N. 35° W.; angle of dip 25°.

A section of rocks between Eagle bridge and Governor Morehead's factory, consists of the following strata:

1. Sandstones and conglomerate, mostly concealed, at the bridge.
2. Flinty black slates, two hundred feet thick.
3. Coal slates, consisting of green and black slates, with posidonia and cypris in great abundance.
4. Red and gray sandstones.
5. Conglomerates.
6. Shaly and green variegated sandstones.
7. Conglomerates and brecciated conglomerates at least three hundred feet thick.

They contain many angular fragments, some of which are very large.

The upper part, which may be observed at Morehead's factory, presents the following strata, which I state more in detail, and in the ascending order:

1. Greenish brecciated trappean mass.
2. Coarse, brecciated mass, intermixed with pebbles only partially rounded, eighty to one hundred feet thick.
3. Greenish slate and shale.
4. Greenish slaty sandstone.
5. Coarse decomposing sandstone, one hundred feet thick.

The first, or No. 1. of this upper part of the series is made up of various rocks, as talcose slates, granite, and masses of feldspar and trap. The size of these angular fragments is from seven to eight inches long, and four to five thick. It is a decomposing mass.

The coarse brecciated mass immediately above this, is a tough, durable building stone of a gray color, and looks like granite at a distance. It contains a large amount of quartz, and the ground or paste in which it is imbedded is less disposed to disintegrate. The dip of this series is N. 30° W.

The upper part of the Dan River sandstone is unlike that of Deep River, unless it is parallel with the rocks at Jones' Falls, which I am disposed to regard as probable, and as the inferior beds of the New Red sandstone There is evidently a change in the deposits indicative of a more important one, connected with a change of the organic remains. This remains to be determined.

The series of sandstones again, which are exposed on Factory Creek, four miles from Madison, on the road to Martin's lime kilns, are interesting, as they are exposed by the denudation of the stream. They are enumerated in the ascending order, and probably begin near the coal shales:

1. Soft greenish slates.
2. Coarse sandstone with pebbles.
3. Red and brown sandstones.
4. Porous red sandstones, or sandstone with angular cavities, similar to those of Deep River, which may have contained a soluble salt.
5. Green and gray hard sandstones.
6. Coarse sandstones, with pebbles.
7. Conglomerates resembling those at Morehead's factory.
8. Marls, reddish and mottled, beneath which are the primary slates in an unconformable position.

The dip in this series is very regular; the angle of dip is twenty degrees, and the distance across them is about half a mile, and every stratum being exposed, there is no danger of committing an error in the succession, or being misled by repetitions. This series is probably equivalent to that which begins at Jones' Falls, upon Deep River; or, in other words, is the upper part of the Triassic system. At the time the examination was made, I noted the succession only, omitting even the approximate thickness of the strata composing the series. Obscure fucoids were observed, but not obtained.

The Thecodont saurian remains were obtained far below this series; and hence, though we find apparent differences in the groups, we may be confident, I think, that the upper and lower parts of the formations upon Deep and Dan Rivers, are the equivalents of each other.

At Madison, the series below the coal slates, as exposed on the east side of Dan River, is made up of the following strata. They rest upon gneiss:

1. Soft variegated micaceous sandstones, two hundred feet thick.
2. Green, shaly and drab colored sandstones, about five hundred feet thick.
3. Red sandstones, with small angular cavities.
4. Green and dark colored coal shales, the latter bituminous.

At Madison, the fossils of the slate are the same as those at Evans' Mills, on Deep River. The conglomerate, which is so conspicuous a member of this formation on Deep River, is very imperfectly developed upon the Dan.

At Germanton, at the extreme south-western extremity of the formation, coal has been obtained. The series is not well exposed, but the relations of the beds are as follows:

1. Slate below.
2. Fire-clay.
3. Coal eighteen inches.
4. Slate, one foot.
5. Coal, eighteen inches.
6. Black bituminous slate, five feet.
7. Sandstone and slate.

Semi-bituminous coal was first obtained about four miles from Germanton. Subsequently only two miles. This coal is not pure at the outcrop. Coal is known at several places between Leaksville and Germanton; but no new discoveries have been made since my report was published. The Leaksville seam has been explored deeper; the slope has been sunk about one hundred feet. The seam had increased; the thickness now being from three-and-a-half to four feet. But, as yet, the investigations of these coal seams have not been sufficiently extended to allow us to express a positive opinion of their value. The coal itself is less valuable than upon the Deep River, inasmuch as it ranks only with the anthracite coals. But the exploration on the plantation of Mr. Wade, at or near Leaksville, becomes more favorable; the coal seam having increased in thickness and improved in quality.

When the lower sandstones and conglomerates

of the two rivers are compared, it is evident that the beds below the coal series are less important upon Dan than upon Deep River. In the latter, the lower sandstones, with their conglomerates, are remarkably thick; and we have seen that the conglomerate is very feebly developed upon the Dan at Germanton, and wanting at Madison; and it appears that in Virginia, the lower sandstones, with their conglomerates, are entirely wanting.

The slates of the coal measures of the two districts are probably equal in thickness; but it appears from facts thus far developed, that the coal and the argillaceous iron ores are less in quantity in the Dan River district.

The series above the coal slates, however, are either better exposed, or else are actually thicker. There is no locality where the upper rocks are so well exposed as upon Factory Creek. Of the identity of the two series there can be no doubt. The fossils of the Dan differ in no respect from those of Deep River.

The Coal Deposits.

[Kerr's Report, 1875.]

The principal coal beds are found on Deep River, in Chatham and Moore Counties. The area of this coal field is given by Emmons as about 300 square miles. The quality of the coal is also discussed by him and by Admiral Wilkes.

The following analyses by Dr. Genth were

made for the Survey, of specimens selected by myself three or four years ago from large heaps newly mined.

Fixed Carbon	63.28	70.48
Volatile Matter	25.74	21.90
Ash	10.14	6.46
Moisture	0.84	1.16
	100.00	100.00
Sulphur	1.35	1.02

It will be seen that these are good coals; they contain a very small percentage of sulphur, much less than many of the coals of Ohio and the West, which are largely used in the reduction of iron ores. The former analysis represents the Egypt coal and the latter that at the Gulf, the Gulf specimens being obtained within fifteen feet of the surface.

In regard to the value of the Chatham coal for gas-making, I have received the following testimony from the Messrs. Peters, of Portsmouth, as to the result of a trial in the gas works of Norfolk and Portsmouth, of a lot mined some three years ago: "Their (the Superintendents') reports are highly favorable to the Chatham coal, both as to the quality of the gas produced and the quantity which a given amount of the coal yielded." And Mr. C. S. Allman, President of the Norfolk Gas Works, says: "Our Superintendent thinks it about equal to the best Clover Hill coal, giving off 14 candle gas, $3\frac{3}{4}$ cubic feet per pound. I have no doubt that fresh mined lump would give much better results."

A sample of a thin seam of coal, which was struck last year in Anson county, in Boggan's Cut, gave, on analysis, (by Hanna),

```
Fixed Carbon......................  63.76
Volatile ....  ....................  23.13
Ash............................... 2.47
Moisture..........................  9.95
                                   ------
                                   99.31
Sulphur...........................  0.75
```

The seam exposed in the cut was only two or three inches thick; but it represents the Chatham coal in its continuation southwestward. There have been no explorations here to determine whether larger seams exist.

The lignite bed on Tar River, near Oxford, in Granville County, is the continuation of the Chatham coal formation in the opposite direction. The thickness of the seam is reported about five or six inches; but no explorations have been made to ascertain either its horizontal or vertical extent.

It is worth while to mention here also the *bituminous shales*, which show themselves in so strong force above the coal in the Egypt section. Dr. Emmons estimates the thickness of the oil-bearing strata at seventy feet, and pronounced them capable of yielding thirty per cent. of their weight in kerosene oil. So that here is an inexhaustible resource for fuel, over and above that furnished by the coal seams.

The other coal in the valley of Dan River, is much less known; but it was mined at Leaksville during the late war, and the coal acquired a very high reputation as a fuel. It is semi-bituminous. The thickness of the only seam explored at this point is about three feet. The longitudinal extent of this deposit is as great as that of the Chatham beds, but it is probably narrower. As stated elsewhere, some recent openings by the iron company operating in Guilford, seems to show a succession of parallel beds more numerous and of greater thickness in places than those on Deep River. These explorations were made four years ago, near Stokesburg. Two analyses by Dr. Genth, of samples of different seams opened here gave, respectively, 75.96 and 76.56 per cent. of fixed carbon, 11.44 and 13.56 per cent of ash, the volatile matter being about 12 per cent. in each. The development of these deposits is a matter of sufficient interest to the State to justify an exploration of the whole length of both these coal areas, and the diamond drill offers a ready and cheap means of tracing out the boundaries and ascertaining accurately the depth, thickness, and all the conditions which will determine their value. And I do not think a few thousand dollars could be more profitably expended.

Of the Ores of Iron.

[Emmons's Report, 1856.]

The midland counties are traversed by three parallel belts of magnetic ore, or, in some places, the ore is changed to a variety called specular ore.

Beginning at the western part of the midland counties, the first belt to be described, passes from six to seven miles east of Lincolnton. It is the prolongation of the King's Mountain ore, in Gaston county. It immediately adjoins or belongs to the belt of sediments which has been described as passing near Lincolnton. At Lincolnton, the rock is mostly a coarse light gray micaceous granite. Beds of slate, limestone and quartzite, succeed it on the east; but between this and the gneiss, a little further east, are the veins of magnetic ore. The position of the narrow belt of talcose slate in which the ore occurs, is below or behind the heavy masses of granular quartz. These masses of quartz, as they are continuous from the South Carolina line to the Catawba, are landmarks for the position of the ore. There is no ore above the quartz, and I do not know that there is any in the gneiss represented as below the veins of iron in the section referred to. The careful consideration, therefore, of such relations, is of great importance; they furnish the clue to the actual position of the veins.

The rocks and ore taken in masses stand in this order, beginning our reckoning on the west:

1. Slate. 2. Limestone. 3. Fire Stone. 4. Quartzite. 5. Slate. 6. Magnetic Ore. 7. Ferruginous Slate. 8. Gneiss. 9. Granite.

The quartz being a rock easily distinguished, becomes a guide to the position of the ore.

These ore beds or veins of which I am speaking, are situated six or seven miles eastward of Lincolnton, and upon the north side of the plank road. The limestone is a mile west of the belt of ore.

The ore is usually near the crest of a ridge, and

here it traverses the parallel ridges, which, however, it crosses very obliquely. There is no instance in which the vein runs precisely parallel with a ridge, or follows it; it makes, in this instance, to the east. This fact should not be lost sight of in tracing the veins; they may be exactly upon the crest in one instance, but in the prolongation northward they will be found to have made to the eastward of the same prolonged ridge.

The direction of bearing, as determined by the harder masses of rock, is N. 20° E.—and what is said respecting the bearing of the ore beds to the east, is true also of the rock and strata in which they occur.

Certain peculiarities respecting the veins of magnetic ore of Lincoln County require a notice in this place.

They are of a flattened oval form, that is, a vein is divided into sections, each of which partakes of this form; the thin edge, perhaps, not making an outcrop at all, but is inclosed between strata and slate, which come together at the surface. This thin edge of ore, with its oval mass, lies obliquely in the slate, widening as it descends, until it reaches its maximum width, where it narrows below to its inferior edge. The thickness of the upper mass may be less than twelve inches. This laps on to the west side of another flattened oval mass, which lies behind the first; but in its descent widens to a greater width than the first.

Some of the veins increase in width in this way, where, at the depth of sixty feet, they are six to eight feet wide. In working these veins, it is important to notice this arrangement, and especially the setting back of each oval mass; it invariably begins behind the upper, and against the foot wall.

The ore of the veins under consideration is usually fine grained, or very rarely coarse; it belongs to the variety which is termed soft; that is, it breaks readily, and may be crushed in the hand. This softness arises partly from the mixture of talcose slate, by which the grains are separated from each other, and their coherence diminished. This fact exerts a favorable influence in smelting, as by it the ore is readily reduced to a size for the fire and the fluxes to act readily upon it. It is also very strongly magnetic. The upper part of the veins have generally undergone disintegration, and the mass of ore is frequently in the condition of a slightly coherent red mass, which readily passes into the condition of a powder. On the outside especially this change has taken place, while the interior of a mass may be still occupied by a black unchanged ore, in the condition of grains. These changes are confined to the upper part of the vein, and only extend to that point where it is constantly wet.

These veins of ore in Lincoln County have been worked for a long period, and they have been and still are celebrated for the good quality of the iron which they furnish, especially when reduced with proper care. The iron has been famous for its toughness and great strength, and the facility with which it is made into blooms.

Messrs. Brevard and Johnston are the principle owners of the depositories of ore in this belt. Being in the interior of the State, the only market which this iron finds is a home market: smiths generally obtaining the necessary supply from them. A much wider range of sale may be anticipated, provided Lincoln County becomes connected with Wilmington and the Seaboard, by means of a railway. The ore being inexhaustible, water power to move machinery being abundant, and more than all, a sufficiency of fuel for charcoal, mades the production of iron cheap. By aid of railways to take it to market, there is no question the iron may compete successfully with northern iron in a northern market. Charcoal iron must always have a preference over all others; and, for special purposes, no other can be used. For all uses where machinery is exposed to great strains, no other will do; especially, in those parts of a vehicle which are liable to break, as the axles of locomotives, etc.

The prolongation of the Lincoln County ore appears in the next place not far from the High Shoals of the Little Catawba.

It preserves the same relations to the slate, quartz and limestone, as those veins which have been already described. The character of the ore, however, in certain places, has changed. Near the High Shoals, or upon the property known by this name, there are three locations called banks, from which the ore has been obtained. The first is known as the Ferguson bank. At this place the ore is brown; it has become peroxidated, and has the color of snuff. The unchanged ore is largely intermixed with sulphuret of iron. It is unfit for bar iron, but may be employed for casting along with better ores; in small quantities it makes a smoother casting than the purer ores. When the Ferguson ore is entirely decomposed, it makes a very good iron in the forge.

The Ellis ore bank, is about three miles from the site of Fullenwider's old furnace. It lies in the direction of King's Mountain. It is a black ore, and the vein is eighteen feet wide. Its direction is N. 20° E. It makes good iron and is inexhaustible.

The Carson ore bank is the most easterly of the three. It is the common black magnetic ore, but is remarkably jointed, and hence breaks into distinct angular pieces. This property, or the High Shoal property, is well provided with the means for manufacturing iron; the water power, the ore and fuel for coal is abundant on the premises. It contains 14,000 acres of land, and the southeast part of which is valuable for tillage.

The belt of ore with the same series of rocks continues to King's Mountain, in the vicinity of which iron has been made for more than half a century. One of the principal veins is forty feet thick. The business is carried on by Mr. Briggs, who supplies the country with iron of an excellent quality. The general character of the belt is preserved still further south. It passes into South Carolina, extending to the Limestone Springs, in the Spartanburg district; or to the Broad River, where iron works have been erected.

In addition to the seams of magnetic ore which belong to this very extensive belt, there are beds of hematite near the top of King's Mountain.

Crowder's Mountain also furnishes the peroxide or specular ore near the top, and is said to constitute a vein six or seven feet wide. This I have not visited. It is evident, from the foregoing statements, that this important ore is widely distributed in Catawba, Lincoln and Gaston Counties. There is no probability, however, that the ore has been discovered at all the accessible points. There is but little doubt, that upon this long belt, extending from the Catawba at Sherrill's ford to the Broad River in South Carolina, at the Limestone Springs, other points not yet found will come to light, which will greatly add to the amount already known to exist. There seems, however, to be so much which is now accessible, that the inducements for finding more are not very imperative, even with those who are engaged in its manufacture.

THE SECOND BELT OF IRON ORE IN THE MIDLAND COUNTIES

may be regarded as beginning in Montgomery County. It passes through Randolph County near Franklinsville, thence into Guilford County, and appears again ten miles west of Greensborough, beyond which I have not traced it; and indeed do not know that on this immediate line of direction iron ore veins are known.

The ore is upon the land of Mr. Deberry, and I believe is six or seven miles in a south-west direction from Troy. The country about it is uncultivated, and covered in the immediate vicinity with the long leafed pine.

The relations of the ore to the surrounding rocks, is as follows :

1. Gold or Talcose Slate.
2. Quartzite.
3. Iron Ore.
4. Agalmatolite.
5. Talcose Slate.

The beds are traversed by a narrow bed of hornblende, which, however, is not in a parallel position.

The mass of ore is about fifty feet wide. It occupies a heavy knoll or hill of moderate height. How far the ore extends in the direction of its strike, I did not determine. It may be traced a quarter-of-a-mile, but being concealed by the *debris*, its extent could not be determined without excavations.

At the surface it is silicious; but subordinate seams of pure heavy ore attest to the purity of the mass, as it will be found below.

This ore is a peroxide at the surface. Its strike is N. 30° E., and dip N. W. at a steep angle. It is jointed and breaks into angular pieces. The ore has never been noticed, and of course no trials have been made respecting the mode in which it will work, or the kind of iron it will make; but being free from sulphuret of iron, it is probable that the quality of iron will be such as to recommend it to the favor of iron masters.

About four miles in a northerly direction from Troy, and in a range with the ore just described, another series of veins are known, and which lie in the neighborhood of the Carter gold mine.

This ore is the magnetic variety, and much of it is in minute octahedral crystals. It is very friable, but is intermixed with talcose slate and grains of quartz, which contributes very much to its softness. The beds of ore differ in composition, but still it is no objection to the view which I have taken of them, viz., that they belong to the same epoch. It sometimes happens that a vein of specular ore lies by the side of a magnetic vein, being separated only a few feet.

In this belt or range the iron ore of Davie and

Stokes Counties should probably be placed. At rather distant points the ore of this belt appears in a range so direct, that there is no doubt of its passing entirely across the State. It lies parallel with the limestones and slates; but I am unable to trace these rocks across Catawba and Davie Counties. We lose, after crossing the Catawba, the guides which I have spoken of. There is some doubt too, respecting the age of the limestone at Germanton; that is, it seems to be different from the King's Mountain limestone, and still, if the iron ore is regarded as an eruptive rock, there will be no objection to combining the Davie and Stokes belts with the King's Mountain belt, which passes through Lincoln County. The continuity of the belt is preserved better in the south than in Davie and Stokes. The ore of Davie presents great advantages for working, in consequence of the water power of the South Yadkin; and as most of the iron used in this and the neighboring Counties is brought from Tennessee, it seems that even a home market is an inducement sufficiently great for the establishment of iron works upon the South Yadkin.

About three or four miles south west from Franklinsville, in an uncultivated part of the country, I found heavy black massive magnetic ore in abundance, lying in loose blocks upon the surface. These masses I found in immediate proximity to a vein of magnetic iron, which appears to be of a superior quality. This vein, though not in an exact geological relation with those of Montgomery County, is still removed only a short distance from the quartzite. Its extent has not been determined, and cannot be, without the sinking of pits or uncovering the ore. I feel satisfied that it is extensive; and as it is near Deep River, its importance is enhanced by this circumstance.

Specular ore was discovered near Trogden mountain many years ago. The seam, however, is too inconsiderable to command attention. A shaft was sunk upon it before the present inhabitants settled this part of the country. The brightness of the ore probably deceived some discoverer, who mistook the ore for silver. Old crucibles and furnaces still attest to the unprofitable industry of some expectant of a fortune in the splendid luster of this specular oxide of iron.

Ten miles west of Greensborough, in Guilford County, on a tract of land formerly owned by Mr. Coffin, two or more veins of magnetic iron of great purity were discovered several years ago. It is black and middling coarse, and has all the external characteristics of a most valuable ore. It is unmixed with any substance which injures the quality of iron, and at the same time sufficiently soft to work easily, and make a tough iron. In New York, in the mineral districts where the magnetic ores prevail, it is regarded as an evidence, and in fact a proof, that an ore which crumbles in the hand, or is easily broken, will make a soft iron; while the hard tough ores, with a bright and shining luster, will invariably make a hard iron with less toughness or tenacity; besides it is not reduced so kindly. The dull looking ores are always regarded as the best; those especially which become red upon the surface. The ore which I am describing is a dull looking ore, but very heavy and free from rock.

The veins to which the surface ore belongs have never been uncovered or exposed. The distribution upon the surface indicates at least two distinct parallel veins. The surface masses become what is known as loadstone. They are not only thoroughly magnetic, but have two or more poles, and of course repel or attract the poles of a common surveyor's needle, according as the poles are north or south; north and south poles attracting, and north poles repelling. I may state in this connection, that a successful method of discovering veins of magnetic iron, is by means of a needle mounted like a dipping needle, but with one pole only. It is therefore made one-half of a thin bar of steel, and the other half of brass. On passing over a concealed vein of ore the needle is attracted; and when immediately over the ore, it points downwards. Its course of direction may be traced by the same instrument.

The ore upon the plantation of Mr. Coffin is between Brush Creek and Reedy Fork. It extends north, and appears on the plantation of Mr. Jos. Harris, and onward to Rockingham County to the Troublesome, upon the plantations of John L. Morehead, Esq., where it is in great force; and south, it crops out on the plantations of Mr. Joel Chipman and John Unthank. Thus it appears to form either another belt distinct from those I have mentioned, or a subordinate one. I mention it here as a subordinate one. The ore of Mr. Coffin's mine, even taken from the surface, worked easily, and made an excellent iron, which is remarkable, for surface ore.

THE EASTERN OR CHATHAM BELT

of iron ore is the least regular, as it now appears from my present information. Four or five miles from the Gulf, on the plankroad leading north, or towards Graham, the specular iron ore crops out on a ridge, on land owned in part by Mr. Evans. It is widely and profusely scattered over the surface, but it also appears in a heavy vein of rich ore some six or eight feet wide. This vein is in a talcose slate, and in connection also with a rock which is regarded as soapstone, but which is by no means magnesian; it is properly the figure stone or agalmatolite, and is known at many other places, in connection with the iron ores. This vein I have traced three-quarters of a mile. It has a compact structure and a fine lively grain when freshly broken, and is entirely free from sulphuret of iron.

It will be seen from the foregoing brief statement, that this vein is an important and valuable one, being within a short distance of the Gulf, upon Deep River. The ground is descending to the river, a short distance only over the sandstone can be regarded as hilly. The raising of the ore too, will be attended with less cost than usual, inasmuch as the excavations may be drained for a long time, and will therefore save the expense of pumping by steam power.

Another seam or vein exists in this vicinity on lands owned by Mr. Glass. It is the crystallized specular ore, but I have seen it only upon the surface. Not far distant is the famous locality of hematite, usually known as Ore Hill. It occupies a knob some two or three hundred feet above the surrounding country. The ore lies in belts, which traverse the hill in an easterly and westerly direction. Quartzite forms the pinnacle of the hill, and as usual, is associated with talcose slate. The ore is more immediately associated with the latter rock.

It is from this place that the ore was procured mainly in the time of the revolution. The old excavations are partially filled. The ore is in large concretions or masses, which, in their general arrangement, lie across the hill. It is not, I believe, in one body, as has been supposed by many. The quantity I am unable to estimate; but appearances go to show that it must be large.

Some of the finest ore of this neighborhood I found upon the plantation of Mr. Headen. It is magnetic, and resembles very closely the kind I have already spoken of in Guilford county, on the plantation of the late Mr. Coffin. I have not, however, seen the vein from which the remarkably fine specimens were derived.

Magnetic ore of a fine quality exists also on the plantation of Mr. Temple Unthank. It is two or three miles beyond Mr. Evans' vein, and about three-fourths of a mile from the plankroad. The vein varies in width from one to three feet. From the foregoing statement, it will be perceived that in this part of Chatham County there is a valuable mineral district; furnishing three species of iron ore, the *hematite, magnetic* and *specular*. These are the principal ores from which iron is obtained. These repositories also contain ore of great purity, differing from each other, however, in richness and other qualities; a fact of considerable importance in the manufacture of iron. It is by a combination of different ores, possessing different qualities, that the manufacture of this metal is facilitated, and by which one possessing the most desirable qualities is obtained. I shall have occasion, however, further on, to add two kinds of ore to the foregoing list; that of the hydrated oxide, mixed with carbonate and the celebrated ore called the black band, which belongs to the coal formation of Deep River. It is this first from which Pennsylvania manufactures her iron principally, though not entirely. Her iron masters also use the magnetic ores. The two kinds are mixed. Experience proves the value of the method. But who would suppose that iron masters, in order to obtain the results they seek for, could afford to transport the magnetic ore from Essex County, in northern New York, to Pittsburg? And yet thousands of tons are annually sent there for this purpose.

Chatham County, however, can furnish within the radius of seven or eight miles, five kinds of ore in abundance. It appears that the ore of this coal field, though less in extent than that of the true carboniferous in Pennsylvania; yet, there has been deposited in this formation, iron ores on as large a scale as in the true carboniferous. Many are slow to believe it, but I do not see any way to avoid the conclusion, seeing that an outcrop of it may be traced thirty miles. These beds, too, have been cut in the great shaft at Egypt, a thousand feet or more within the outcrop. But this is not the place to enter into a statement of details concerning this great deposit of iron ore. I shall give all the facts respecting it, when this formation comes up in its proper place for consideration.

But, one word more respecting facilities for

THE MANUFACTURE OF IRON

upon Deep River. It has been supposed that Pennsylvania must enjoy a monopoly in the manufacture of this indispensable metal, in consequence of the extent of her possessions, and the vast amount of anthracite which she can employ. Of the extent of her resources in this respect no one can doubt. She can make iron cheaply by her anthracite, but no cheaper than it can be made on Deep River by bituminous coal or coke; and coke-made iron will be as good as that made by charcoal, in consequence of the purity of the bituminous coal on Deep River. And in the manufacture of coke, I believe, products of distillation may be obtained which will more than pay the cost of making the coke. But this is a matter to be tried, and does not properly come in for consideration now. What I wish to say is, that in the coal of Deep River, the manufacturer has all the material he can want for this purpose; and if a better article of iron can be made from coke than by anthracite, then, in a district of equal extent, North Carolina has advantages over Pennsylvania, for the manufacture of iron. In proof of this, I repeat that she has: 1st. The peculiar ore of the coal fields; 2d. The magnetic, specular and hematitic ores of the primary and paleozoic rocks in immediate proximity; 3d. The use of coke by which to make the iron; 4th. A fine agricultural region for the cereals, and 5th. A milder climate and rivers both for moving machinery and transportation, which is unobstructed in the winter. The cost of living, and the means for conducting the business, will be much cheaper. These advantages are too obvious to require comment or further explanation.

Iron ore may exist in districts where it can be of little value only; there may be a destitution of fuel, or a want of water-power, though with respect to the latter, it can be dispensed with when there is an abundance of the former.

In the first belt described, that which belongs to the King's Mountain belt, there is yet timber and wood for a supply for many years, I know not how many. The country is yet thinly settled, although it was cultivated before the day of the famous battle of King's Mountain. Oaks, chestnut, pine and hickory yet cover the ridges and plane-grounds of the Great and Little Catawbas. The water-courses furnish all the power required for moving machinery. It is strictly a district created for manufacturing purposes, supplying in itself all that is wanted to conduct the various manipulations required in creating what may be termed the raw materials for the arts.

The second belt, that which begins in Montgomery County, and passes through Randolph and onwards in a north-eastwardly direction, is also supplied with timber and wood, and water-power. The forests of the long-leaved pine, still untouched by the boxing-ax and scraper of the turpentine merchant, are certainly the finest in this or any other State. The hills of Randolph are still clothed with trees.

The third belt, that which belongs to Chatham County, but which also passes into Orange in the direction of Red Mountain, to which the belt of iron ore is prolonged, has its forests of long-leaved pine, as well as its oaks, ash and hickory timbers. Rocky River, Deep River, Haw and New Hope, furnish all the mechanical power required for moving machinery.

It is evident, therefore, after a careful examination of the premises in each belt, or district, that there is not lacking any thing which is necessary for the successful prosecution of the iron business, except capital. The great highways are being opened to market, and I see no reason why capitalists may not now step in and reap the harvests.

Carbonate of Iron, or Steel Ore.—The localities of this mineral are rather numerous in North Carolina. It is not yet determined, however, whether they possess any value as iron ore, for the production of iron. That it is frequently valuable as a flux for smelting copper is conceded, or has been proved by trial. The drawback upon this species of ore, for the production of iron or steel, lies in the presence of copper pyrites. It is not in beds, but an associate of other metals or ores, and is their vein stone, and hence is more or less intermixed with them. But in parts of several mines, as the North Carolina copper mine, the copper is absent, and it is only intermixed with quartz.

In the vicinity of Gen. Gray's, upon the head waters of the Uwharrie, carbonate of iron is a very common substance. Upon the plantation of Mr. Johnson, a vein composed mainly of this substance has been exposed, by sinking two or three shafts, for the purpose of testing it for gold. This vein is pure enough for making iron. It carries gold in its quartz, but the quantity of the sulphurets is inconsiderable. I observed it at several places in this district. It is not, however, expected that this ore will be used by itself in the manufacture of iron. But where it exists in the vicinity of other ores, it will form an excellent addition as a flux, while it will also control the quantity of reduced iron, in the ultimate result.

Recapitulation of the leading facts respecting the Ores of Iron.—1. The ores of iron, although they do not make an extraordinary show upon the surface, yet, it will be seen from the foregoing statements, that they constitute an important source of wealth.

2. These ores embrace those which are known to be the most important ones for the production of iron, and embrace the brown oxides, or hematites, the specular and magnetic, or black oxide of iron.

3. They are distributed in the midland counties in belts, and though it cannot be shown that they form continuous masses or veins, still they lie in certain ranges, through which they may be traced, and upon which they appear at the surface at intervals.

4. They belong to both series of rocks, the pyrocrystalline and sedimentary; in both they occur in veins, which, of course, proves that they belong to a later period than that to which the rock itself belongs.

5. Those veins which belong to the sediments appear to hold a fixed relation to the quartzite or sandstone near the base of the Taconic system, being, so far as yet known, behind or beneath it, in slates which may be termed the bottom rocks of the sediments.

6. The hematites accompany, in several instances at least, the quartz rock already referred to; and they bear the marks of having been derived from pre-existing ores.

7. Experience has proved that the magnetic ores make a superior iron. The specular has not been tested in the furnace or forge, but their purity is a sufficient guarantee of their value.

The Ores of Iron.

[Kerr's Report, 1875.]

The ores of iron are very widely distributed in this State, their occurrence being not only co-extensive with the area of the Archæan (or Azoic) rocks, but extending over a part of the Mesozoic, and even into the Quaternary. And these occurrences include all the principal kinds of ore, Magnetite, Hematite, Limonite and Siderite, and most of their varieties and modifications. But as many of these forms occur in association or close proximity, it will avoid confusion to consider them by districts,—to group them geographically. We begin with the most easterly occurrences. But for the benefit of those who are not familiar with the mineralogy of the subject, and who may not have access to authorities, it may be worth while to state that Magnetite, (*magnetic iron ore, gray ore, black ore,*) a granular, hard, dark to black, heavy mineral, contains, when pure, 72.4 per cent. of iron; Hematite, (*specular iron, red hematite, red iron ore,*) 70 per cent.; Limonite, (*brown hematite, brown iron ore, brown ochre, bog iron ore, etc.,*) very nearly 60 per cent.; Siderite, (*spathic ore, carbonate of iron,*) 48.28 per cent. These ores are never found in a state of purity in workable beds, but contain various impurities, earthy or rocky, in different proportions,—alumina, silica, lime, magnesia, manganese, etc.; so that practically that is considered a good ore which yields 40 to 50 per cent. of iron in the furnace.

Limonite Ores of the East.—The clayey, sandy and earthy accumulations of the eastern section, which have been previously described as Quaternary, contain in many places a rough brown ore, more or less earthy, or sandy, either in beds 2 to 3, or 4 feet in thickness, or more frequently in sheets, or layers of irregularly shaped lumps or nodules. One of the most considerable of these deposits occurs in the southern end of Nash County near the Wilson line. It is in the form of a horizontal, continuous bed, of a loose, spongy texture and rusty brown color, except in a few points, where it becomes more compact and of a submetallic lustre. It lies on the margin of Toisnot Swamp. The thickness is 2 to 3 feet, and its extent horizontally about 50 yards by 150. It is known as the Blomary Iron Mine, from the fact that iron had been made from this ore in a Catalan forge, a few miles south, during the war of 1812. Iron was also made here during the Confederate war in a furnace erected on the spot. Mr. W. H. Tappey, one of the proprietors, informed me that "the iron made was of excellent quality, soft and very strong." And there is a tradition in the neighborhood that the forge iron, previously referred to, was a sort of natural steel. The following is the analysis of what appeared to be a fair sample of the bed, selected lately:

Silica,	15.06
Alumina,	0.55
Sesquioxide of Iron,	60.74
Protoxide of Iron,	0.24
Sulphide of Iron,	0.06
Oxide of Manganese,	1.56
Lime,	11.43

Magnesia,	1.54
Sulphuric Acid,	0.03
Phosphoric Acid,	0.11
Organic Matter and Water,	15.58

Which gives Iron 42.73 per cent. This analysis places the ore among the best of its class.

A second deposit, reported to be abundant in superficial nodules and irregular lumps, is found in the southern part of Duplin County near Wallace, on the farm of D. T. Boney. The following is a partial analysis of an average specimen from a box of about 50 pounds sent to the Museum:

Silica,	7.59
Oxide of Iron,	77.03
Sulphur,	0.05
Phosphorus,	0.02; giving
Metallic Iron,	53.93

The ore is often in quite large and tolerably compact lumps, of a reddish-brown color, and slightly magnetic.

Another bed of the same character and appearance, except in the size of the nodules, which are rather small, occurs in a field about 2 miles north of Rocky Point in New Hanover.

Specimens of the same sort have been frequently sent to the Museum from other points east,—Edgecombe, Pitt, Halifax and Robeson, for example; showing that this kind of ore is of common occurrence in that region.

Hematites of Halifax and Granville.—On the hills fronting the Roanoke, less than a mile below Gaston, are several outcrops of hematite ore. There are two principal beds, of which the lower only has been opened. The ore is granular, for the most part, and of the variety known as specular, but contains a considerable percentage of magnetic grains disseminated through it. On the south side of the river, the bed has been exposed for several rods on the upper slope of the hill, at an elevation of about 100 to 150 feet above the surface of the water. The ore is generally slaty, impregnating and replacing the argillaceous and quartzitic and chloritic strata which constitute the Huronian formation at the locality. This lower bed is double, another parallel outcrop appearing at the distance of about 100 yards. The strike is N. 20° E., and the dip eastward 80°. The principal bed is about 20 inches thick at the surface. There is a re-appearance of it on the other hill front about a mile distant, on the north side of the river, the ore being of the same character, but a little less slaty. It gave on analysis 63.76 per cent. of Iron, and 0.09 of phosphorus.

The analyses of both these beds are added below:

	3	4
Silica,	9.10	10.12
Alumina,	6.18	
Oxide of Iron,	83.96	
Lime,	0.22	
Phosphorus,	0.00	0.05
Sulphur,	0.03	0.08
Metallic Iron,	58.73	53.31

The upper bed, last described, is represented by No. 3, the lower by No. 4. About 5 miles southward from the above locality the same bed makes its appearance on the farm of Mr. Hines; here, however, it is highly magnetic, fine grained and dense, although still showing the decidedly slaty structure of the first of the Gaston beds. At this point it is reported as 3 to 4 feet thick.

These ores are of conspicuous purity and obviously adapted to the manufacture of the higher grades of iron and of steel. And there is evidently a range of ore-beds here of considerable extent.

In Granville County, about a mile north of Tar River, and the same distance eastward from Fishing Creek, is an outcrop of a coarse, granular, somewhat slaty magnetic ore, having very much the appearance of that of the upper bed at Gaston. The rock is a feldspathic talco-quartzitic and chloro-quartzitic slate. This bed is revealed only by the numerous fragments scattered over the surface through the forest for several rods along the roadside. This ore is in a small triangular patch of Huronian slates, intercalated between the older rocks of the region. It is reported that there are other outcrops of iron ore near Rainey's Mill, and also in the neighborhood of Lyon's Mill, but I have not seen either of them.

Iron Ores of Johnston and Wake.—There is, according to Dr. Emmons, "a large deposit" of limonite four miles west of Smithfield; the specimens brought to the museum by Mr. Guest, owner of the land, resemble very closely the bog ore of Duplin; they are more or less sandy and earthy, irregular lumps, or nodules.

Another "bluff" of limonite is referred to by Emmons as found at Whitaker's, seven miles southwest of Raleigh, in Wake County. These last two are in the Huronian slates. And hand specimens of very coarsely crystalline magnetite of ten to fifteen pounds weight, associated with syenite, are found within a mile of Raleigh; and compact hematite also occurs in veins in the same vicinity. These and other specimens of these species and of limonite are from different parts of the County, and are from the surface, as no openings have been made; but they indicate the very common occurrence of this mineral.

Iron Ores of Chatham and Orange.—One of the best known and most important iron mines of this region is on the borders of Harnett, the *Buckhorn Mine*. It is about seven miles below the forks of the Cape Fear, on a hill nearly 200 feet high, overlooking the river from the left bank. The ore occurs as a bed, capping the hill and sloping from the river, with a dip of 20° to 25° towards the northwest. It is massive at the outcrop, and breaks out in large angular blocks. The lower portion of the bed, which contains much manganese and less iron in proportion, is of a mottled gray and dull reddish color at the summit, and at the distance of two or three hundred yards along the slope, is a light colored and gray and spotted (black and dirty white,) ferriferous, manganesian slate. Occasional sheets of laminated black oxide of manganese occur, one or two inches in thickness. Some parts of the bed are slightly magnetic. The thickness is about 36 feet at the outcrop, and diminishes to 20 at the lower quarries, 200 to 300 yards distant.

The ore is properly described as specular; it is of a dull, dark gray to blackish color, subcrystalline structure, and uneven fracture. The streak is dark red. Occasional fragments of the ore show a tendency to lamination, and in such cases the divisional planes are commonly coated with mica crystals. The character of this ore is very like that of the Iron Mountain, Mo., and its extent and mode of occurrence strongly suggest the Pilot Knob. It is at least equal to either of these notable iron ore deposits in quantity, and is equally pure, and has the advantage of both in the presence of large percentages of manganese, and the capacity to produce *spiegeleisen* without admixture of other ores. It is not difficult to foresee that this must speedily become the nucleus of a large iron manufacturing interest ; especially when the remarkable facilities for manufacturing, in the way of water power, (heretofore noted,) and the proximity of coal in abundance, are taken into account.

The rocks of this region are slaty, gray gneiss and mica slate, with occasional patches of massive light gray granite.

The rock which underlies the ore is a light-colored, feldspathic slaty gneiss, which readily decomposes. The neighboring hills, at the distance of half a mile, both north and south, are reported to show many scattered fragments of the same ore on the surface ; and on the right bank of the river, on nearly the same level with the Buckhorn Mine, at the distance of about one mile southwest, is the *Douglass Mine*. This is a recurrence of the Buckhorn bed, on the scale and with the features of its lower exposures, being more schistose in structure, some of the strata being in fact simply gneiss and mica slate, with disseminated grains and laminæ of hematite (and magnetite), and the lower strata passing into a slaty manganesian silicate. The thickness, not very well exposed, seems to be ten to twelve feet. Angular fragments of dark, dense, granular ore, with a black, manganese stain, are scattered over several acres of the hill top, indicating a wide extension of the bed. From the facts stated, it will be apparent that these different beds are mere remnant fragments of an ancient and very extensive deposit which has been almost entirely removed by denudation, and carried away by the erosive action of the river.

About one mile north of the Buckhorn Mine is a small vein about one foot thick, of a highly magnetic ore. Its strike is N. 60° and dip eastward 30°. The gangue is an epidotic quartzite. There are two openings on the vein, called the Pegram Mine. An analysis of this ore for the owners by Mr. C. E. Buck, gave 56.57 per cent. of iron and 1.51 of titanic acid. This group of mines is worked by the American Iron and Steel Company, who have erected a charcoal furnace, the first of eight proposed, at the Buckhorn Locks, nearly two miles above the ore bank. They have already expended upwards of $300,000 in opening the navigation of the river for a distance of some forty miles above the ore bank, through the coal deposits, and they have also repaired the Endor furnace and put it in blast, and have been making a very superior car-wheel iron. The product is mostly a spiegeleisen, of which the following partial analyses by Mr. Lobdell, will show the peculiarities:

	5	6	7
Manganese	4.573	6.50	4.88
Silicon	0.233	0.14	0.38
Sulphur	0.015	0.009	
Phosphorus	0.051	0.12	0.095

The copy of these analyses was accompanied by the remark, "The above samples were made while the furnace was running on ordinary iron, no attempt having been made to produce spiegeleisen. The phosphorus and sulphur were reduced from the fluxes employed, as the Buckhorn ore used contained only very slight traces of these impurities."

The origin of this peculiar and valuable product, which was altogether accidental, will be apparent on the inspection of the analyses given below. These were made for the company in the course of their operations, by G. G. Lobdell, of the firm, and C. E. Buck, of Wilmington, Del., and by the Chemist of the Pennsylvania Steel Company.

	8	9	10	11	12
Silica	14.45	5.65	12.80	30.50	7.50
Alumina		0.80	5.20	19.20	8.49
Oxide of Manganese		trace		22.80	7.52
Phosphorus	trace		trace	0.02	0 04
Sulphur	0.06		trace	0.03	0.02
Iron	56.70	66.50	54.15	18.41	55.00

Of these, Nos. 8, 9 and 10 are from the upper and main portion of the Buckhorn bed, and No. 11 from the lower manganesian section. This last analysis suggests the presence, in this part of the bed, of the mineral knebelite, a characteristic ore of the most famous Swedish spiegeleisen mines. No. 12 is the Douglass ore, on the other side of the river.

Besides the localities already mentioned, a number of additional outcrops of ore have been noted, mostly magnetic; one for example, two miles north of Buckhorn, (at Dewar's) yielding 57.77 per cent. of iron, (no phosphorus or sulphur), and three or four others in a southwest direction, for ten miles, to the head waters of Little River,—at McNeill's, Dalrymple's and Buchanan's; analyses as follows, respectively:

Iron	52.90	36.47	53.25
Sulphur	0.05	0.05	0.04
Phosphorus	0.12	0.11	0.57

Near Haywood, in the angle formed by the junction of the Haw and Deep rivers, in the red sandstone of the Triassic, there has been opened a series of parallel beds of a red-ochreous earthy ore, on the lands of Dr. Smith. The only bed exposed at the time of my visit, was 20 to 25 inches thick, dipping southeast with the sandstone, 20° to 30°. The ore has a rough likeness to the "Clinton" or "Fossil ore" of New York, etc., and the "Dystone" of Tennessee, but has a much coarser and more irregular texture, and is composed of rounded concretionary masses of various sizes from that of the Clinton grains to $\frac{1}{2}$ and $\frac{3}{4}$ inch and upward. It is commonly more or less compacted into conglomeritic masses, often of the entire thickness of the bed, but frequently it is loosely and slightly compacted, and when thrown out, crumbles to a heap of very coarse gravel. The ore is partly limonite, but seems to be largely changed to red hematite. The following analyses of samples taken from different parts of the beds, whose outcrops extend over an area of several acres, will exhibit the character of the ore:

	13	14
Silica...		23.50
Alumina...		2.54
Sesquioxide of Iron...	69.73	67.50
Protoxide of Iron...	0.84	
Bisulphide of Iron...	0.17	
Phosphoric Acid...	0.10	
Lime...		0.90
Magnesia...		0.24
Water and loss...		5.03; giving
Iron...	49.56	47.25

The second of these analyses represents the ore as it occurs on the lands of Mr. Richard Smith, adjoining the preceding. This ore makes its appearance again about a mile from Sanford, some 12 miles distant, where it was opened and worked to some extent during the late war. Only one bed was exposed here, which is about 20 inches thick. The ore is easily dug and shoveled from the bed and crumbles into a heap of very coarse, reddish-brown gravel, a rough sort of *shot ore.* The preceding analyses will nearly enough represent the composition of this also.

The next ores demanding attention are the *Black Band* and *Ball ore*, or "kidney ore" of the coal measure. These are earthy and calcareous carbonates of iron, imbedded in the black carbonaceous shales which enclose the coal, or interstratified with the coal itself. These ores seem to be co-extensive with the coal on Deep River, outcropping every where with it, and at several places outside of its limits. Two seams are shown in the sections, and there is a third in the bottom shales, not penetrated at the Gulf, but shown in the Egypt section, as accompanying the lower coal, 30 feet below the main seam.

Emmons also speaks of another seam of argillaceous carbonate as occurring at the depth of 230 feet in the shaft at Egypt, and four occurrences of it are indicated as ball ore in the Egypt section. Emmons says of this argillaceous carbonate, "It contains 33 per cent. of metallic iron; the surface ores being altered contain 50 per cent.," and he describes it as occurring "in balls, or in continuous beds." About the Gulf it occurs in rounded flattish masses, 5 or 6 to 8 or 10 inches in diameter. They are dense, uncrystalline and heavy, of a light gray to drab color, and are pretty thickly distributed in parallel layers of one to two or three feet thickness. An analysis by Prof. Schæffer, as given in Admiral Wilkes' report to the Secretary of the Navy in 1858, is as follows: protoxide of iron 40 per cent., silica 13, earthy matter 13, carbonaceous matter 34. This is evidently a black band ore. The following is an analysis (by Buck) of the ball ore proper, as it occurs at the Gulf, and such as was used extensively and successfully as a flux during the late war:

	15
Silica	6.04
Alumina	0.48
Protoxide of Iron	14.51
Sesquioxide of Iron	1.63
Lime	29.57
Magnesia	6.51
Carbonic Acid	38.30
Phosphoric Acid	0.92
Sulphuric Acid	0.19
Organic Matter	1.45
Water	0.40

Which gives 52.80 per cent. of carbonate of lime, and 13.60 of carbonate of magnesia. Its adaptation to the purposes of a flux is obvious.

There are many outcrops of ferriferous limestone in the neighborhood of Egypt (and the Endor furnace), among others this, near Dowd's Saw Mill:

Lime,	31.68
Magnesia,	0.79
Sesquioxide of Iron,	9.60; no sulphur or phosphorus.

But oyster shells from the Tertiary bluffs below Fayetteville, and limestone from the Eocene beds about Wilmington, have been also used as fluxes in the furnaces of the region, and on account of their greater purity and abundance, and their ready accessibility and cheap transportation, will doubtless become the chief resource for fluxing.

The seam of *black band* between the main coal beds in the Egypt shaft, is stated by Wilkes to be 16 inches, the lower one to consist of two thicknesses of 3 feet each, separated by a thin seam of coal between. He adds, "This ore is readily distinguished from a slate by its brownish black color." The analysis of this ore by Dr. Jackson, published in Emmons' report, gives:

Carbon,	31.30
Peroxide of Iron (Protoxide?),	47.50
Silica,	9.00
Volatile Matter,	8.81
Sulphur,	3.39

Emmons adds, "The roasted ore gives sulphur 0.89 per cent." An analysis by Schæffer for Wilkes, gives only 17 per cent. of iron, and 42 of carbonaceous matter; specific gravity 2.12.

The following analyses of samples selected from a recent opening at the Gulf, have been just completed for the survey by Mr. Hanna:

	16	17	18	19
Specific Gravity,	2.361	3.150	2.110	2.110
Silica,	9.154	7.089	34.380	5.188
Alumina,	4.244	0.127	19.638	4.060
Protoxide of Iron,	19.419	33.802	12.361	9.614
Sesquioxide of Iron,	0.000	1.755	1.430	0.938
Sulphide of Iron,	10.485	2.145	2.023	7.146
Oxide of Manganese,	1.750	1.980	0.995	1.500
Lime,	9.520	12.672	3.100	14.040
Magnesia,	1.490	1.170	1.220	0.863
Alkalies,	0.000	0.000	0.000	0.000
Sulphuric Acid,	trace	0.170	trace	0.152
Phosphoric Acid,	4.960	6.820	0.730	6.300
Volatile Matter,	22.065	27.215	14.913	15.009
Carbon,	16.213	4.726	6.562	34.473
Water,	0.700	0.300	2.588	0.717
	100.000	00.000	100.000	100.000
Ash, or Roasted Ore,	60.475	72.070	76.902	48.571

Of which the composition is as follows:

	20	21	22	23
Silica,	15.137	9.849	44.740	10.684
Alumina,	7.018	0.178	25.527	8.359
Sesquioxide of Iron,	46.360	56.562	20.922	33.252
Sulphide of Iron,	0.909	0.000	0.788	0.530
Oxide of Manganese,	2.895	2.749	1.294	3.089
Lime,	15.742	17.585	4.108	28.914
Magnesia,	2.464	1.624	1.587	1.777
Sulphuric Acid,	1.273	1.989	0.085	0.421
Phosphoric Acid,	8.202	9.464	0.949	12.974
	100.000	100.000	100.000	100.000
Which give:				
Metallic Iron,	33.032	39.593	14.645	23.619
Sulphur,	0.839	0.800	0.319	.360
Phosphorus,	3.581	4.131	0.474	5.664

The quantity of phosphorus which these beds contain is very notable, and is, of course, due to their highly fossiliferous character. And yet not only were there no fossil bones visible, as in the Egypt beds, but no identifiable organisms of any description, not even a shell. Of course the high percentage of this element excludes these ores from the manufacture of wrought iron. They must await the perfecting of the new industry of "phosphorus steel;" or the discovery of a practicable method for the elimination of this injurious ingredient. With this exception these ores are well constituted, containing the necessary amount of carbon, of flux and of manganese, for the manufacture of iron very cheaply, by judicious mixing of the ores obtainable in the immediate neighborhood. It is not probable that this phosphatic fossiliferous character will follow the ore-beds and appear at the other outcrops in the same force; it is a character likely to be local. An investigation of these beds at other points is therefore very important and will be instituted as soon as practicable. Such ores are, however, valuable for casting. Outside of the line of outcrops of the coal, and within a few rods of it, is a bed of limonite belonging to the underlaying shales. The thickness is 2 to 3 feet, and it is traceable for a considerable distance along the surface. Probably it is the result of the weathering of some of the argillaceous carbonates already described. And a similar outcrop has been noticed, and the bed partly stripped, at a point $1\frac{1}{2}$ miles southeast of Egypt, on Pretty Creek, known as the McIver ore-bed. It is 20 inches thick. This is a very slaty and somewhat shaly limonite, with occasional masses of ore of considerable size, and is embedded in shales. It is obviously the result of the oxidation of one of the black-band or argillaceous carbonate seams already described, but it is in the forest, and its exact geological relations are concealed, as well by vegetation as by overlying earth. An analysis of a sample of this ore, by Buck, for the Company above refered to, gives the following result:

              Metallic Iron,.................. 47.59
              Sulphur,........................ 0.14
              Phosphorus, ... 0.94

The Evans vein is about 6 miles north of the Gulf, on the Graham road. It is 6 feet thick. This ore is a hematite, non-crystalline, scarcely sub-metallic, hardness 6 to $6\frac{1}{2}$, jaspery, non-magnetic, dark gray to bluish black, streak dark-red, fracture sub-conchoidal. The country is (Huronian) talcoid and chloritic argillite, which is a sort of spotted slate conglomerate, in the hill a few hundred yards beyond. Wilkes gives the following analysis, (by Schæffer):

Peroxide of Iron,	96.4
Silica,	2.1
Earthy Matter,	1.5

The ore is scattered abundantly in fragments over the surface of several acres. Emmons traced the vein three quarters of a mile. He speaks also of another vein of hematite (specular, crystalline,) on the neighboring farm of Mr. Glass, which was revealed only by surface fragments; and also of "a magnetic ore of fine quality on the plantation of T. Unthank, two or three miles beyond the Evans place;" and another of the same class at Headen's, near Ore Hill. Another locality is noted by both Emmons and Wilkes as containing a bed of reddish-brown ore, which is magnetic. It is represented as 2½ feet thick at the Tysor place, and as occurring at various other points. The analysis quoted by Wilkes from Emmons, gives:

Peroxide of Iron,	79.72
Carbon,	7.37
Silica,	4.00
Water,	8.80; containing
Iron,	61.

But the most noted iron locality in Chatham County is known as *Ore Hill*. The rock is a talco-quartzose slate, knotted and toughened with much tremolite. The ore is limonite, with the exception of one vein near the top and back of the hill, which is a hematite, (in part specular), and much resembling the Evans ore. There is much of this ore on the surface in scattered fragments, indicating a vein of considerable extent, which, however, had not been exposed. Most of the other veins have been opened, but the pits and tunnels were so much filled and fallen in that no accurate measurements could be taken at the time of my visit last year. But it was easy to see that two or three of them were very large,—10, 15 feet and upwards. The ore is very spongy, porous, scoriaceous, botryoidal, mammillary, stalactitic, tabular, foliated, dendritic, and of many fantastic and nondescript forms. The workmen state that there are large cavities (vuggs) in some parts of the veins.

The analyses below are of samples from the 90 feet shaft, nearest the hematite vein, and may be considered as fairly representative:

	24	25
Silica	1.42	3.79
Alumina		
Sesquioxide of Iron	82.02	83.69
Protoxide " "		0.11
Lime	1.19	
Magnesia	0.11	
Phosphoric Acid	0.00	trace
Sulphuric Acid	0.00	0.77
Water	15.26	
	100.00	
Metallic Iron	57.41	58.67

The first of these analyses was made by Chatard, for Dr. Genth, the second by Mr. Hanna. This ore was worked on a considerable scale during the American Revolution, and again during the late civil war, and the iron is reported to have been of good quality; and it is obviously an ore very readily smelted. The presence of the hematite vein and the proximity of the ball ore, which was successfully used as a flux in the last working of the furnace, furnish admirable conditions for advantageous iron manufacture. And it is gratifying to be able to state that there is a prospect of the immediate development of the property by the Philadelphia and Canadian capitalists who have lately come into possession.

Besides the ores above described, there are many others, of which specimens have been brought or forwarded to the Museum, from various parts of the County and region, magnetite, hematite and limonite, representing veins and deposits of whose extent I have no information. It is worth while to mention two of such specimens, one from Chatham, (between Lockville and Endor), and the other from the adjoining County of Moore, Governor's Creek, as they are almost the only examples of the species of ore called *jaspery clay iron stone* yet found in the State. The former contains 48.92 per cent. of iron, phosphorus 0.39.

A fine quality of magnetic ore, dense, metallic and very pure, is found on the east side of Haw River and about 2 miles distant, at the foot of Tyrrell's Mountain, on the farm of Mr. Snipes. The vein has not been fully exposed, but is reported to be 3 or 4 feet. It is in syenite, and has an epidotic gangue.

The analysis (made by Lobdell) is as follows:

Silica.	1.62
Alumina.	6.60
Magnetic Oxide of Iron.	88.41
Manganese.	0.56
Lime.	trace
Magnesia.	0.85
Phosphoric Acid.	0.00
Sulphur.	0.13
Metallic Iron.	63.49

A very fine micaceous hematite is found near

the mouth of Collins' Creek, a few miles above, in Orange County. It has not been explored, but surface fragments are reported to be abundant.

But the most notable ore bank yet opened in this County, is that at Chapel Hill. It is a very dense, steel-gray, hematite, (specular in part), with slight magnetic indications. The vein is found on a hill one mile north from Chapel Hill, and more than 200 feet above the creek at its base. The rock is a gray granite and syenite, but the vein is carried by a much-jointed, fine grained, ferruginous, slaty quartzite of several rods' breadth, the iron-bearing portion of it, the vein proper, being 7 to 10 feet at the main shaft, and suddenly enlarging near the summit of the hill, just beyond the second shaft, to 25 and 30 feet. The hill top is covered with angular fragments of the ore of all sizes, up to more than 100 pounds weight.

The character of the ore is shown by the following analysis:

	26
Silica	2.63
Alumina	1.68
Protoxide of Iron	2.45
Sesquioxide "	91.24
Oxide of Manganese	0.34
Lime	0.56
Magnesia	0.00
Phosphoric Acid	0.04
Sulphur	0.11
	99.05
Iron	65.77

The ore is of notable purity, and the practical tests to which it has been subjected have confirmed the indications of the analysis, that it is an ore of high grade; and the quantity is very great. The vein has a dip to the west at an angle which is a little short of 90°. A second vein of the same character, 5 or 6 feet thick, crosses the main vein near the first shaft. The ore becomes poorer as the vein is followed beyond the summit of the hill northward, until at the distance of 150 yards beyond the upper shaft, the quartzite predominates and the ore becomes poor.

There are surface indications on the neighboring hills, both north and south, for several miles, which show that this vein has a considerable extension; and in fact it may be considered as a continuation of the hematite veins of Deep River. And a magnetic ore makes its appearance about 20 miles northeastward, 3 miles beyond the upper forks of the Neuse River, in the southeast corner of Orange County, on Knapp of Reed's Creek, on the farm of Mr. Jos. Woods. The rock here is clay slate, more or less chloritic and quartzitic, and thin bedded. The ore is slaty, and is in fact an impregnation of the chloritic argillaceous quartzite with granular magnetite and hematite. The ore is very extensively scattered over a succession of hills, for about a mile, in a northeast direction. The ore bed outcrops at one point for a few rods, where it appears to be about 3 feet thick, and has a strike N. 40° E., and dips at an angle of 70° to the northwest. The bed seems to be duplicated towards the northeastern termination, another line of fragments marking the course of a parallel vein several rods to the east of the former. This last is associated with a bright vermilion red, and a banded, black and red jasper. The ore is of good quality, as will be seen by the following analysis by Dr. Genth:

	27
Silica	20.38
Magnetic Oxide of Iron	75.69
Magnesia	1.26
Phosphoric Acid	0.05
Water, &c	2.62
Metallic Iron	54.81

; which gives

An analysis of another sample (by a different chemist), gave iron 56.50.

Hand specimens of very fine magnetite and specular ore have been brought to the Museum from many other parts of Orange County, but no information has been received as to their quantity.

At Mt. Tirzah, in the southeast corner of Person, near the Orange line, there is a vein of hematite, (specular) from which iron was made to some extent during the war. The vein is described as about 6 feet thick. The specimen sent to the Museum indicates a very fine ore, resembling that at Buckhorn.

The ores of Montgomery and Randolph belong properly (geologically) to the Chatham range; they are found in the same great slate belt (Huronian), that constitutes the most notable feature of the middle region of the State, both geologically and mineralogically. The best known of these ores is found near Franklinsville, Randolph County. And another vein has been opened near Ashboro, both of specular hematite. Some of the strongest and most highly prized iron obtained during the war came from this locality. It was all devoted to the manufacture of shafts and other machinery for the Steam Rams (ironclads) and the like. Dr. Emmons describes an occurrence of hematite of apparently considerable extent 7 miles southwest of Troy, in Montgomery County; he says it is free from sulphur and a very pure ore. Another occurrence of ore,—magnetite, is noted by him 4 miles north of Troy. It is found with talcose slate, and is soft and friable, and contains seams of hematite.

Iron Ores of Guilford County. One of the most remarkable and persistent ranges of iron ore in the State crosses the County of Guilford in a northeast and southwest direction, passing about 10 miles northwest of Greensboro, near Friendship. It extends from the head waters of Abbott's Creek, in Davidson County, entirely across Guilford to Haw River, in Rockingham, a distance of some 30 miles, making its appearance on nearly every plantation, and indeed almost every hillside in the range.

The ore is granular magnetite, and is everywhere titaniferous. It is usually rather coarse grained and frequently associated with crystals of chlorite in small seams and scattered bunches. The ore is in the form of beds, which partake of all the foldings and fractures and irregularities of bedding to be expected in a region where only the oldest metamorphic rocks are found. The deposits lie along, and just west of the line of junction of what is provisionally set down as the lower and upper Laurentian series of granitic rocks. There is a second, but much more interrupted range of ore parallel to the one just described, and lying a few miles to the northwest. I visited this region in 1871, in company with Dr. F. A. Genth, who was at that time Chemist and Mineralogist to the Survey.

The entire range was taken into the tour, and specimens carefully selected from many points by Dr. G. for analysis, so as to ascertain the average character, as well as to eliminate the local peculiarities of the beds. Fortunately, an association of Pennsylvania capitalists, the North Carolina Center Iron and Mining Company, had invested largely along this range of ores, and had recently had the beds opened by trenching, at a great many points, so as to expose very well the general features of the deposits. And still more fortunately, the Company had procured the services of Dr. J. P. Lesley, now the Director of the Pennsylvania Geological Survey; and this distinguished Geologist had recently made a very careful study of the whole range, in all its bearings. I have before me his report, and shall give some of the more important points of his results. Whatever is found below on the subject of this range of ores, in quotation marks, is taken from this report, unless it is otherwise stated.

It is questioned by many geologists whether all our North Carolina metamorphic rocks are not altered Silurian and Devonian, like most of those of New England. I am glad to have the support of so eminent an authority in the view presented in the map published some two years ago and maintained in this report, that these azoic and crystalline rocks of Middle North Carolina are Archæan of the most ancient type and date.

"This part of North Carolina is occupied by some of the oldest rocks known; the same rocks which hold the iron ore beds of Harford County, Maryland, and Chester County, Pennsylvania, and the gold ores of Georgia, North Carolina, Virginia and Canada. The gold mines of Guilford County, N. C., are opened alongside of, and not more than ten or twelve miles distant from, the Tuscarora iron belt. Both the gold and iron range continuously, (with one break in New Jersey,) all the way from Quebec, in Canada, to Montgomery, Ala. The gold and iron bearing rocks are: Granites, gneissoid sandstones and mica slates, all very much weathered and decomposed; and to a depth of many fathoms beneath the present surface. The solid granites are decomposed least, the mica slates most. All contain iron, which has been peroxidized and hydrated, in the process of decomposition of the whole formation, and dyes the country soil with a deep red tint. The surface of the country is a smooth, soft, undulating plain, broken by gentle vales, the bottoms of which are never more than 100 feet below the plain, and commonly not more than half that depth."

The length of the outcrops, air line measure, is 28 miles.

"The beds were deposited like the rest of the rocks in water; deposited in the same age with the rocks which hold them; are in fact rock-deposits highly charged with iron; and they differ from the rest of the rocks only in this respect— that they are *more highly charged with iron*. In fact all our primary (magnetic and other) iron ore beds obey this law. They are merely certain strata consisting more or less completely of peroxide of iron, with more or less intermixture of sand and mud, which when crystallized, fall into the shape of feldspar, hornblende, mica, quartz, etc., etc.

"The belt of outcrop of ore-bearing rocks has a uniform breadth of several hundred yards, and I believe a uniform dip towards the northwest or north-northwest.

"The map, however, shows *another ore belt*, running parallel with the former and at a distance of three miles from it. This is called the Highfield or Shaw outcrop. Beyond Haw River the two belts approach each other, and are believed to unite in Rockingham County. This and other considerations make it almost certain that the Shaw belt is the northwest outcrop of a synclinal basin, three miles wide, and that the Tuscarora belt is the southeast outcrop. If so, the Tuscarora ore-beds descend with a northwest dip to a depth of a mile beneath the surface, and then rise again as ore-beds at Highfield's and Shaw's.

"The locality of the ore beds is indicated by the occurrence of fragments of ore scattered over the surface; and these are the indications by which nearly all iron ore deposits are discovered. Large pieces on the surface are the best evidence we can possess that the beds are of good size, for they have come from those portions of the bed, which have been destroyed in the general lowering of the surface of the country. There is no reason why the parts of the beds left under the present surface should not yield as large masses as the parts which have moldered away."

As will be readily understood, from what has been stated above, the number of ore beds in the cross-section will be likely to vary from point to point along the range. "A large number of rock strata will become ore-beds locally. But there will always be a particular part of the formation more generally and extensively charged with great quantities of iron than the rest. In other words, the iron of the formation as a whole, is concentrated along one or more lines. This is evidently the case with the Tuscarora Ore Belt, as is shown in the almost perfect straightness of the outcrop of the Sergeant Shaft ore bed, where its outcrop has been opened for half a mile northeast of the shaft. There are two principal beds cropping out on the Teague plantation, at the (southwest) end of the belt, both vertical, and about 300 yards asunder." And not only does the number of ore beds vary, but they are often very irregular in position.

"Similar irregularities are noticeable everywhere. The miners say that the pitch of the outcrop of the ore bed worked in the Sergeant Tunnel and Shaft, was southeast for some distance down, after which it took its regular northwest dip, such as it now has in the shaft and tunnel at the depth of 100 feet. Besides which, there are in fact two beds cut in this shaft-tunnel, the smaller bed underlying the other, and with a dip which would carry the two beds together at some distance beneath the floor."

"Another instance occurs on the Trueblood plantation, where the two ore-beds appear to be only 200 yards apart at their outcrops and seem to dip different ways, which I explain by reference to the false surface dip of the Sergeant Shaft and bed."

The sections made at the Shaw plantation (Shaw range) furnish a further illustration of these irregularities. "The ore-bed is full six feet across, solid ore,—a very green, chloritic, mica slate, rock-ore. In this run of 800 yards there are *apparently two hundred thousand* (200,000) *tons above water level*, in the one six foot bed. The outcrop runs along the top of a hill about 100 feet above the bottom of Haw River Valley. There are apparent variations in the dip, some of the outcrops seeming to be vertical, whereas the principal part of the mining has already shown a distinct dip towards the southeast and south." The average dip of the ore-beds of this second range was observed by Dr. Lesley to be considerably less than that of the Tuscarora beds.

The *quantity of ore* which this remarkable range is capable of yielding is obviously immense. The number and extent of the beds have been noted. Their size varies greatly. "They consist of strings of lens-shaped masses, continually enlarging and contracting in thickness, from a few inches to 6 and 8 feet. The principal beds may be safely estimated on an average of four feet, and in the best mining localities the average yield of a long gangway may reach five feet." "It is evident that centuries of heavy mining could not exhaust it, for each of two or three principal beds may be entered and mined at fifty places."

The *kind of ore* has been stated in general terms as titaniferous magnetite. More particularly, not only titanium, but chromium and manganese are uniformly present, as will be seen from Dr. Genth's analyses, given below. "The ore belongs to the family of primary ores, the same family to which the Champlain (or Adirondack) ores, the Marquette (Lake Superior) ores, and the ore of the Iron Mountain in Missouri, belong. It is very similar to the New Jersey ores, which are so extensively mined for the furnaces on the Lehigh River. It is a mixture of magnetic crystals and specular plates of sesquioxide of iron, with quartz, felspar and mica, in a thousand varying proportions. Sometimes the bed will be composed of heavy, tight, massive magnetite (or titaniferous magnetite), with very little quartz, &c.; at other times of a loose, half-decomposed mica-slate or gneiss rock, full of scattered crystals of magnetic iron. The ore is, in fact, a decomposable gneiss rock, with a varying percentage of titaniferous magnetic and specular iron ore, sometimes constituting half the mass, and sometimes almost the whole of it."

Dr. Genth, who made a special chemical and mineralogical study of these ores, says in his report, published in the *Mining Register*, "All the ores consist of mixtures of magnetic iron with titaniferous hematite, or menaccanite, probably also with rutile (titanic acid), mixed with a chloritic mineral, or a silvery micaceous one resulting from its decomposition. Some of the ores contain alumina in the form of granular corundum, in one or two places in such quantities that they become true emery ores. None of the constituents could be separated in a state of such purity that in all cases their true mineralogical character could be verified by analysis."

But besides these characteristic ores of the beds described, Dr. Lesley mentions beds of ochre of various sizes, "as one of the constituent elements of the whole formation. What the exact relationship of these ochre beds to the magnetic ore-beds, I do not know. But the ochre outcrop seems to be always in the immediate vicinity of the ore-beds. The largest exhibition of ochre which I saw, is on the I. Somers plantation, on Brushy Creek. Here an ochre bed twenty feet thick rises, nearly vertical, out of a gully in a hillside covered with small pieces of fine, compact ore. The whole aspect of this place gives an impression of an abundance of ore beneath the surface, but no openings on the beds which have furnished these fragments have been made."

The following table presents the analyses of

sixteen samples, collected, as stated, by Dr. Genth, along the whole length of this range of ore beds in 1871:

	28	29	30	31	32	33	34	35	36
Silicic Acid,	0.76	5.68	0.40	1.84	1.76	1.30	12.75	1.30	26.80
Titanic Acid,	13.52	11.67	11.95	13.28	12.35	13.60	15.35	1.27	16.20
Mag. Ox. Iron,	79.53	72.74	81.89	77.62	77.90	76.04	57.93	93.63	30.90
Ox. Man. and Cobalt,	0.81	0.64	1.02	0.95	1.10	0.96	1.15	0.93	1.55
Ox. Chromium,	0.46	0.48	1.07	0.65	1.10	0.72	1.25	1.43	0.43
Alumina,	1.68	5.08	1.06	2.30	2.54	4.26	5.17	0.55	8.87
Magnesia,	2.79	2.61	1.99	2.01	2.41	2.33	4.14	0.75	10.30
Lime,	0.45	0.76	0.24	0.58	0.51	0.60	0.90	0.14	1.40
Water,		0.34	0.38	0.77	0.79	0.18	1.36		3.55
	100.00	100.00	100.00	100.00	100.00	100.00	100.00	100.00	100.00
Metallic Iron,	57.68	52.68	59.03	56.21	56.41	55.06	41.95	67.60	21.63

	37	38	39	40	41
Silicic Acid,	0.50	1.80	0.74	1.39	0.98
Titanic Acid,	12.27	14.46	13.92	0.78	2.42
Mag Ox. Iron,	79.16	74.81	76.80	42.77	46.29
Ox. Man. and Cobalt,	1.21	1.53	1.30	1.00	1.27
Ox. Chromium	0.57	0.97	1.07	0.30	trace.
Alumina,	3.62	2.66	3.82	52.24	44.86
Magnesia,	2.04	3.09	1.80	0.68	3.27
Lime,	0.63	0.69	0.55	0.84	0.91
	100.00	100.00	100.00	100.00	100.00
Metallic Iron,	57.32	54.17	55.61	30.97	33.52

The following are Dr. G.'s notes in part: "Nos. 28 and 29, K. R. Swain, Davidson County. The ores on this place are both massive and granular magnetite, with small admixtures of greenish chlorite, mostly between the fracture plants, partly altered to the above-mentioned silvery-white or brownish-white micaceous mineral, and those in which the latter forms a conspicuous constituent. Both kinds were analyzed; 28, the massive ore; 29, the micaceous.

"No. 30. Elisha Charles, Guilford county.

The ore is granular, iron-black, with small quantities of the silvery micaceous mineral.

"No. 31. Widow Cook. The ore is similar to the last, although a little more chloritic and micaceous in little patches throughout the mass.

"No. 32. John Clark. The ore closely resembles that from the Widow Cook's plantation.

"No. 33. Widow Stanley, Sergeant Shaft. The ore is compact, granular, iron-black; it shows rarely octahedral crystals of magnetite, and is associated with dark green, foliated chlorite, especially on the fracture planes.

"No. 34, 35, 36. Widow McCuisten. The greatest variety of ores exist at this plantation. They are peculiar but highly interesting and important. No. 34 is the soft micaceous ore: 35, the magnetic portion of 34; 36, the non-magnetic portion.

"No. 37. W. A. Lewis. Very fine granular ore, with very little admixture of chlorite.

"No. 38. Levi G. Shaw, Rockingham. Fine grained, black, slightly micaceous; shows a somewhat stratified structure.

"No. 39. P. Hopkins (Alcorn Farm), Rockingham. Very fine-grained, black, fragile ore, with little admixture of foreign substances.

"No. 40. Granular, reddish ore. It has much the appearance of a granular reddish-brown garnet, for which it has been mistaken, until the analysis proved it to be not a silicate, mixed with granular magnetite, but *corundum.*

"If this and the next should be found in quantity, they would be of considerable value, as a good quality of *emery.*

"No. 41. Granular grayish ore. This is of a

similar quality, and is found at the same locality; the minute grains of corundum have a yellowish or brownish-white color. and show in many places cleavage fractures, which give it the appearance of a feldspathic mineral.

"From these analyses it is seen that the average of the ten specimens of original iron ore, which represent the whole range for a distance of nearly 30 miles, is: Iron 54.61 per cent. Titanium 8.07 =13.24 per cent. of titanic acid. The ratio between titanium and iron is=1 ; 6.77.

"All the ores were examined for sulphur and phosphorus, and were found to be entirely free from these substances."

As there seems to be an unfavorable impression of the titaniferous ores in some quarters, it is worth while to quote Dr. Lesley on the subject of the effect of titanic acid in iron ores, as there is no higher authority in this country : "This kind is difficult to smelt in the high-stack blast furnaces ; but makes the best iron in the world, when smelted in the Catalan forge ; and is of great value for the lining of puddling furnaces. It serves the same purpose as the Lake Superior ore, which is brought in large quantities to Pittsburg and the surrounding district of Eastern Ohio and Western Pennsylvania, for lining puddling furnaces and to mix with poorer ores in the blast-furnaces.

"The titaniferous magnetic ores of the Ottowa region, in Canada, are also brought by a long and expensive route to Pittsburg, to mix with Pennsylvania ores. These Canada ores are of the same geological age, and of the same mineral character as the Tuscarora ores under consideration. There cannot be a question that these Tuscarora North

Carolina ores will command a high price at the iron works of Eastern Pennsylvania.

"The trial of the ore has been made by Mr. Nathan Rowland, at his works in Kensington, Philadelphia. Five tons were forwarded for trial as lining to puddling furnaces. Mr. Rowland expressed his opinion that it stood up three times as long as the Champlain ore, which he uses for that purpose. The difference is due to the superior compactness of titaniferous magnetite over that of pure crystalline magnetite. I believe that mining operations here would be successful, if they were entirely confined to this one branch of the business, so great is the demand for the best puddler's lining ores." Dr. Lesley says that these ores are "essentially like those of Northern New Jersey, as to age, situation, consistency and general composition," but unlike in this titaniferous quality. "The New Jersey ores seldom possess this property, and in any case, only in a low degree. The Canada ore and the ores of South Sweden hold large quantities of titanic acid; even as much, sometimes, as between 30 and 40 per cent. A small,—very minute quantity of titanium in pig iron, is believed to add greatly to its value, increasing its hardness and firmness, and its ability to stand wear. The Canadian ores were introduced to the Pittsburg iron works for this end."

It has been stated above that these titaniferous ores are difficult to smelt, "requiring a much higher heat in the stack to decompose, than oxide of iron does." But they labor under another disadvantage, of suffering a loss of iron in the process of smelting; the reason of which is that "the only solvents of the titanic acid are the double silicates of *iron* and lime, or *iron* and alumina and lime, or *iron*, potash and lime, etc." And of course the more titanic acid, the greater the waste of iron in the slag. These Guilford ores, therefore, "have the advantage, that, while many of the Canada ores hold 25 and 30 and 35 per cent. of titanic acid," those contain less than 14, on an average. And at the same time "they have all the advantage which the presence of titanium affords: 1st. Making the ore so firm that it is the best possible for lining puddling furnaces: 2nd. Making the iron tougher and harder, like the best Swedish iron: 3d. Imparting a certain quality, (the cause of which is not yet understood), which adapts the iron especially for the manufacture of *steel*." "The titanized iron is found to be exceedingly strong, and is used in Europe for armor plates, commanding three times the price of ordinary pig iron." Muchet's steel is made from titaniferous ores, for the manipulation and utilization of which, in the manufacture of steel and high grade iron, that gentleman has taken out no less than 13 patents in England, where Norwegian ores containing 41 per cent. of titanic acid are successfully employed, as stated by Dr. Lesley on the authority of Osborne.

"There is no question that titanium in iron ore favors the production of iron peculiarly suited to conversion into steel. The English steel trade has always largely depended on Swedish iron; and I believe that the titaniferous ores of the United States, (and they are far from abundant), will become annually more and more valuable, on account of the demand increasing for the best iron for steel making purposes."

Dr. Lesley refers also to the fact that the

ochre-beds already described as accompanying the iron ore range, furnish a superior flux for these ores. "The ochre must become a fluid double-silicate, without robbing the ore, and will carry off the excess of titanic acid."

An analysis by A. A. Fesquet, which he gives of "this ochre, which forms large beds on the outcrops of the more ferruginous feldspathic rocks," is added:

```
Sesquioxide of Iron..............................19.43
Silica...........................................34.12
Alumina..........................................33.21
Water, etc., etc.................................13.24
```

So that this ochre will furnish more than enough oxide of iron for the slag, and will therefore increase the run of iron.

I add a few of Dr. Lesley's general conclusions as to the quality, quantity, uses and value of these ores.

"The quality of ore, although various and suited to at least two branches of the iron manufacture, is of the very first rate—none better in the world.

"The soft ores will smelt easily and make magnificent iron; absolutely the very best; perfectly malleable, tough and strong.

"The hard ores will command a high price for puddlers' linings; will be in demand for mixing with poorer ores of other regions," as are those of Canada and the Champlain; "and will have an especial value for the Siemens and the Bessemer processes, and the steel manufacture generally."

"The quantity of the ore is limitless."

"It would be the best policy to bring the ores

to nature on the spot. Small charcoal blast furnaces and groups of Catalan forges, are possible in a country so well provided with wood, and where any amount of labor can be got at the lowest price. The geology is all right; the mineralogy is all right; the region is a good one; population numerous; food plenty; labor abundant and cheap; railroads at hand." The range is crossed by two lines of railroad, and portions of it lie within 5 miles of a third.

Another probable advantage is the proximity of the Dan River coal. Although no satisfactory exposures of this coal have been made, yet there are good reasons for believing that it is both abundant and of good quality, from some explorations recently made by the North Carolina Centre Iron and Mining Company, about Stokesburg, and from the results of the trial of the coal from the shaft near Leaksville, during the late war.

The views of Dr. Lesley have been presented at some length, not only because, being from another State, and that a large iron manufacturing State, his opinions may be supposed to be given without bias, but chiefly because of his eminence as a geologist, and especially as the highest authority in this country in everything connected with the geology, mineralogy and metallurgy of iron.

Any one who has the least knowledge of the present drift of the iron industry of the world, and of the controlling importance of high grade ores, is prepared to realize the immense value of such deposits as those just described in Guilford and in Harnett, Chatham, Orange and Halifax. For the manufacture of the common qualities of iron, England has unequaled advantages in her wonderful Cleveland beds of fossil ore, and her clay iron stones and black band ores, mined in unlimited quantities from the same pit with the coal by which it is smelted. But for ores of the better class, adapted to the Bessemer and other processes of steel-making, and for the better kinds of iron, England is confessedly dependent, in a large measure, on other countries. Her principal domestic resource is the Cumberland red hematites. And nothing could be more precarious than the supply from this source. This hematite is compact and mammillary, of a brick-red color, and occurs in pockets and irregular masses, of the most uncertain forms, distribution and magnitude. In fact the masses are simply the fillings of cavities of the most irregular and lawless shapes and forms which had been dissolved out of the paleozoic limestones in which these ores occur. So that each mass or pocket has to be sought for and mined independently. And but for the introduction of the American Diamond Drill, it is difficult to understand how profitable mining could be carried on, after the exhaustion of the comparatively few masses which happen to make an outcrop. These ores are of very fine quality and commanded the remarkably high price of $9.00 a ton at the pit's mouth at the time of my visit in 1873. And the largest heaps of ore to be seen at the furnaces of Scotland and England, where malleable iron or steel is made, are Spanish red hematites, to procure which English capital has penetrated by rail a hundred miles from the coast, into the province of Bilboa. I happened also to hear of a transaction of the day before, by which a Scotch firm contracted for three millions of tons of the famous hematites of the island of

Elba, so popular with the old Romans, twenty centuries ago. And it is well known that English capitalists and iron associations are sending their experts and foremost iron manufacturers to investigate the iron resources of this country. The ores which fix the attention of these experienced scientific and practical Englishmen, are chiefly of the class under consideration,—the better class of iron and steel ores,—the Marquette region, the Iron Mountain, etc. It is only necessary that the numerous deposits of such ores in this State become known. If we could have a full report (such as the above) by Dr. Lesley, on each one of half a dozen iron ore ranges in the State, capital would not be long in finding a way to utilize them.

This Guilford range of ores has not been traced to its termination in either direction, and doubtless other valuable beds will be discovered; and there are already indications that there are outcrops of the same kind of ore as far northeast as Caswell County, some very fine specimens of magnetite having been brought to the Museum from that county.

There are also other iron ore localities in Rockingham, which do not belong to this range; for example, near the Virginia line, in a northeast direction from Madison; and again two miles below the mouth of Smith's River, (Morehead's Factory), there is a bed of red hematite iron ore, about ten inches thick at the outcrop. It is very dense, heavy and hard, uncrystalline, and almost jaspery, and is no doubt a good ore, judging from its appearance.

Iron Ores of Mecklenburg and Cabarrus.— No iron mines of any extent have been worked in these counties, but ore has been found in a number of localities. Hand specimens of magnetic ore of great purity are frequently brought to the Museum, and a systematic search would no doubt reveal workable beds. Fragments of a very heavy, black metallic ore are found in considerable quantities on the farm of Mr. Geo. Phifer, three miles from Concord, and some little search was made during the war, but not enough to reach any satisfactory conclusion. A few trenches of one or two feet depth exposed only small seams of ore, but of the best quality. Some explorations were made also in the southern part of Mecklenburg at the same time, in the Sugar Creek neighborhood. Numerous blocks of a remarkably pure granular magnetic ore were found scattered over several acres of surface of an old field, and along the public road; and several trenches were cut, which exposed two or three veins of one to three and four feet thickness. Adequate search would no doubt bring to light still larger veins, judging from the size and number of the surface fragments. Some twelve or fifteen miles north of Charlotte, in the Hopewell neighborhood, a very notable quantity of surface fragments of large size are found in an old field and skirt of woods adjacent. This is a specular ore in a gangue of quartzite, not unlike the Chapel Hill Ore. No exposures of the vein, however, have ever been attempted. Specimens of a very fine micaceous hematite have been brought from the upper end of this county also, but no information of precise locality or extent.

The ores of the southern end of this county and of Cabarrus are found in the syenite, so prevalent in the region.

Iron Ores of Gaston, Lincoln and Catawba.—
In these counties is one of the most extensive ore ranges in the State. It is also the best known and best developed of them all, and has been the principal source of our domestic supplies of iron for a hundred years. Some of the furnaces of the region were put in blast during the Revolutionary war. The ores are predominantly magnetic, with a variable percentage of hematite, and are found in the belt of talcose and quartzitic slates, (supposed Huronian), called elsewhere the King's Mountain slates. The direction of this range of ore beds is coincident with the strike of the slates, and is about N. N. E. from King's Mountain on the southern border of the State, to Anderson Mountain, near the Catawba River, in Catawba County. These ores are mostly of a very slaty structure, and friable. In fact they may be generally described as magnetic and specular schists, being talcose, chloritic, quartzitic or actinolitic schists impregnated with granular magnetite and hematite (itabirite). These beds have a westerly dip, with the rock strata, at a very high angle, usually nearly vertical. The general range of the beds is accompanied and indicated by a line of quartzose slaty ridges, or knobs, the quartzite lying usually to the west of the ore-beds, but occasionally on the east and sometimes on both sides. To Mr. G. B. Hanna, who has lately made an examination of many of the beds for the Survey, I am indebted for several valuable observations. He states that for a considerable part of the range there are two parallel beds, the more westerly being generally the larger and more productive, their thickness running from 4 feet (and sometimes as low as 2 feet) to 12 ; the

interval of 12 to 20 feet between them being occupied by talcose and chloritic slates, with a little ore in layers. The beds generally occur in lenticular masses, or flattish disks, which thicken at the middle and thin out toward the edges, having nearly the same dip with the bed; but they do not succeed each other in one plane, their edges overlapping so as to throw the upper edge of the lower behind the lower edge of the upper. The ore has been generally mined in a very rude and wasteful fashion, the operations seldom penetrating beyond water-level, 50 or 60 feet, and generally limited to surface openings. The range naturally divides itself into two groups of beds, the northern and the southern, the one lying mostly in Lincoln, and the other in Gaston. The most considerable of the Lincoln beds and the one which has been longest and most extensively wrought is known as the *Big Ore Bank*. This is situated 7 or 8 miles north of the C. C. Railroad, and, as is usual with the outcrops of these beds, is on a hill or broad ridge. There are several beds evident, but the scattered and partially filled openings do not furnish the means of arriving at a satisfactory notion of their exact relations. The quantity of ore, however, seems to be very great, the thickness of the beds at some places being estimated at about 18 feet. The surface of the hill is still covered with a coarse dark magnetic gravel, after all the large fragments have been emoved, and several crops of the gravel also as they weather out in succession. Several furnaces and a number of forges have been supplied with ore from this point for a long period. Following the compass course of the outcrops, about N. 20° E., a succession of ore beds is encountered at intervals of one or two miles, to the southeastern base of Anderson Mountain,—the Brevard Ore Bank, the Robinson Ore Bank, the Morrison Ore Bank, which last extends into Catawba county. The latter of these was not much opened until the late war, when the Stonewall furnace was erected in the neighborhood, and a considerable quantity of iron manufactured. The thickness of the beds is given by Mr. Hanna in the general statement quoted above, as ranging from 4 to 12 feet. The quality of iron manufactured from this range of ore beds has always been good; and all the furnaces on this part of the range were put in blast after the war, for the purpose of supplying a high grade charcoal-iron for the northern market.

Limestone for fluxing is found convenient, in the range of beds which accompanies these slates, one to two miles to the west, from King's Mountain to a point several miles beyond Anderson Mountain.

A few miles northwest of the last named mountain is a bed of limonite 5 or 6 feet thick, which was opened during the war, and furnished ore for a Catalan forge erected on a small stream near by.

Several miles further, in a north-westerly course,—7 miles south-west of Newton, there is a series of ore deposits, known as the Forney Ore Bank, whose mineralogical character and geological relations are entirely different from those of the ore-beds of Lincoln County. They occur in the syenitic belt which will be noted on the map, as lying in a narrow zone of 3 to 5 miles, parallel to the slate belt, across these counties, from the great bend of the Catawba River nearly to S. C. The ore is a remarkably pure magnetite, heavy, black, metallic and non granular, for the most part. It occurs in irregular masses,—*pockets*, which seem to be scattered very disorderly through the massive syenitic rock. So that the proper way to seek for it is by the miner's compass. The iron manufactured from it in the forges of the neighborbood, particularly at Williams', was in much request before and during the war, being very malleable, tough and strong. All the blooms which could be procured at the naval works in Charlotte during the war were used for the manufacture of shafts for ironclads and bolts for the cannon of the coast forts. At a point 6 or 7 miles north-easterly from this, is the Barringer Ore Bank, which is some two miles southeast from Newton. This ore is of the same character and geological relationships as the last. Some of the ore is more granular and it is occasionally disseminated in grains in a light colored, granitic gangue. Several thousand tons of ore were mined here during the war. The openings which extend in a double line about 100 yards, did not penetrate more than 15 to 20 feet; so that no proper development of the deposit has been made. The vein is apparently nearly vertical, but was not sufficiently exposed at any point, on account of the filling up of the pits, to give an opportunity for measurements of size or dip. But the ore is of the best quality; and the distance from railroad is only about 2 miles. There is also another deposit in Lincoln County which does not belong to the series of beds above described. It lies about two miles east of Lincolnton on the plank road, and is traceable some hundreds of yards through the forests by the surface fragments, which are widely scattered. The ore is limonite. No exposures of the deposit have ever been made, but the quantity must be considerable. Magnetic ore, no doubt belonging to the regular ranges of ore-beds, is found at other points in this county, notably on Major Graham's place, 4 or 5 miles north of the railroad, but no mining has been done here.

The lower part of the great iron range under consideration is mostly found in the southern half of Gaston, as the upper was mainly limited to the northern part of Lincoln. The ore-beds which have been opened and wrought are all found south of the South Fork of Catawba, and of its principal tributary, Long Creek, in the neighborhood of King's Mountain and its spurs, and affiliated ridges. The rocks here are the same body of slates,—talcose, argillaceous, quartzitic (itacolumite of Lieber), which carry the ores of Lincoln. And the most prominent ore-beds of the King's Mountain region are of the same character as those of the same range already described,—granular, slaty, but with a larger admixture of hematite, and so having a decidedly red streak. These ore-beds appear to constitute a double parallel range, the divisions much more widely separated than in Lincoln. The *Yellow Ridge Ore Bank*, on the most southerly outcrop, at the western base of King's Mountain seems to belong to eastern division. The bed here, which has been extensively wrought, and was penetrated to a depth of 120 feet, is reported by Mr. Hanna and others to be 16 feet thick (occasionally 40), with a steep westerly dip. Hanna says of the ore, "it is notably magnetic but more highly peroxidized than that class of 'gray ores' generally." It is finely disseminated in a talcose gangue, being strikingly like the ores of Lincoln County. At the western base of Crowder's Mountain, in a northeasterly course, on this range, is the Fulenwider ore-bed, on the headwaters of Crowder's Creek, and near the forge; and still further in the same direction Mr. Hanna speaks of a field which is covered thickly with fragments of ore, although no bed has been exposed.

There is also a notable succession of parallel beds of magnetiferous arenaceous slates in a nearly vertical position and with a northeast strike, on the summit of Crowder's Mountain.

The following analyses of several samples of these Crowder Mountain ores have been furnished by Hanna:

	42	43	44	45
Silica,*	11 02	23 14	9 27	2 58
Peroxide of Iron,	72 00	58 36	75 17	84 53
Protoxide of Iron,	2 03	5 40	2 68	1 30
Sulphide of Iron,	0 09	0 12	0 20	0 02
Sulphuric Acid,	0 02	0 12	0 01	0 01
Phosphoric Acid,	0 05	trace	0 02	0 07
Loss by heating,	1 65	2 78	4 02	11 88
Metallic Iron,	52 02	45 13	54 80	59 29

These analyses show a high grade of purity.
No. 42 is from the slaty beds of the Pinnacle.

There are other beds or veins of iron ore on the east side of Crowder's Mountain, one of which, about a mile distant, a friend reports having traced two miles by its outcrops; but no openings have been made here.

There are three notable ore-beds on the western division of this part of the range, on the lands

---

*And a small percentage of Titanic Acid.

known as the "High Shoals." They are the *Ferguson*, the *Ellison* and the *Costner* ore banks. The first is the most southerly. It is a granular magnetic ore, with much iron pyrites, which has been superficially changed to limonite. This bed has been long worked, but the sulphur has always lowered, more or less, the quality of the iron made from it. The Ellison ore bank is about a mile northeasterly on the range. This has been worked for a great while, and has furnished an immense amount of ore. Its quality is very high.

The heavy iron castings for the Rolling Mills at High Shoals were made from the furnace hearth, and, after seven years use, show scarcely a sign of wear; and car wheels made of this iron were very extensively used during the late war, and were found by all the railroads which used them, "equal to the best manufactured from the Salisbury iron," as testified by the Superintendents and other officers of the most important lines, on some of which "as many as 2,000 car wheels, made principally from this iron, were in use" at one time. "In castings where strength and durability are specially required," it is pronounced by several of those officers most familiar with it, as "having no superior." This ore is a slaty granular magnetite, with much hematite, and generally has a very red streak. The slate contains actinolite, as well as some chlorite and talc. The bed has the strike of the inclosing slates, N. 20° E., and a steep westerly dip, nearly vertical, and a thickness of twelve to eighteen feet; it has been worked to a depth of more than 100 feet, and at this level is eighteen feet thick.

The *Costner Ore Bank* is about three miles in a northerly course, on the same line, and one mile east of the furnace ("Long Creek"). This has more of the seeming of a vein, from its associations and general character. The rock is granitic and syenitic, and one wall is a bed of crystalline lime stone, twelve feet thick. The ore is a very dense, metallic and subcrystalline magnetite, and is very free from impurities, as will be seen from the analysis below; and the bar iron made from it is very tough and strong. The vein is ten to twelve feet thick; and it is reported by the miners who last penetrated it, at a depth of over 100 feet, to be above twenty feet thick.

There are two other important ore beds on this tract,—"High Shoals," but they do not belong to the regular range of ore beds which we have been considering, being out of their line to the west, and of a very different character. The ore nearest to the line of the deposits last described is the *Mountain Ore Bank*. It is on a high ridge, or mountain spur, (Whetstone Mountain) 2 or 300 feet above the level of the general level, and some two miles west of the Ferguson Ore Bank. It is a regular vein of limonite, fibrous, radiated, mammillary and cellular; a portion of it a dirty bluish-black, earthy mass, with a disposition to break out in small angular fragments,—evidently manganiferous and derived by decomposition from the carbonate of iron. The vein is four to eight feet thick, associated with a heavy quartz vein, in a quartzo-argillaceous slate, and has a strike N. 35° E., and which does not vary more than 1° to 5 from the vertical (towards the west). It is remarkably pure and will no doubt become valuable in the manufacture of *Spiegeleisen*. The second vein, the *Ormond Ore Bank*, is in the slate belt also, and is probably a vein, (no exposures of it were visible on account of the filling up of the pits). It has been worked quite extensively before and during the late war; and the iron has a high reputation in the region. It is specially preferred for wagon tires, and is said to outlast those made from any other iron. The vein is reported to be 8 to 15 feet thick. The strike is N. 35° E. The ore is fine granular, of a dirty brownish-red color, and much of it is friable and easily falls to powder. This ore is manganiferous like the last, and is a hematite, which is partly hydrated and limonitic, (turgite?).

The following analyses, by Dr. Genth, will show the high character of these ores:

	46	47	48	49	50
Magnetic Oxide of Iron	92 18	69 64	82 14	86 66	88 56
Sesquioxide of Iron....		4 30			
Oxide of Manganese....	0 28		0 53	5 12	5 17
Alumina................	0 44	0 96			
Magnesia...............	2 23	1 30		0 27	0 30
Lime...................	0 35			0 25	0 37
Silica and Actinolite....	4 34	23 80	4 47	1 42	0 84
Water..................	0 18		12 86	6 28	4 76
Iron...................	66 75	53 44	57 50	60 66	61 99

Dr. G. adds: "These ores contain neither sulphur nor phosphorus." No. 49 contains a trace of cobalt. No. 42 is the Costner ore; No. 43 the Ellison; Nos. 48 and 49 represent the fibrous limonite, and "manganiferous limonite, resulting from the decomposition of siderite," of the Mountain Mine; and No. 50 is the Ormond ore.

There are five furnaces on this range of ores, one on the High Shoals tract,—the southern part of it, and four on the northern. One of these has been in operation between 90 and 100 years, the others 80, 60 and less, down to 12 years for the last and most northern,—the Stonewall, at the base of Anderson Mountain, built during the war. These are all charcoal-furnaces, of a capacity ranging from 3 to 6 tons. And there are many Catalan forges, both in these and the adjoining counties, which have long supplied the local market, and with a much better quality of iron than could be gotten in the general iron market of the country. The belt of limestone, which forms an unfailing term of the King's Mountain slates through their course, lying generally about a mile west of the iron ore-beds, and the abundance of timber and water power have furnished the most favorable conditions for the cheap production of good iron. And the itacolumitic sandstone of the series furnishes excellent material for hearths, a "firestone" much superior in durability to any fire bricks procurable.

Iron Ores of Yadkin, Surry and Stokes.—The ores of this region occupy a relation to the Pilot and Sauratown Mts. similar to that of the Gaston and Lincoln ores to the King's Mountain range. They are found along the base and among the spurs and foot hills of the range. And like them too, these deposits divide themselves into two groups, geographically, one in Stokes and the other in Surry and Yadkin. They are all magnetic and granular, but differ, in the two groups, in their mode of occurrence. In the latter case the ore is disseminated in grains, for the most part through mica slates and gneiss rocks, and the earthy and rocky matter often bears a large proportion to the ore and requires to be separated by stamping and washing before it is sufficiently concentrated for the forge. The rock is generally decomposed to a great depth and the grains of ore are easily separated by very rude and cheap means. The ore-beds of this group have been long known, and have been used to some extent as a source of local supply of iron. They were described by Dr. Mitchell in 1842, as follows: "There is a series of beds extending in a northeasterly and southwesterly direction from the Virginia line to the Yadkin River. There are also some beds on the south side of the river." An example of this magnetiferous gneiss, and of the mode of occurrence and the method of mining, concentrating and reducing the ore is seen on Tom's Creek, in Surry county, a few miles northeast of the Pilot Mountain. The decomposed gneiss of the ore-bed has little appearance of an iron ore, and is in fact distinguishable mainly by its superior weight, the grains of magnetite merely replacing, in varying proportions, the mica and hornblende of the rock. And consequently the beds are not defined at all; the rock is worked in any direction where it is found to pay, and the excavations are made in the most irregular and undefinable fashion.

Another ore-bed and two forges (Hyatt's), are found on the west side of Ararat River, near the mouth of Bull Run Creek. This ore-bed is nearly west of the Pilot, in a light-colored slaty gneissoid sandstone. A third ore-bed, which has been worked for many years, known as Williams', is four miles northwest of Rockford. The rock is a hornblendic gneiss, and the mode of occurrence of the ore is very much as on Tom's Creek, but it is more disposed to gather into bunches and pockets and solid masses. The iron made from the ores of Surry has a good reputation in the region; they are apparently very pure. On the south side of the river, there is a series of ore-beds running from the river in a southwesterly course to Deep Creek, nearly across the county of Yadkin. There are a number of mines here, the most noted of which are the *Hobson Mines*. The ores are very much like those on Tom's Creek, but the beds are better defined, and the ore more concentrated in definite strata. The analysis below, by Dr. Genth, will show the character of the ores of this county:

	51	52	53	54	55	56	57	58
Mag. Oxide of Iron	93.61	55.87	56.13	71.68	74.48	87.39	70.61	79.75
Ox. Man	0.11	0.86	trace	trace	0.04	trace	0.48	0.81
Oxide of Copper	0.10	0.09	0.05	0.10	0.04	0.09	0.15	0.13
Alumina	0.20	0.45	1.88	2.46	0.98	0.75	0.66	1.20
Magnesia	0.86	1.94	0.19	0.10	0.25	0.77	0.90	0.98
Lime	0.45	3.14	0.36	0.57	0.60	0.70	1.34	0.82
Silica, Actinolite, Epidote, etc	4.62	37.24	40.60	24.62	23.16	10.83	24.28	14.46
Phosphoric Acid	0.05	0.05	trace	trace	trace	0.09	0.12	0.10
Sulphur		0.02	trace	trace	trace			
Water, etc		0.34	0.79	0.57	0.45	0.38	1.46	1.75
	67.79	40.46	40.65	51.83	53.93	62.55	51.13	57.75

The Hobson ores, several beds, are represented by Nos. 53, 54 and 57. These ores have been used in the forges of the neighborhood for many years. The ore-beds are in the northern part of the county, but others are found southward of them, and are represented by the other analyses; and the ores have also been used in the blomaries of the neighborhood for a long while. The other beds represented in the table are the Sand Bank (51), Black Bank (52), Hutchins' (55), Upper Bank (56), and Shields' (58). At East Bend also is an outcrop of magnetic ore, which is coarse, granular, and more free of rocky matter than most of the other deposits; but it has not been operated.

This range of ore-beds extends southward across the South Fork of Yadkin River into Davie

County, where the ore still preserves the same characteristics as in the above mentioned Counties, but of the extent of the beds and their distribution, I have no definite information.

The northern or Stokes group of the range lies on the east, (north) side of Dan River, and within 2 and 3 miles of Danbury. These are collected for the most part in a group of parallel beds in a dark to black and greenish-black micaceous and hornblendic gneiss, the beds being very well defined, and the ore concentrated in certain definite strata, and in the case of the Rogers Ore Bank, it is aggregated into considerable masses of pure granular ore, of very coarse grain. This bed is 8 feet thick and has been worked on a considerable scale; and an excellent iron was smelted in the furnaces at Danbury during the war. Another bed reported to be ten feet thick has been opened about half a mile east of the last, and two beds, (one of them 4 feet thick, the other not opened), have been discovered at different times within 300 and 600 yards of it, on the west. The ores are all magnetites, with sometimes a small admixture of hematite. The folowing Analyses are by Dr. Genth:

	59	60	61	62
Oxides of Iron,	92.47	85.09	79.71	67.66
Oxide of Manganese,	trace	trace	trace	trace
Alumina,	trace	0.70	2.27	0.17
Magnesia,	0.20	0.16	0.17	0.23
Lime,	0.13	0.29	0.31	0.19
Phosphoric Acid,	0.00	0.00	0.00	0.00
Actinolite, &c.,	7.20	13.76	15.66	31.75
Water,			1.88	
Metallic Iron,	65.34	61.74	57.13	49.03

The purity of these ores is conspicuous. Phosphorus is wholly wanting. Some samples contain a small percentage of pyrites. Manganese appears as only a *trace* in the analyses, but it must exist in larger proportions in some parts of the bed, as spiegeleisen is occasionally an accidental product. The above specimens of ore are all from the Rogers Ore Bank. There is also a small outcrop of limonite in the vicinity of the Rogers bed, of which Dr. Genth's analysis gives the peroxide as 31.36 per cent.; phosphoric acid 0.44. There are other outcrops of magnetic ore in the county, a notable one on the south side of the Sauratown Mountains, among the head waters of Town Fork of Dan River. It is evident that here is an important iron range which must become a centre of manufacture for the higher grades of charcoal iron whenever transportation shall have been provided, either by railroad or by the opening of the navigation of the Dan, which is very feasible. The proximity of the Dan River coal beds is another advantage, which may prove of the highest importance, whenever these beds shall be opened.

There are in the Museum several very fine specimens of magnetic ore and micaceous hematite, from (Forsyth County,) the neighborhood of Salem, south and west, which make it probable that there are valuable ore deposits in that section; but no definite information of their extent is in hand.

Iron Ores of Burke, Caldwell, etc. There are many valuable beds of limonite in a range extending in a northeast direction from the northeastern foothills of the South Mountains into the Brushy Mountains,—from Jacob's Fork of Catawba River, near the eastern border of Burke, across the Catawba, and by way of Gunpowder Creek, to the waters of Middle Little River near the eastern border of Caldwell; and beyond, near Rocky Creek, in Alexander, and even on the northern slopes of the Brushy Mountains in Wilkes, the same ores occur, being undistinguishable in appearance, and of identical lithological relations. These ores are associated with the peculiar kyanitic hydro-mica schists, and purplish paragonite schists, which characterize the region.

There is a bed near the town of Hickory, reported to be 5 or 6 feet thick; and 3 miles west, at Probst's, are a number of pits, from which a quantity of ore was obtained during the war; and at the distance of 6 miles, on the lands of Mrs. Townsend, a bed was opened some thirty years ago, and the ore, in considerable quantities, smelted in the Shuford furnace in the neighborhood. The beds are not exposed in either of these cases, the pits being filled up. The ore was mixed with the magnetite obtained from the Barringer Mine near Newton (already referred to), and the iron so made is reported to have been of good quality.

Iron was also made on Gunpowder Creek, Caldwell County, 30 or 40 years ago, from a similar series of limonite beds. The quantity of ore is reported as large. The beds on Middle Little River, 12 miles southeast of Lenoir, were worked nearly 50 years ago, and the ore hauled 7 miles to Beard's furnace, on the Catawba River. The outcrops are traceable on the slopes of McIntyre's Mountain and Bald Mountain, near Mr. White's on Miry Branch, for a distance of 2 to 3 miles, the outcrop on the former being about 3 or 4 feet, and on the latter 8 or 10; and it is reported that at some points the thickness is more than double the above figure. There is every surface evidence of abundance of ore. Being a mountainous region, timber for fuel is abundant, and water power also; and the proximity of magnetites and hematites, to be presently mentioned, completes a very favorable combination of circumstances for the establishment of iron manufactures.

Specimens of magnetic ore are of frequent occurrence in Burke County, and the western part of Catawba, of which there are several very fine examples in the Museum,—sent, one from a point near Hickory, and another from near Morganton, etc., but nothing is known to me of the quantity or special mode of occurrence. On Steele's Creek also in the northwestern part of Burke County, there is an outcrop of magnetic and hematite ore of the best quality. The bed or vein has not been exposed, and the quantity cannot be safely conjectured. It occurs on a spur of Brown Mountain on the land of Mr. Estes. Limonite also occurs in Brindletown, among the spurs of the South Mountains.

A bed of superior magnetic ore occurs on Warrior Creek, not far from Patterson, Caldwell county, and within a mile of the bend of the Yadkin River. It is traceable hundreds of yards by large surface fragments of a fine grained heavy metallic ore, remarkably free from rocky admixtures; and a similar ore is reported as occurring in large mass a few miles west on Mulberry Creek. Another very fine ore, a shining metallic, slaty hematite, of great purity, is found a few miles above on the spurs of the Blue Ridge, flanking the Yadkin River, in a cove known as Richlands. The smooth faces of the slaty masses of ore, as well as of the walling slates, are sprinkled quite thickly with small shining octahedral crystals of magnetite, many of which have been converted into hematite, constituting a fine example of *martite* schist. The bed at this point outcrops only a few inches in thickness, among the thin bedded and shaly, argillaceous and arenaceous micaceous slates of Linville, which show themselves in force along the flanks of the Blue Ridge in this section. The analysis of this ore, by Hanna, is as follows:

	63
Sesquioxide of Iron	96 14
Sulphide of Iron	0 08
Sulphuric Acid	0 01
Phosphoric Acid	0 00
Manganese	trace
Silica	2 25
Alumina	0 87
Water, etc	85
Metallic Iron	67 32

In the same neighborhood, on the farm of Mr. J. Curtis, on the banks of the Yadkin River, 7 or 8 miles above Patterson, is a heavy ledge of titaniferous iron ore in a massive, granular, talco-chloritic gneiss of a light greenish-gray color. The ledge is exposed in a cliff rising sheer out the river, and again in the steep face of a hill 150 yards distant. The exposure is not less than 12 to 15 feet thick, and the surface is covered with heaps of angular fragments of all sizes, up to a hundred pounds or more. The bed also contains a small proportion of a sesquioxide of chromium, amounting, according to Hanna, to 0.10 per cent.

Some 10 or 12 miles northeast of this point, on the flanks of the Blue Ridge, near Cook's Gap, in the edge of Watauga county, occurs another outcrop of the specular (martite) schist of Richlands. The bed at this locality, which is called Bull Ruffin, is reported to be 3 to 4 feet thick at the outcrop, and the neighboring and enclosing rocks, granular quartzose schists and other characteristic schists and slates of the Linville belt are often impregnated, as well as the ore schist itself, with fine to coarse crystals of magnetite and martite. The ore so exactly resembles that at Richlands that it is impossible to distinguish them. There is also an outcrop of limonite near the same point, of which the Museum contains a specimen, but I have no information of its extent. The quality of this ore is so high as to justify an exploration of this promising outcrop, and indeed of the whole range; which however does not stop at this point, but follows the line of the Blue Ridge for a distance of 75 miles, showing itself in the notable magnetiferous and martitic schists of Fisher's Peak, near the Virginia line, on the Surry-Alleghany border.

In McDowell county there are several beds of limonite. These are mostly aggregated along the top of Linville Mountain, southern part, and the western slope, near the foot, and in the spurs of the southern end. One of these ore-beds was worked by Mr. Conolly twenty-five or thirty years ago. Another bed, Fleming's, was opened also, 2 or 3 miles south of Linville, on the slope of Graveyard Mountain; the thickness appeared to be 2 to 3 feet. These Linville limonites made an inferior iron when worked alone; but mixed with the magnetites and hematites of the region, they would become available for the manufacture of good metal. There are ores of the last named species in the Linville River region, of which however, I have seen hand specimens only.

The limestone beds of the same belt, in North Cove and along the flanks of Linville, are conveniently located for furnishing a flux, and the forests of these mountains will furnish indefinite quantities of fuel.

Ore Mountain, one mile west of Swannanoa Gap, (and therefore just over the Buncombe line), is named from the occurrence on its flanks of a bed of limonite, which doubtless belongs to the iron ore range of Linville. The bed is not well exposed, but 3 or 4 feet of thickness are visible on the steep escarpment, and large masses which have broken off, are fallen down to a lower point on the slope.

Iron Ores of Mitchell and Ashe.—In Mitchell county is found one of the most remarkable iron-ore deposits in North America. It lies on the western slope of the Iron Mountain, (a part of the Great Smoky range), in the northeast corner of the county, 3 miles from the Tennessee line, about a mile from the rapid torrent of Elk River, the principal affluent of the Watauga. It has been long known as the Cranberry Ore Bank, from Cranberry Creek, which flows at the foot of the steep mountain spurs, on which it outcrops. The prevalent and characteristic rock of the mountains in this locality is hornblende slate and syenite, and it is on the northern margin of a mountainous ledge of such rocks, that the ore-bed occurs, gray gneisses and gneissoid slates coming in beyond in immediate succession and association, in part.

The ore is a pure magnetite, massive and generally coarse-granular, and exhibits strong polarity.

It is associated with pyroxene and epidote, in certain parts of the bed. The steep slope of the mountain gorge and ridges which the bed occupies, are covered with blocks of ore, often of hundreds of pounds weight, and in many places bare vertical walls of massive ore, 10 and 15 feet thick, are exposed, and the trenches and open diggings, which are scattered without order, over many acres of surface, every where reach the solid ore within a few feet of the surface. The length of the outcrop is about 1500 feet and the breadth 200 to 800. A large quantity of ore has been quarried and smelted here during the last two or three generations, but no *mining* has been done, the loose and partly decomposed and disintegrated masses of ore and magnetic gravel mixed with the surface earth, having been preferred by the ore diggers, as being more easily obtained, and much more readily stamped and granulated for the forge fire. The quality of the ore will best be seen by reference to the following analyses :

	64	65	66	67	68
Magnetic Oxide of Iron	94 37	91 45	85 59	80 77	91 89
Oxide of Manganese	0 26	0 06	0 24	1 42	0 32
Alumina	0 42	0 77	0 11	0 52	1 03
Lime	0 43	1 01	0 72		1 06
Magnesia	0 36	0 53	0 33		0 23
Water		0 44	1 53	8 21*	1 15
Silica, Pyroxene, etc.	4 16	5 74	11 48	9 08	4 02
Sulphur					0 25
Phosphoric Acid					trace
	100 00	100 00	100 00	100 00	99 95
Metallic Iron	68 34	66 22	61 98	58 49	66 53

The first four of these analyses are by Dr. Genth, who says " the first three samples contain neither titanic acid, nor phosphorus and sulphur; the fourth contains a trace of phosphoric acid."

No. 68 was made in 1869, by Prof. Chandler, of Columbia College, New York city, who remarks: "This is the best iron ore I have ever analyzed. It is very rich in iron and very free from sulphur and phosphorus." The smiths and farmers of the region will use no other iron, if the Cranberry can be had, and they willingly pay fifty per cent. more for it than any other in the market. The softness and toughness of this iron is very remarkable, and its tensile strength, as tested by the United States Ordnance Department, ranks with that of the best irons known. The blooms from the Cranberry forges have been extensively used in Baltimore for boiler iron, and commanded fifteen dollars a ton above the market. In quality it is unsurpassed by any iron in the world. And in regard to quantity, the bed much exceeds the great deposits of Missouri and Michigan, and at least equals anything in the Champlain region. So that it has not probably an equal in this country.

There are other magnetic ore-beds in the neighborhood of less extent. One is said to occur along the face of the same (Iron) mountain between one and two miles eastward; and several others at the distance of six to ten miles in a southeast direction. Northwestward also, beyond the State line and within a few miles of it, is a number of ore beds, mostly magnetic—one limonite; indeed it is evident that there is an extensive range of iron ores in this region, which are of the highest quality, and must one day attract a large capital for their development. Deposits of ore are also found in other parts of the county; but like the last named, they are known only by their outcrops. One of these is a bed of magnetite, on the lower slope of Little Yellow Mountain, at Flat Rock. The ore is quite like the Cranberry, of equal purity apparently, and strongly polaric. Some large blocks are found on the surface, weighing several hundred pounds, but no vein or bed of more than one or two feet, has been exposed by the slight effort at trenching recently made. Frequent specimens of menachanite are also found at the same locality.

A bed of limonite occurs three or four miles northwest of Flat Rock, recognizable by a profusion of surface fragments, but no explorations have been made. On Rock Creek, beyond Bakersville, at the foot of the great Roan Mountain, are also several beds of magnetic ore, of which hand specimens resemble the Cranberry ore, and the geological associations are also the same. Of the size of the beds I have no definite information, except in regard to one near the mouth of Big Rock Creek, where a little trenching has been done, and a few small veins or beds of irregular shape, and one or two feet thickness, were touched. The rock is gneiss, syenite and dolerite, much decomposed superficially. Other larger deposits are said to exist near the head of the same stream. Near Bakersville, also, I have seen small outcrops of limonite.

In Ashe county, in the northwest corner of the State, there are some important ore deposits, on the waters of North Fork of New River. They lie chiefly north and northeast of Jefferson, on Horse Creek, and Helton Creek. On the former creek there are two beds of ore, both coarse, granular, highly magnetic and polaric, in gneiss and syenite. The gangue is largely pyroxene and epidote. One is on a high mountainous ridge, some 500 feet above, and on the west side of the creek, and two miles from the river, at Hampton's; the other on the east side, at Greybill's. Both are traceable many rods by numerous surface fragments which indicate beds of considerable extent.

On Helton, six or eight miles east of the last, are still larger deposits, of very pure magnetic ore, which has been long used in the forges of the neighborhood. The ore is a coarse-grained and very pure magnetite, one of the beds of which is reported to be eighteen feet in thickness and another nine feet. This is manifestly an iron region, and worthy of a thorough investigation.

There are many other localities in this region from which hand specimens have been brought to the Museum; as for example, Cove Creek in Watauga, which has furnished both magnetite and limonite, and the neighborhood of Flat Top Mountain, where a titaniferous ore is found.

Iron Ores of the French Broad.—There are several localities on the western slopes of the Black Mountain, on the head waters of Ivy, in the eastern edge of Madison, where magnetite is found in considerable surface masses, though no explorations have been made. A bed also of titaniferous iron occurs here near the public road, and about midway between Asheville and Burnsville. The prevalent rock of the region is gneiss, with much hornblende slate and syenite. There are many fragments of this ore of considerable size along the steep slope of a mountain spur. It is very hard, lustre resinous, color black, fracture subconchoidal. The analysis is as follows (Hanna):

Titanic Acid	37.88
Protoxide of Iron	37.06
Sesquioxide	11.03
Sesquioxide of Manganese	0.89
Alumina	9.51
Lime	2.57
Magnesia	0.93
Sulphur	0.09
Phosphoric Acid	trace
Water	0.15
Silica	0.83
	100.94

On Bear Creek below Marshall, near the French Broad, there are surface fragments of magnetite in hornblende slate, but no vein or bed has been exposed. On the eastern fork of Big Laurel there is a large outcrop of a slaty granular magnetite at Mrs. Norton's, and near Jewel Hill a bed or vein of specular hematite in a reddish felspathic gneiss, the ore said to be abundant. About 5 miles west of Asheville a bed of limonite of several feet thickness has been opened. There are hand specimens of magnetic ore in the Museum, brought from the eastern part of Buncombe county, but no outcrop has been reported to me. There is a range of limonite ore-beds associated with the limestones of this county, which follow them from Cane Creek across and up the French Broad into Transylvania.

In *Haywood* county, there is a large massive outcrop of granular magnetite; it is in the northeastern part of the county on Wilkins' Creek. The bed is no doubt large, from the boldness of the outcrop, which projects in large masses above the surface.

There are also magnetites and hematites in various localities of Jackson and Macon counties, some of which are represented in the Museum by very fine specimens, and the deposits are reported to be extensive, but as no iron has been made in those counties, there has been no occasion for their development.

Iron Ores of Cherokee.—There is no other county in the State which contains so much iron ore as Cherokee. It is all, however, of one species, limonite. The marble beds of Valley River and Notteley River are everywhere accompanied by beds of this ore. There seem to be generally 2, 3 and 4 parallel beds of it, one or two of which are frequently slaty and micaceous,—a limonitic mica slate, and the others cellular concretionary, etc., and (the most western, generally) ochreous. The breadth of this iron and marble range is 2 to more than 3 miles. The trough which has been scooped out by the rivers, in a northeasterly and southwesterly direction, owes its existence to the destructible beds of limestone, and their associated soft mica-schists and hydro mica slates and shales, which occupy this tract. The direct valley range is about 24 miles in length; and there is bifurcation of it, at a point 6 or 8 miles above Murphy, one branch pursuing a more southerly course, by way of Peachtree Creek and Brasstown Creek, making the whole iron range of the county above 30 miles.

The most common and characteristic terms of the series, in cross section, are, counting from the northwest, slaty gneiss and mica schist, limonite, steatite, marble, limonite, slaty quartzite, slaty limonite, mica-schist and slaty gneiss.

At several points there are two or three reduplications of the marble, and there are commonly intercalations of mica schists and hydro-mica slates between the different terms of the series. The section at Valleytown shows two parallel beds of limonite on the slope of the mountains to the south, these beds being sometimes not more than 100 to 200 yards apart; the marble lies in the valley, and the slaty talc beds to the north side of the valley, and a bed of ochre north of that, outcropping in Paint Creek, 6 to 10 feet wide. There are here two or three parallel beds of marble. Lower down, at the Parker Mine (gold), and across by the Taylor place, are, first, the 2 beds of limonite, some 200 yards apart; then the valley, with its marble and steatite, with an outcrop of limonite to the north. This is nearly half way between Valleytown and Murphy. At Colbert's, the quartzite ridge appears with iron beds on both flanks. This is 6 to 7 miles above Murphy, where some rude mining has been done for iron ore quite recently, and much more and more systematic mining in ancient times, by no one knows whom or for what purpose. There are still visible shafts more than a hundred feet deep, which are said to have been approached by drifts, of which some signs of the entrance still remain. The marble here comes next the iron, to the northwest, and then the steatite. The latter appears of unusually fine quality in a large bed near by, at Mrs. Leatherwood's. At Mrs. Hayes', the quartzite appears with its northern bed of limonite, followed by the marble, talc and another bed of limonite. At several points between this and Murphy the same terms of the series are discoverable. About one mile north of Murphy the quartzite forms a high ridge, having the two beds of limonite, one on either flank, that on the northwest very fine and 25 feet thick. From this point much ore has been obtained for the supply of the neighborhood forges, chiefly the one on Hanging Dog Creek. The iron was reputed of very good quality. Beyond this bed of ore in the same section, is the marble and talc of "No. 6."

At one-half mile below Murphy there seem to be four limonite beds with a small outcrop of the quartzite, the marble occupying the middle term of the section. One of these beds may be seen in the streets of Murphy; but half a mile below, are two outcrops, indicating the presence of immense quantities of ore. Taking the course of the Notteeley to the southwestward, the two limonite beds, with intervening quartzite, appear near the Ducktown road about 5 miles from Murphy, and there is a large outcrop also at the bridge, 6 miles from Murphy. There is a large quarry of steatite within the same distance. Ascending the Hiwassee from Murphy, on the south bank, at the distance of about 2 miles, and after passing a heavy bed of slaty gneissoid quartzite, is a large bed of limonite; and beyond this, other quartzose gneisses, much-veined; then a second bed of the ore, after which come hydro-mica slates, and at 3 miles, (Martin's), white marble. Half a mile beyond is a fine bed of limonite 10 to 12 feet thick, which has been worked to some extent, and a few hundred yards farther, is a bed of blue marble, which is reported to occur also on Brasstown Creek. The steatite does not show itself in this section, being concealed by superficial deposits, but in another section a little north (less than 2 miles), it comes in as a brown spongy decomposed massive talcose rock just west of Garrison's, the marble and iron ore appearing on both sides of it at Garrison's, and west of the ledge; this last being an ochreous bed, associated with quartzite. Eastward of Garrison's, on this section, at Williams', the marble appears, and at Southard's, both marble and limonite; and the marble and iron are reported as outcropping again at Coleman's, on Little Brasstown Creek, the marble here having a greater thickness than at any other point, many hundreds of feet. The last outcrop in this direction of the marble and limonite is near Peachtree Creek, between 7 and 8 miles from Murphy. So that here the beds must have suffered much and rapid folding or faulting.

These beds of ore are traceable northwards to within two miles of the Valley River beds near Mrs. Hayes'. The quantity of ore in this county is therefore immense, and very widely distributed, and the forests of the mountain slopes furnish unlimited supplies of fuel, while the marble is at hand everywhere for fluxing. The quality of the ore may be inferred from the following analysis by (Chatard for) Genth, of a large mass obtained from the open cut a mile north Murphy:

Sesquioxide of Iron	85 69
Silica	1 50
Water	12 81
Metallic Iron	59 98

This completes the description of the North Carolina iron ores, as far as my investigations and information have gone. There remains much to do to complete the chapter; there are many blanks to fill, and whole counties, of which little is known, except that they contain iron ores. My work has been necessarily limited to the study of such ore beds as have happened to be opened, and of course these are but a small proportion of the whole, in a region always wholly devoted to agriculture and studiously eschewing all sorts of manufacturing.

Deep River Timber and Minerals.

[Colonel Laidley's Report.]*

NORTH CAROLINA ARSENAL,
April 29, 1856.

COLONEL: Following out your suggestion made to me in December last, to visit the country of the Deep River, with a view of examining its capability of furnishing timber for ordnance constructions, I proceeded on the 15th instant to visit several of the best timbered localities that I could hear of in the counties of Moore, Chatham, and Randolph. This region of country is rich in mineral wealth, and its growing importance, and the proposition of establishing a national foundry on the Deep River, determined me to embrace in the objects of my visit the examination of the coal and iron, and whatever else might be useful for ordnance purposes.

Taking the plank road, the first point reached on Deep River is the Gulf, distant from this place

---

* Printed by order of the U. S. House of Representatives, June 10, 1856.

forty-nine miles. Its elevation above Fayetteville is 150 feet. The coal and iron both crop out here; the former has been used from this mine for a longer time than from any other place in the coal-fields, and was known, and reported upon, at the time of the Revolution.

No machinery has ever been put up for working the mine, as wood is so abundant that the demand for coal is confined to the different blacksmiths' shops in the neighborhood.

At Egypt, five miles east of the Gulf, preparations for mining the coal have been made on a large scale. On a broad plain, more than 500 yards from the river, a shaft has been sunk, cutting the coal at 425 feet from the surface of the ground. Permanent buildings have been erected and a steam-engine of forty horse-power has been put up to raise the coal, and a similar one is soon to be used to keep the mine free from water. At this shaft the top bench of coal is four feet in thickness, underlaid by a vein of slate eighteen inches thick, which separates it from the lower bench, which is twenty-two inches thick. There is a vein of coal seven inches thick under six inches of slate, but this is not at present worked. The entire thickness of coal is, therefore, six feet four inches. I descended the shaft and examined the coal in place. When first mined it is clean and lustrous, scarcely soiling the fingers, and very free from earthy matter. Its qualities have been summed up by Professor Emmons, who has examined it critically. He says of it, "it is scarcely equaled for fineness and excellency in this country; it is highly combustible, easily ignited, and burns with a bright flame; it is rich in bitumen, and contains but very little sulphur; it furnishes an excellent coke, and is well adapted to the work of reducing metals, inasmuch as its flame is free and durable; it is admirably adapted for steamings; and for forge use it is not surpassed by any coal in the market. For the manufacture of gas no coal is superior to it."

At the Egypt mine I witnessed its fine qualities for driving the engine. It is used exclusively for this purpose, though wood is abundant, close at hand, and worth only the cutting and hauling.

In sinking this shaft four strata of iron ore were penetrated, varying in thickness from ten inches to three feet, amounting in all to six feet. Fire-clays in abundance were also met with.

I visited also the the coal mines of Farmville, about five miles east of Egypt. This is a surface mine, and *has* been worked, though it is not at present. Permanent buildings have been erected, and a steam-engine put up for raising the coal and pumping out the water from the mine; rail track and cars are provided, so that they can go to work on an extensive scale as soon as transportation is provided to take the coal to market.

Taylor's mine, two miles west of Egypt, has been worked, but no buildings or machinery have been erected. I found specimens of iron ore at this place also.

These are all the mines that I visited. There are others that are opened and worked to some extent, though the principal ones are those I visited. At Hornesville, Dye's, Fooshee, Wilcox, Chalmers, Sinclair, and others, coal has been taken out, covering a space of about thirty miles in length. The quality of the coal at these localities is much the same, except at Wilcox's, and one or two other places, where it is semi-anthracite.

Iron ore of the coal formation is found in quantities all along the out cropping of the coal. A different ore, the pure oxide, is found in a large vein, about six miles north of the Gulf, where it has been traced for several miles, east and west. It has never been worked. About five miles further north lies the Iron Mountain or Ore Hill, several hundred feet high, and about two miles long, composed almost entirely of a rich iron ore —the red hematite. About the time of the Revolution this ore was worked, and the remains of the old furnace, the slag, etc., still exist where the smelting was carried on. Some specimens of the specular iron ore have been found in this vicinity.

In the immediate neighborhood there is an abundance of wood to make charcoal for the manufacture of iron, and the nearest coal mines are only ten or eleven miles distant.

The valley of the Deep River is generally cleared of its timbers, and is under cultivation: the hills and the valleys of many of the small creeks have still their primeval growth upon them, and in many places there are oaks, poplars, ash, hickories, and gums of fine size, and well adapted for the construction of gun-carriages. On Indian creek, about three miles above the Gulf, I found some fine trees—none of the largest size.

On McLennon's Creek, a tributary of Deep River, about eight miles above Carbonton, there is some very large timber, capable of furnishing pieces of the greatest required dimensions for the heavy seacoast carriages.

I also found on Crawley's Creek, a branch of

McLennon's, some fine white-oak timber; trees from two to three feet in diameter. The large trees are found, in all cases, in the low, wet valleys, which have been fertilized by frequent overflows; the timber cannot be so good as that which grows in higher and drier places.

On Crawley's Creek there is fine sandstone for building purposes, and also grit, suitable for grindstones, of various degrees of fineness.

In this vicinity there is also soapstone in abundance, which can be had in large blocks.

There are mill-seats on all of the many creeks, many of which are already improved, and sawmills are to be met with every few miles.

From McLennon's Creek I passed on to Randolph County, in the vicinity of Ashboro', and examined the timber on Uwharrie River, which empties into the Pedee. The valley of this river being generally fertile and well adapted for agriculture, it is mostly cleared, and under cultivation. There are some small tracts, however, where the timber has been permitted to stand, and there the growth is of large size. The same remark is applicable to Sandy Creek, which flows into Deep River, just below Franklinsville. I went up this creek twelve miles before finding a tract of any size that was uncleared. Timber of the largest dimensions can be furnished from this county, but it will be by taking a tree here, and one there, wherever they can be found. I found on Mill Creek, about three miles from Franklinsville, a few large trees from three to three and a half feet in diameter.

There are no extensive tracts, that I could hear of, where there was an abundance of timber of large and thrifty growth, but there is the greatest abundance of white oaks of moderate size, from eighteen inches to two feet in diameter, suitable for wagons and field-carriages. The best, for this purpose, that I have seen, is in the vicinity of Franklinsville. The country is hilly, the soil a stiff red clay, with many quartz-rocks scattered over it; the timber is firmer and tougher than that which grows on lighter soils, or in the sandy country. In this opinion I am confirmed by the experience of some of the wagon and carriage makers, whose opinions I have heard expressed.

About three miles from Franklinsville, I visited a shaft, sunk about sixty feet, passing through a vein of specular iron ore the greater part of that distance. The ore has never been worked. There is also magnetic ore found in the vicinity.

In this part of the country I find that white oak is never used for the naves or fellies of wagons. For the former, black gum, red elm or post-oak, is invariably used; and for the latter, the willow-oak. They all possess the advantage over the white oak of not splitting so readily.

The willow-oak is a coarse-grained wood, growing in moist places, tough and hard, and possessing great strength; it is always used for plow-beams and such like purposes, where strength and stiffness are required.

White-oak timber is not very valuable, being used mostly for making spirits of turpentine barrels. Near Ashboro' I found it was used for laying the plank road, though the pine is still plenty: the oak is heavier to haul, but lasts longer.

The carriage and wagon makers pay from twelve to fifteen dollars per thousand for their white oak, delivered at their shops, sawed through and through the log, into boards from one and a half to two and a half inches in thickness. The transportation from Ashboro' to this place is estimated to cost fourteen dollars per thousand feet. The road is planked the entire distance, eighty miles.

There is a locality on the east side of the Cape Fear, about sixty or seventy miles distant, on the New Hope River, which is said to abound in white-oak timber of large size. The valley of this river is represented as low and wet, and has not, in consequence, been cleared of its forest growth for agricultural purposes. It was from the headwaters of this stream that a contractor, four years ago, endeavored to furnish timber for this arsenal, but was compelled to abandon the contract in consequence of the great expense of transportation, being obliged to haul his timber some sixty or seventy miles through the sand.

Since that time the navigation of the Cape Fear has been improved, and water transportation for forty miles can now be had in place of wagoning. After farther improvements in the river, this timber may become available for ordnance purposes at this arsenal.

There is timber on Crane's Creek, thirty-three miles from here, but not of the large kind, and its quality is granted to be inferior to that of Franklinsville.

White-oak timber can also be had from the valley of the Cape Fear, within fifteen miles of this place, and farther up; but the samples that I have seen are inferior in quality, being light and brash.

I have made some trials of the strength of the white oak of this section of country, and give below the results. The timber was cut in 1852, and was from the counties of Randolph and Orange.

The pieces were two feet long between the bearing points; their cross-section was an inch and a half square. The bearing points were knife edges, and the breaking weights were applied to a knife-edge resting equidistant from points of support. Weights were added till the piece gave way.

NO.	WHERE FROM.	BREAKING WEIGHTS.	REMARKS.
1	Franklinsville....	920 lbs. bent .75 in.	Grain, diagonal.
2	Same tree, Franklinsville.....	952 " " .75 "	" perpendicular.
3	..............do............	952 " " .75 "	" parallel.
4	..............do............	920 " " .75 "	" oblique.
5	Same tree,.....do...........	906 " " .75 "	" "
6	..............do............	873½" " .75 "	" diagonal.
7	Orange Co., (near Chapel Hill)	1,085 " " 1.50 "	" oblique tough.
8	Same tree,Or.Co.(nr.Chap.Hill)	1,184 " " 1.50 "	" perpen'r tough.
9	..........do..........do.....	1,284 " " 1.50 "	" parallel, tough.
10	..........do..........do.....	754 " " .5 "	" diagonal.
11	..........do..........do.....	794 " " .6 "	" "
12	..........do..........do.....	973 " " .75 "	" parallel.

Experiments, similar to the above, were made at the Washington arsenal several years since, to test the effect of Dr. Earle's process, but I have not been able to procure any record of them to make a comparison between this and the oak of the middle States.

I enclose, herewith, a map of the coal region, and a sketch of the places visited.

Very respectfully, I am, colonel, your obedient servant,

      T. T. S. LAIDLEY,
         Brevet Major.

Col. H. K. CRAIG,
  Ordnance Office, Washington, D. C.

The Deep River Region.

[Admiral Wilkes' Report.*]

Washington, *December* 30, 1858.

Sir: In obedience to your order of the 21st of July, appointing a commission, to consist of myself, Chief Engineers Henry Hunt and D. B. Martin, and Naval Constructor S. M. Pook, to make a thorough examination of the Deep river country in the State of North Carolina, and to report upon the expediency of establishing, at some point in that State, machine and work shops for the construction of engines, boilers, etc., for naval vessels, as embraced in a resolution of Congress, April 13, I have the honor to submit the following reports:

Before entering into the details of our examintion of the Deep river district, it may be proper to give the extent of the sandstone formation of this part of North Carolina in which the coal measures lie.

Professor Olmstead, of Yale College, was the first to define this extent, in 1824, and more recently it has been examined by Professor Emmons. They both agree that its northern terminus is near Oxford, in Granville county, where it comes to a point. It passes from thence in a southwesterly direction across the State for 120 miles, and has its terminus about 6 or 7 miles within the boundary of South Carolina. The breadth of the formation varies. Between Raleigh

---

*Printed by order of U. S. Senate, Feb. 9, 1859.

and Chapel Hill it is reported as being 18 miles. On the Cape Fear I found it less than five, which continues for some ten miles to the southward and westward. It then suddenly enlarges to 12 miles, embracing the whole valley of the Deep river district, and is then continued, contracting gradually, till it passes out of the State, near Wadesborough.

The rocks which bound this sandstone formation are the metamorphic slates, gneiss, and granites; on these the formation reposes. Their outcrops are seen with a great dip to the northwest, giving a well defined outline of this sandstone deposit.

A particular description of the geographical position of the Deep river country is deemed necessary from the fact that but little is known of it even in the capital of North Carolina.

The Deep river district is situated 30 miles southwest from Raleigh, 15 miles south from Pittsborough, and 50 miles north from Fayetteville. It occupies the very center of the State, and comprises part of the counties of Chatham and Moore. It forms an extensive valley, bounded by the Pittsborough hills on the north and east, the Buckhorn hills on the south, and the Carthage hills on the west.

This area lies between the Cape Fear river on the east and the Hancock mills on the west, the head waters of the creeks flowing to the Deep river from the south, and those which take their rise toward Pittsborough on the north. This district is about 25 miles in length by 10 in width, and embraces an area of some 250 or 300 square miles. To this our examination was confined.

The Deep river takes its rise in the county of

Guilford, flows to the southeast through the county of Randolph, with a descent of some 500 to 600 feet in some 60 miles, until it enters the county of Moore, in the neighborhood of Hancock's Mills, towards which its current is rapid; thence its general direction is to the north of east for 30 miles, pursuing a very tortuous and sluggish course, with a fall of 27 feet, and joins the Haw river, at that distance, coming from the northwest to form the Cape Fear river.

The country which it drains comprises an area of one thousand miles, affording an abundant supply of water for its slack-water navigation and for milling purposes. It is subject, occasionally, to great freshets in the lower part, which overflow its banks to the depth of ten or twelve feet, but owing to the sluggish flow of the current, it passes off without damage to the crops and farms.

In our examination of the coal and iron of this district I must refer to the geological formation, and, for the purpose of more clearly illustrating and understanding the limits, will treat it as an independent formation, (for such it may be regarded, being unconformable to the primitive rocks,) under its three natural divisions, viz:

First. The conglomerate and lower red sandstone.

Second. The coal measures, including the sandstones of a drab color, bituminous shales, and slates.

Third. The tertiary and drift.

These three occupy the depression, or basin, of the primitive formation, the outline of which may be recognized a short space beyond the outcrops.

In every part of the coal field we have evidence that the conglomerates rest upon the metamorphic slates, gneiss, or granite. The effects of upheaval, as well as diluvial action, are visible in many places throughout its extent.

In order to define the extent of the basin I found it necessary to search not only for the outcrop of the coal but also for the outcrops of the underlying as well as the outlying rocks; and, assisted by information derived from reliable authority, I succeeded in tracing it from one locality to another, until I had obtained what I deemed sufficient evidence of the margin of the basin or trough.

The following is the course which it follows:

The line of outcrop of this coal has been traced, beginning near Dye's, to the eastward of the plantation of Evander McIver; thence westward some two miles, near the house of McIver, turning there to the north-northwest of his plantation; thence towards the northeast for two and a half miles, and then to the westward, crossing the Deep river at Mr. Wicker's plantation, from which place to the westward, passing through the Farmville plantation in nearly a straight line, touching the river near the bend opposite Egypt, and continuing beyond through the Taylor, Haughton, Tysor, and Palmer plantations, a distance of seven miles.

From the latter to the Bingham plantations its course is west-southwest five miles, and thence it passes on a more westerly course, through the Murchison and Fooshee plantations three miles, again crossing the river, and is covered up near the latter by the overlying debris of the rocks.

On the south the coal does not outcrop, owing to thick covering of the debris of the rocks, which has been deposited over it. We have therefore to refer to the outcrops of the conglomerates and red sandstone, and the dip and strike of the slates and sandstones overlying the coal measures on the western end, to assist us in arriving at the form of this basin.

The conglomerates are seen to extend beyond the coal at the southwestern end; several quarries have been worked on Richland creek, where the millstones have been sought for and found. Their direction changes towards the south and southeast, across the range of the sandstone formation of the State. This is also observed of the slates and sandstones, the dips tending towards the axis, while the strike conforms to the margin of the basin. The slates are generally argillaceous and destitute of fossils; the sandstones are fine, with ripple marks resembling those which lie beneath the coal of the Egypt shaft.

The rock which has been termed the upper red sandstone I have nowhere encountered, except beyond the margin or a short distance within the basin, as an upper deposit. I think it has no place in the formation of this trough or basin; but it is of recent origin, probably of the tertiary. It lies unconformably to the rocks of the basin, and the beds of pebbly quartz, which in certain localities are found near it, appear to be accumulated drifts from the older and outlying rocks.

In all cases where the conglomerate crops out we find the lower red sandstone accompanying it.

The lower rocks are seen on the south side along the courses of the creeks which flow towards the Deep River, where they crop out with a dip towards the northwest and a strike to the northeast and southwest. The southern outcrops are not so distinct or continuous as on the northern sides, yet they offer abundant evidence of the limit to which the coal must be circumscribed. The rocks have a less and opposite dip, but the strike conforms to the basin. These rocks lie in contact with the primitive formation of metamorphic slates, gneiss, and granite, along the Buckhorn range, the whole surface of which is strewn with fragmentary quartz.

These outcrops have been further traced to the northeastward to Gilmore's mill, on Pattison's Creek; to the north at Evander McIver's mill, on the Great Buffalo creek, and at the Little Buffalo church; thence to the eastward, again outcropping on the head waters or branches of Lick creek, near Kelly's mills, at the "Sisters" and "Wooley Rock;" thence to below the mouth of Lick creek, and about a mile above the junction of the Buckhorn creek with the Cape Fear river.

The conglomerate on the north side is seen at House's quarry, then near Jones' falls, dipping to the eastward, and (thence is traced to Ellington's by Professor Emmons; then to the southwestward to near Y. Wicker's plantation, where it makes a turn to the northwest toward's M. Wicker's,) passing between his house and the Deep River; crosses the Deep River near George's creek, and pursues a course to the westward a short distance to the north of the outcrops of the coal, and nearly parallel to its curve.

Thus I have traced the peculiar outline of the basin or trough, and thereby determined its length and width.

It will thus be seen that from Evander McIver's to Ellington's the north and south conglomerates, with the red sandstones, approach nearest to each other, and have almost a parallel direction, with opposite dips. They are not separated more than two and a half miles.

It is therefore evident that the older rocks have narrowed the depression, though perhaps not lessened the depth; consequently, some of the overlying rocks may be wanting, or thin out, as they are observed to do near this locality.

The topography of the country shows that the outcrops of the conglomerates conform to the highest ridges, and follow them almost at a uniform height, leading to the conclusion that at some remote period the whole was deposited at the same time and derived from the same source.

It is apparent, also, that the debris of the rocks in the upper or most western part of the valley have been carried by the water towards its easttern termination and deposited; thus the valley or lake (if such it was) has been gradually filled up and the river finally confined to the channel it now occupies, winding with little fall through the alluvial or drift, from ten to fifteen feet below the surface of the valley.

Although the deposit of coal in the Deep river district will not bear a comparison to the vast fields of that mineral in the western States, yet, owing to its position, proximity to market, and adaptability to many purposes in the arts, and connected as it is with extensive beds of iron ore, it may be esteemed of great value and interest to the State as well as of national importance.

The shaft which has been sunk by the Governor's Creek Coal and Iron Company, at Egypt, affords the most reliable evidence of the perpendicular section of the strata, to the depth of four hundred and sixty feet below the surface, and includes the lower coal seam.

This shaft has fully established the existence of several veins of coal as well as veins of valuable iron ores, lying in juxtaposition with the coal. It is situated fifteen hundred feet within the outcrop of coal, to the south and perpendicular to its trend.

The strata in the shaft of Egypt, however, cannot be taken as a true development of the coal field. At short distances from it, both east and west, we find the sandstones in thicker masses, and replacing some of the slates exhibited in the section, which shows but a limited development of them. It will be seen that the first sandstone met with is at the depth of 323 feet, 100 feet above the coal, and but one foot in thickness.

There are two lower seams, separated by a strata of black slate, with iron balls 405 feet deep, and one foot ten inches, and three feet in thickness.

By this section we are assured of the depth at which the underlying seams of coal are found. Five are seen at the outcrop, which unite as they descend and form but four in the shaft. The large or six feet wide seam in the shaft, at Egypt, is 423 feet deep. Between the coal seams are found carbonates of iron, known by the name of the "Blackband."

I think every one must be satisfied, from its regularity and the diminution of dip in the distance from the outcrop, (some eight or ten degrees) that its seams tend to conform to the shape of a basin or trough.

It appears that the greatest depth of this coal basin is on the northern side, giving cause to be-

COAL AND IRON OF NORTH CAROLINA. 155

lieve that this valuable mineral does not extend below *such* depths as to render its mining both profitable and easy.

We may acquire some approximate estimation as to the quantity of coal this basin may contain by taking the data which our results give of the extent of the basin, viz: some 75 square miles, which there is every probability is underlaid by the veins of coal, from which the value of this mineral·wealth, locked up in this district, may be readily calculated.

There is no anthracite coal in this field. In some places it is debituminous, viz: at Tysor's, Palmer's, and Wilcox's, where it has undergone, with the slates and beds of iron ore, much disturbance, probably by an upheaval, and afterwards been denuded by the action of the river, which has removed the debris of the rocks and exposed to view the shales and slates as far as the plantations of Mr. Alston and Mr. Clegg.

Through the heat of the trap dyke which has been injected near by, its volatile matter has been driven off, leaving it in a debituminized state, or nearly a natural coke. It corresponds in fracture with the coals of other localities in the field, and is known under the appellation of "dry coal;" but I have seen none with a concoidal fracture, which the true anthracites have as their distinguishing mark. The "Wilcox seam" is of this character; its outcrop corresponds in thickness with the upper coal seam.

In the neighborhood of the Wilcox place small seams of natural coke are found to crop out in juxtaposition with veins of iron ore. In some parts these have undergone great heat, sufficient to change them to scoria.

The coal lying to the northward of the Wilcox outcrop is, however, unaltered, and similar to the best kind of coal, affording evidence that the heat of the trap dyke has been confined to a limited space, and effected only a local change in the character and position of the coal along the line of its strike, which passes through the Evans, Tysor's, Palmer, and Haughton plantations, in a E.NE. direction.

There also appears to have been a disturbance near Evander McIver's, and an injection of trap, which, however, does not appear to have changed the coal, as at Wilcox's. Here we find the outcrops of the black slates and ripple marked sandstones lying within a few hundred feet of each other, with opposite dips and strikes. The position of this outcrop is 150 feet above the plain of Egypt.

The sandstone, traced round to the southward of the black slate, is found of great thickness near the conglomerates in the neighborhood of McIver's mill, on the Great Buffalo creek.

This sandstone has larger ripple marks and is more argellaceous than that which underlies the coal in the shaft at Egypt, 450 feet below the surface, but otherwise resembles it.

It will be observed that these two strata, which we find in the shaft at Egypt underlying the coal, are here noticed to the southward and eastward of the northern outcrop, and apparently overlying it; but it is readily seen that they must be the sandstone and black slates of the southern side of the basin.

This disturbance probably took place before the injection of the "trap dyke."

The black slates pursue a direct course on their

strike, and, after a considerable distance, disappear under the debris of the rocks. It is this locality where the two conglomerates approach nearest to each other.

I am strongly impressed with the belief that coal will be found within the area between McIver's and Jones' Falls, or to the eastward, beyond where its outcrop is seen to end.

Nearly the whole of this space is now covered with forest, and a deep deposit of drift overlies it, so that no outcrops of the recent or older rocks appear.

The conglomerates consist of quartz pebbles of various sizes, most of which have undergone much attrition, some round, others oblong. These are intermixed with disintegrated slates of the older rocks, consolidated by a cement under great pressure.

In some localities the cement is mixed, more or less, with marly clays, colored red by the oxide of iron, which diminishes their hardness. With this exception, on the north and south sides, the conglomerates are alike.

At the west end the cement is the strongest, and the rocks are quarried for mill stones.

The red sandstone lying above the conglomerate is of a dark, purplish color, approaching that of a burnt brick. Its texture is even, composed of fine grains of quartz, is a good freestone, and has few marly layers.

The black slates lie next above the red sandstone, and is the rock in which the shaft at Egypt ends.

Above, in the series, they alternate with the argillaceous slates, and contain deposits of argillaceous iron ore. They are from fifteen to forty feet in thickness; this is the strata in which the fossils in the series are found, consisting of posidonia, cythere, etc.

The drab colored sandstone, known by its ripple marks, is a fine and compact kind. In color it is of a dirty buff or greenish yellow, and the surface is not unfrequently marked with marine plants. It is suitable for grindstones, and might be used as a firm and solid material for building.

The bituminous shales in connection with the coal are very inflammable, and burn with a white flame. They contain nearly 30 per cent. of volatile matter, and about 20 per cent. of fixed carbon; they will probably be used for the preparation of kerosene oil, though they do not yield the quantity that is obtained from the coal in the west. At the present price it can be manufactured from the shales at a profit. I have seen samples of it which had been well clarified. The bituminous shales all lie above the coal and in strata, alternating with the argillaceous slates. The fire clays do not occur, as in other coal fields, immediately below the coal seams; but the sandstone partakes somewhat of this character. They are interstratified with the slates. According to Professor Emmons, organic remains traverse them vertically; the plants are different from other coal fields, and the sigillaria have not yet been discovered.

The calcareous shales are greenish in color and resemble somewhat magnesian limestone. These contain no fossils, and in thickness vary from four to twenty-five feet.

The upper red sandstone differs from the lower in being soft and perishable, from its marly nature. In color it is of a light red, occasionally a light brown, mottled with green spots and often variegated. The outline of these is distinct. In it are found many cavities of irregular shape, around which is generally perceived, during the summer season, a white efflorescence; this proved to be common salt, (chloride of soda.) It was found more abundant on the western end of the coal field, where this red sandstone overlies the formations. In some cases wells which are sunk in this rock have brackish water; but where they go deeper than 30 to 35 feet the water is pure. In the deep shaft at Egypt the water is entirely free from saline taste. In my inquiries I was not able to learn of the existence of any salt springs. The upper red sandstone bears a resemblance to the lower in its lithological character, but there is a marked difference in their fossils.

The plant bed of Professor Emmons, I think, gives evidence that this upper red sandstone is totally distinct, and more recent than the coal formation of the valley of the Deep river.

It will be seen, from the foregoing remarks, that I am of opinion that this formation of coal belongs to the new red sandstone, and, as far as my observations have gone, the fossils appear to prove it.

The coal of the lower seam lies, as will be seen, between two seams of black band ore, and more or less partakes of their character. It is consequently unfitted for use as a fuel, but is well adapted to the reduction, by roasting, of this ore for iron.

The three upper seams of the bituminous coal are well adapted for fuel, cooking, gas, and oil. It is a shining and clean coal, resembling the best specimens of Cumberland. It ignites easily, and burns with a bright, clear combustion, and leaves a very little purplish gray ash. It swells and agglutinates, making a hollow fire ; is a desirable coal for blacksmiths' use, for the parlor, and superior to most coals for the production of gas, for which it is likely to be in great demand. Its freedom from sulphur is another of its recommendations.

It is thought not to readily disintegrate by exposure to the atmosphere. Its coke is light and porous. When rapidly burned it inclines to melt and flow ; but when under slow combustion it does not exhibit this tendency, which is owing to the presence of a large quantity of bitumen.

I was, at first, determined to have the iron ores of this district tested both by an assay and by chemical analysis. The former, it is believed, affords a more practical test of their value ; but as it could not be obtained within the time, the chemical analysis was alone made. The ores and coal were submitted to Professor George C. Schaeffer, of this city, whose ability and care in this operation are well known, and who has afforded me full data of the results and the manner of conducting the analysis.

COAL FROM EGYPT SHAFT.

The mode of analysis was as follows : The coal was dried and coarsely powdered, and ignited in a covered crucible until all inflammable matter had been driven off.

The quantity of sulphur was determined by digesting the finely pulverized coal in fuming nitric acid, to which, from time to time, chlorate of potassa was added; by which process most of the carbon was oxidized. The sulphur was then estimated in the usual way—from the quantity of sulphate of baryta precipitated. The result was, sulphur, 1.3 per cent.

The large quantity of inflammable matter that the coal contains led to a slight variation in the results, as in one case the vessel was found lined with carbon deposited from the gas coming in contact with the highly heated surface.

The first specimen gives—
Bituminous matter as gas.................. 30.
Fixed carbon, (coke)....................... 70.

Second specimen—
Bituminous matter as gas.................. 34.
Fixed carbon, (coke)....................... 66.

The ash in first was 5.3 per cent.; second, 5.4 per cent. The composition of this coal is, therefore, as follows:

	Per cent.
Bituminous matter given off as gas	32.7
Fixed carbon, (coke)	60.7
Ash	5.3
Sulphur	1.3
	100.0

Specific gravity......... 1.28 } 1.278 mean.
Another specimen...... 1.277 }

The coal is a light, highly bituminous coal, yielding a shining and very porous coke and purplish ash, an excellent coal for making gas or for burning. It absorbs only $\frac{1}{2000}$ of its weight of water, after having been immersed for some time.

From Professor Johnson's able report we have

several analyses of this coal, from the Farmville estate, which give the mean results as follows:

Carbon	59.25
Volatile matter	30.53
Earthy	10.21
	99.99

Specific gravity 1.409.

The dry or debituminized coal has less than one-quarter of the volatile matter that the bituminous coal contains. It is thought that it cannot compete with the true anthracites of Pennsylvania in the northern markets. It is, however, adapted for stoves, and for the reduction of iron ores in roasting.

I have heretofore stated that there is but a small quantity of this coal in the basin, and that it has been produced by a change in the bituminous, effected by the heat of the trap dykes.

Professor Schaeffer remarks on this description of coal from the Wilcox vein, that it has a cubical fracture, as is seen in some specimens of anthracite, with a metallic lustre. When it is heated to a high degree it decrepitates with violence, falling into thin plates.

The loss, after intense ignition in a covered crucible, was, in one experiment, 3.1 per cent., and in a second, 3.8. This loss is not imputed to the escape of bituminous matter, nor from enclosed, uncombined water; for both specimens were well dried. On an average the composition of this coal may be stated as follows:

Water and volatile matter	3.75
Fixed carbon	87.75
Ash	8.50
	100.00

Specific gravity 1.8.

The quantity of ash varies considerably, from 7 per cent. to 10 per cent.

When this coal has a cross fracture at right angles to its laminæ, various substances, in solution, seem to have been introduced, particularly oxide of iron. This affects its quality.

The specific gravity and the increased quantity of ash confirm the supposition that this coal is, like the bituminous, deprived of its volatile matter by heat, while under pressure, and that the decrepitation may be due to a constrained condition of its particles.

The large quantity of carbon it contains will render it serviceable in some metallurgic or manufacturing process, but as a fuel it cannot well be used, from the decrepitation it undergoes.

Professor Johnson gives the analysis of this coal, the mean of three experiments, viz:

Fixed carbon	83.13	83.36	87.18 =	84.56
Volatile matter	8.28	6.64	7.35 =	7.42
Earthy matter	8.60	9.60	5.47 =	7.89
	100.00	100.00	100.00 =	99.87

Mean specific gravity 1.49.

IRON ORES.

Professor Schaeffer was directed to examine the iron ores, with particular reference to a determination of their commercial value, or if they were combined with any injurious substances, especially phosphorus and sulphur. The method of analysis he reports as having adopted is as follows, viz: The ore was reduced, in an agate mortar, to an impalpable powder; a part weighed, then dried, and ignited in an open crucible to drive off water and burn all carbonaceous matter, and the quantity thus driven off and consumed determined.

It was digested in hydrochloric or nitro-hydro chloric acid, according to circumstances, until everything soluble was taken up; the solution was then, after dilution, filtered, and the residue insoluble in acid determined. This was mainly, if not entirely, silica. The acid solution, containing more or less of peroxide of iron, was then acted upon by a current of washed sulphurated hydrogen, or by its solution in water, until sulpho-cyanite of potassium gave little or no color, evidencing that all of the peroxide of iron had been reduced to a protoxide. The solution, smelling strongly of sulphurated hydrogen, was then boiled until every trace of this gas had disappeared.

The quantity of iron present was then determined by the quantity of a solution bichromate of potassa required to convert the protoxide to peroxide, as ascertained by testing with a solution of ferricyanide of potassium. The solution of bichromate was made according to the equivalents required. It was more than once tested by solutions of known quantities of pure iron, so that there might be no doubt as to the results. When any variations from this mode of analysis were adopted it will be noticed under the respective ores. All the ores were tested for the presence of sulphur and phosphorus. The test for sulphur was by the action of chloride of barium upon the acid solutions. The presence of phosphorus was determined by an acid solution of molybdate of ammonia in excess. This test gave a negative result, except in one case. The presence of either of these substances was only ascertained in the ores in which it is mentioned.

The *black band ore* is said to have been first noticed at the Farmville pits, where it crops out. It appears not to have been suspected as being similar to the black band of Scotland. At its outcrop it resembles the argillaceous carbonates, but the change it undergoes was thought to be owing to the influence of the weather. When found in the coal fields it invariably accompanies the coal seam. There is a seam lying between the two upper seams of coal of sixteen inches thick, and two others, each three feet in thickness, below the sandstone or fire clay, having a thin seam of coal between them. With this seam of coal they may be mined with great advantage.

This ore is readily distinguished from a slate by its own brownish black color. It has an even fracture, slightly concoidal, massive and compact. After being roasted, it is strongly magnetic; it is easily converted into pig metal, and the coal mined with it is almost sufficient for this purpose. The iron produced from it is highly valued to mix with other ores for castings, but for forging it is deficient in strength and never used.

Professor Schaeffer remarks upon this black band ore, that it has a slaty structure, and is highly bituminous. The iron is present in the form of carbonate of the protoxide; there is also some carbonate of lime and the usual earthy matter in such ores. It loses when burned with access of air 39.9 per cent., 24 per cent. going off as gas; sulphur was present in considerate quantity, but not estimated. In its analysis the large quantity of bituminous matter had at first prevented the complete solution of the iron. This was discovered on igniting the silica after a prolonged digestion, when it was again digested in acid, and the whole of the iron obtained.

The composition of this ore is as follows, viz:

	Per cent.
Bitumen, carbonic acid, given off as gas	26.0
Fixed carbon	15.9
Earthy matter soluble in acid	28.4
Silica	12.5
Protoxide of iron	17.2
	100.0

Specific gravity, 2.12.

This small per cent. of iron led to the examination of another portion of this ore. It was first ignited, again pulverized and digested in acid. The result, however, was nearly the same as the above. The quantity of iron is too small to make this a good ore. It is more bituminous than the well known "black band," to which it bears a great resemblance.

The composition of this "black band" ore, according to the analyses of Dr. Jackson, is much richer, and gives—

Carbon	31.30
Peroxide of iron	47.50
Silex	9.00
Bitumen and water	8.81
Sulphur	3.39
	100.00

The specimen analyzed by Professor Schaeffer

contained, undoubtedly, much less iron than the general run of the vein, and much more bitumen, and, as he remarks, it might be used for making gas. He is of opinion it would bear the expense of transportation to be used for this purpose, (it furnishes, at least, one-fourth its weight of volatile matter,) as the sulphur is not given off until after the gas has escaped.

The presence of phosphorus was detected in this ore in considerable quantity, probably owing to the (coprolites) animal matter it contains.

Many coprolites are found in the black band, and fossils are also more abundant than in the slates. Professor Emmons found the Saurian teeth in great abundance in the seam, which intervenes between the upper coal beds.

Specular ores occur outside the sandstone formation, about six miles to the northward of the Gulf, on the road towards the town of Graham. It is said to be in abundance, and the plank road passes not far from it. The analysis of the ore by Professor Schaeffer is as follows, viz:

Peroxide of iron	96.4
Silica	2.1
Earthy matter soluble	1.5
	100.0

This is nearly pure peroxide.

The "heading ore" is also of this kind, and situated not far from it. It contains, viz:

Peroxide	98.2
Silica	1.4
Soluble in acid	0.4
	100.0

Specific gravity, 5.09.

Prolonged ignition produced no appreciable loss in weight. Few ores are as pure as this, and none but the nearly pure magnetic oxide are richer in iron.

The hematitic ores are some distance beyond, and 9 miles from the Gulf, on a hill known as Ore Knob. It is elevated about 300 feet above the surrounding country, and covers about 350 acres. The ore is a red one. It is visible everywhere. A massive vein appears to bisect the hill, and continue beyond to the southwest. Some specimens of fibrous ore were observed. The hill is well situated for mining, and has been opened in several places, and we were informed was worked in the revolutionary war. Some castings are said to have been found, which were made then, and proved, on examination, to be of great strength and toughness. The analysis by Professor Schaeffer is as follows, viz:

Peroxide of iron	74.3
Silica,	10.6
Earthy Matter	5.6
Water	9.5
Sulphur, a trace	0.0
	100.0

The quantity of iron makes this a valuable ore.

Magnetic Iron Ore.—Its color is reddish brown; it lies in regular strata; is 2½ feet in thickness. It is found in various places, but was observed especially at the Tysor place. Its analysis by Professor Emmons gives, viz:

Peroxide of iron	79.720
Carbon	7.368
Silica	4.000
Water	8.800
	99.888

Contains 61 per cent.

When reduced to powder, this ore becomes of an olive brown color and attracted by the magnet. It is here that a company are erecting a Catalan forge for the production of blooms.

The "ball ore" resembles the ore of the other coal formations. It has also been analyzed and found to contain, viz:

By Professor SCHAEFFER.		By Professor EMMONS.	
Protoxide of iron	40	Peroxide of iron	32.40
Silica	13	Silica	40.00
Carbonic acid and carbonaceous matter	34	Carbonate of lime	4.72
Earthy matter	13	Carbonic acid	18.21
		Volatile matter	4.66
	100		99.99

There is another locality of iron ore lying without this coal formation, and rising through the older slate rocks, on the Cape Fear River, at Buckhorn Falls. Although it was not immediately connected with the district to which our examination was directed, yet it was visited. It lies some nine miles below the junction of the Haw and Deep Rivers, immediately on the east bank of the Cape Fear River. This ore hill rises about 300 feet in height. It passes in a southeast direction for nearly a mile, and covers a surface of over 300 acres. It is somewhat dome-shaped, and appears to be one mass of very rich ore, having a solid vein of pure peroxide, which is 8 feet in width, while ores containing manganese and silicious matter extend beyond it on each side.

This remarkable ore was first discovered by Mr. Wm. McClane, but a few years since, and it probably has not its equal as a deposit of iron in this country short of the Iron Mountain of Missouri. Professor Emmons says it is similar to that ore, as well as to that found on Lake Superior. It is a massive peroxide of iron, in composition similar to the well known specular ore; it is of a dull reddish brown color, has a bright red streak, is not crystallized, but very heavy, tough but not difficult to break. He gives its analysis as follows:

By Professor Emmons.		By Professor Morfit.	
Peroxide of iron	95.20	Peroxide of iron	92.96
Silica	4.79	Silica	3.60
		Manganese	1.14
		Lime, magnesia, and alumina	2.32
	99.99		100.00

Specific gravity, 4.952.

Professor Emmons found neither alumina, manganese, or lime, nor was he able to detect sulphuret of iron, and does not believe the ore contains any foreign substance that would be injurious to its manufacture.

The specimens of which the above is the analysis were no doubt taken from the central part of the vein.

The specimen submitted to Prof. Schaeffer was taken from beyond the vein, as it contains silex and manganese in some quantity. Professor Morfit's analysis of another portion exhibits nearly the same result:

By Professor Schaeffer.		By Professor Morfit.	
Peroxide of iron	56.4	Peroxide of iron	42.00
Silica	26.4	Silica	27.20
Manga'e and earthy matter	17.2	Metallic manganese	7.99
		Lime, magnesia and alumina	18.13
		Oxygen with iron	15.69
	100		99.82

Specific gravity 4.52 and 4.42.

It is quite evident that the above specimens were taken from different parts of the vein, and therefore the impurities appear. The first determination is to be taken as to the analysis of the pure ore, and the latter as that lying beyond the vein.

Professor Schaeffer found this ore excessively hard; sufficiently so to scratch glass, and difficult to pulverize. Some traces of a metal were precipitated from the acid solution by sulphurated hydrogen, which he believes was lead.

This ore can be transported for manufacture on the Deep river, or sent down the Cape Fear to Wilmington to be shipped to a northern market.

Thus it will be perceived that there is no want of iron ores of the finest kind for manufacturing the best quality of iron, and all that is required is limestone; but this is not to be found in the coal field of sufficient purity to be used. There are hydraulic limestones found in the shaft at Egypt, but they contain a great deal of magnesia. Analyzed by Professor Emmons, I find its contents as follows:

Silex	16.20
Carbonate of lime	42.600
Carbonate of magnesia	16.004
Iron	19.380
Alumina	0.750
Water	2.
	96.934

A limestone bed occurs at Evander McIver's, but it does not appear to contain much lime, and slacked very slowly; none of it is crystallized, and from the analysis of Professor Emmons, it contains a larger proportion of magnesia than the foregoing obtained from the shaft at Egypt, as follows:

Carbonate of lime	46.00
Carbonate of magnesia	28.70
Silex	10.40
Water	2.40
Protoxide of iron	5.60
Bitumen loss	0.00

A strata of magnesian limestone crops out in the neighborhood of Evans' mills. Its strike is to the northward and westward.

Although there may be no limestone in this valley suited for the fluxes of the ores of iron, yet it can be readily obtained by the return boats from some of the deposits on the Cape Fear river, below Fayetteville, where shell lime exists in great quantities.

The composition of the calcareous shales, according to Professor Emmons, is as follows, viz:

Carbonate of lime	35.50
Magnesia	9.25
Alumina and protoxide of iron	15.70
Water	2.59
Insoluble	36.88
	99.93

Copper.—Several copper mines, lying on the northeast, near Rocky river, coming up through the metamorphic slates, have been discovered, and have proved very rich. I did not visit the localities, but saw a large number of barrels on their way to the north. It was the yellow and gray sulphuret, they informed me.

In speaking of the manufacture of iron, I must mention that *charcoal* can be had in any quantity and at a very low price, as the virgin forest yet exists in the neighborhood of the Deep River district; and those engaged in the use and manufacture of iron know that the best kinds of iron cannot be produced without this article, and that neither the anthracite nor bituminous coals, nor coke, can compare with it.

It is thought by those who have great experience in the manufacture of iron that there is no locality on the eastern side of the Alleghanies where a better article of iron can be produced than in the Deep River district, and at less cost. Its proximity to market gives it great advantages for becoming a large manufacturing district, which must be the case, from the weight and bulk of the coal and iron and its cost in transportation; besides, it will prove far more economical and profitable to manufacture articles on the spot.

I am of opinion that very little, if any, coal will be sent to market from this district, unless for use in generating gas, which may be able to afford the price it will command for the manufacture of iron.

There are few places to be found in our country where there is such a concentration of material, and which can be mined with so little toil and expense; an abundance of the best fuel, consisting of charcoal, and the mineral coals susceptible of being advantageously coked, and in great quantity and variety for all purposes of the arts, as well as domestic uses; fire clays for refractory furnaces; building materials of sandstone, gneiss and granite; millstone grit, and fine sandstone for grindstones; clays and sands for the manufacture of glass and porcelain. Of the latter class there is a large tract near Jones' Falls—a part of the plantation of Captain Bryan.

Steatite, or soapstone, and agalmatolite are found in extensive masses in Chatham county, near Hancock's mills, in alternate beds with the metamorphic slates. The latter is of exceedingly fine and compact grain, and has a very soft and soapy feeling, and is of a greenish white color. It is different in composition from the steatite or soapstone, and is of a much finer grain. It can be applied to the same uses; but that which has been quarried in Chatham county has been ground at Stuart's mills, on the Deep river, to a powder as fine as flour, and exported to New York, where it is used for clarifying sugar. It sells for $18 or $20 a ton; but in Carolina I was told that it was believed to be used for the adulteration of paints or soaps, and for a cosmetic. Its composition is given by Professor Emmons from an analysis of Jackson, as follows:

Silex	73.00
Alumina	18.76
Potash	2.00
Water	3.55
	97.21

Roofing slates are found on Rocky river, near the residence of Mr. Johnson. Specimens were brought me of some size and suitable thickness. They were of a light slate color, compact, and appeared to split smooth and even.

I had no time to visit the quarry, but learned from reliable authority that it was well situated near the forks and above water level, and could be easily obtained.

Timber.—The Deep River country is the dividing line between the alluvial and primitive formation. The change of vegetation has a well-defined outline, the long leafed pine lying on the south, and the oaks and other timber on the north. Our examination of the timber extended not only over the Deep River country above described, but over many miles surrounding it. This examination proved conclusively that there was but a small quantity of large oak and other timber required for naval purposes. There are considerable quantities of the middle size, which is well adapted for the construction of vessels and machinery.

Most of the country has been cleared, and the large timber cut down or fallen; the few left standing are partially decayed and useless.

As the country is becoming more settled, and improvements are progressing, this timber will fast disappear. On the south the virgin pine forest yet exists, of which kind of timber there is an abundant supply of all sizes.

In the examination of this district the water-power claimed much of my attention. It has been previously mentioned that the Deep River has been dammed, to effect its slack-water navigation. These dams are five in number, with a fall of thirty feet, and the water is set back at the upper pool as far as Woomble branch. Beyond this is the Hancock mills, which is the only one I shall include in the Deep River district. The last dam is at Evans' Bridge, where there is a lock, and several mills for grain, etc. The next dam below is at the Gulf, and has a large flour mill, as well as carding machines, owned by Mr. Lawrence Haughton The third is at the bend of the river, below Egypt, where the fall is about seven feet. There is no mill yet erected at this place. The fourth is at Clegg's, below the Rocky River, and the fifth and lowest is at Jones' Falls. Here they are improving the water power, and several mills are being repaired and constructed. This fall is two and a half miles from the Cape Fear river. This slack-water navigation is uninterrupted, as will also be the mills, during the entire year.

Besides this water power on the Deep River, there are very many sites on the Haw, Rocky, and Cape Fear rivers; and on most of the creeks leading into the Deep River, there are mills for grinding the cereals and sawing the timber, of great convenience, as well as of advantage, to the country.

We now come to the consideration of the accessibility of this district or the ways and means of transporting its materials to the markets of the world.

The first which claimed my attention was the slack-water navigation of the Cape Fear and Deep rivers. This is effected through the construction of nineteen dams and locks, from Jones' Falls, on the Cape Fear, to above that at Evans' bridge, the pool of which latter reaches the Woomble branch of the Deep River. The whole distance is ninety-eight miles, and the height overcome 204 feet.

Below Fayetteville, some eight miles, the shoals of the Cape Fear river are encountered. When drought prevails there is not a sufficiency of water over these shoals to float a steamer drawing more than eighteen inches water.

These shoals it is thought could be avoided by a canal around them or deepened by a sluice.

COAL AND IRON OF NORTH CAROLINA. 177

The river is navigable for ten months in the year, and boats used on the river and slack-water navigation can then pass free from all detention,

Steamboats ply daily between Wilmington and Fayetteville, a distance of 100 miles in twelve hours, and those of small size will be employed to tow the barges on the slack-water navigation.

Besides their slack-water navigation the citizens of Fayetteville have undertaken to construct a railroad direct to the coal fields, with the intention of carrying it on to the junction with the Central road, near High Point, and have pushed its structure with great energy and perseverance.

Other improvements are projected; among them a railroad from the coal fields to Raleigh, a distance of some thirty miles. The route is a most favorable one, and will make another connection with the Central road, also with the Gaston and Raleigh, and through it with the Seaboard and Roanoke, which will place the coal fields into direct communication of a few hours with Norfolk.

Besides the above, there will be a connection with the harbor of Beaufort, by the Central road to Goldsboro', and thence, by the Newbern and Morehead City, to that point. The distance of both the above routes is less than 200 miles. There is also a connection talked of between Fayetteville and Warsaw, on the Wilmington and Weldon, and from the latter, by a branch road, at Kinston, which will give another route.

On leaving the Deep River district I took the plank road from the Gulf to Fayetteville, a distance of fifty miles, in a southerly direction. The country is very sparsely settled, and is generally covered by the virgin forest of long leaf pine. But few of the trees have been "boxed." The country rises until the plantation of A. Schermerhorn is reached, where it is four hundred feet above the level, and forms the dividing line of waters flowing north and south. Here the Gulf plank road joins that from Fayetteville to Ashboro', in Randolph county.

From Schermerhorn's to Wilmington there is a regular series of undulations, not unlike the ground-swell of the ocean, extending to within a few miles of Fayetteville, and these undulations tend east and west and appear to extend over this whole section of country; lie directly across the line of railroad, running nearly north and south; consequently require heavy, deep cutting. In one of these, about ten miles from Fayetteville, the substratum has been reached, corresponding to the surface undulations, and exposing to view the tenacious and unctuous blue clay of which it is composed.

The country, to within a few miles of Fayetteville, continues to be well wooded with the long leaf pine; the soil is sandy, though occasionally we passed over some of the sandstone, or the "hard pan rock," of the country, (and which frequently caps the undulations spoken of above). It is of a dark brown or reddish color, is used in building, and is a cheap and easy wrought material, but cannot bear exposure to heat.

Fayetteville is well situated on the north side of Rockfish creek, some 72 feet above the level of the Cape Fear river, when at its lowest stages. During freshets the river rises 50 feet, but these pass off rapidly. On the Rockfish creek and the streams there is excellent water power, on which a number of mills have been established for the manufacture of cotton, paper, etc.

Having given the details of the examination of the Deep river country, its coal, iron, and timber, I shall consider that part of the resolution of the Senate relative to the "expediency of establishing, at some point in the State, machine and workshops for the constructing of engines, boilers, etc., etc., for naval vessels." The contents of this report fully establish the fact that there is an abundance of the raw materials for the manufacture of iron of the very best description, for use in the construction of engines and boilers for naval vessels; that, with the exception of the largest size of timber, there is also an abundance of that material for use in the construction of implements of wood employed on naval vessels, and there is no doubt that all these materials can be obtained at less cost and of superior quality than elsewhere in the eastern section of the United States. This could be accomplished either by the government erecting furnaces for the reduction of the ores, or by encouragement offered for the best kinds of iron, etc., for these purposes.

There can be no doubt of the expediency of having the indestructible materials used in our steam navy, of the very best kind, constantly on hand, to meet the wants of the steam service; and I can see no difficulty in the government establishing machine and workshops for the construction of all the parts of the engines and plates for boilers, as well as workshops for the making of implements required, of wood, in the naval service.

As to the expediency of establishing these at some point in the State of North Carolina, you will be able to come to a correct conclusion upon the subject, now that all the facts are laid before you.

Our attention being specially directed to the Deep river country, we have a better knowledge of it than any other part of the State; and we believe that no other portion of North Carolina can offer so many advantages for the manufacture of iron as the Deep river district. Besides an abundance of raw material, there is both water and steam-power at command. The climate is salubrious and the country healthy ; all kinds of provisions abundant and cheap. The agricultural products consist of wheat, corn, rye, and oats. Vegetables and fruits are to be had in their season, in plenty and of fine kinds.

The great advantages it offers to the miner and manufacturer of iron will insure a large population of those engaged in these pursuits. It is also desirable for the agriculturist; finer crops are seldom seen than those which fell under our observation, on the bottom lands, bordering the ravines and creeks, and they seldom fail.

The temperature neither partakes of the extremes of winter or summer; and those who have passed many years there enjoyed excellent health. Although constantly exposed during the months of August and September, in the hottest weather, I felt little inconvenience and no debility from the effects of heat after I reached this district. The navigation of the river is never closed by ice, and travel on the railroads rarely interrupted.

The distance from Washington is less than 24 hours by rail, and when the contemplated improvements are finished there will be means of transportation north, south, east, and west.

I herewith submit copies of the reports of Chief Engineers Hunt and D. B. Martin, and Naval Constructor S. M. Pook, to me, relative to the fulfillment of the duties assigned them in the examination of the Deep river district. It affords me pleasure to state that their duties were performed to my entire satisfaction.

I annex a map of the Deep river district, prepared by myself, to which reference has been made in the body of this report.

I have the honor to be, with great respect,
CHARLES WILKES,
Captain United States Navy, Chief of Com'n.
Hon. Isaac Toucey,
Secretary of the Navy, Washington.

PART II.

COAL AND IRON COUNTIES

OF

NORTH CAROLINA.

Piedmont and the Mountains.

[As seen by a New Englander.]

There are two sections of North Carolina especially worthy the attention of those citizens of the temperate zone, who for any cause wish to change their place of residence. One of these is the Piedmont, the other the Mountain region. If the reader will draw a line on the map from Virginia through Raleigh to the Georgia border, all the country lying west of that to the Blue Ridge Mountains may be considered the first division, while all that extensive territory beyond the Blue Ridge to the Summit of the Unaka or Great Smoky Range, comprises the Second or Mountain Division. In these two vast sections of the State are to be found grander opportunities for the safe investment of capital that will speedily prove largely remunerative, and for the planting of colonies of farmers and mechanics, than any where else in the United States. While the Piedmont Region is well settled by a thrifty and prosperous people, it is by no means crowded. Tens of thousands of acres of virgin soil and numerous extensive tracts of woodland await the coming of purchasers who will improve them. The cities, towns and farming settlements are inhabited by a sensible, energetic and neighborly race of Americans, most of whom have made themselves prosperous by their own thrift and industry, aided by the salubrity of the climate, the excellence of the soil, the abundance of unfailing water powers, and access to market over perfected systems of railways. Wheat, corn, rye, oats, barley, cotton and tobacco, are among the staples of agriculture, while apples, peaches, apricots, plums, cherries and small fruits flourish there with much greater certainty of annual crops than in any State north of Maryland. As compared with Springfield, Massachusetts, the climate of Charlotte is from six to eight weeks earlier in the spring, and the frosts of fall are two or three weeks later. The Piedmont railroad and its connecting lines afford quick transit for passengers and freight to the cities of the Gulf States, to the mountains by way of Asheville, and to Charleston, Wilmington, Richmond and Norfolk, as may be desired. There is scarcely a railroad town in New England, New York or Ohio that is not within forty-eight hours journey of all the railway stations of this Piedmont region. In the principal towns are good schools and academies; religious privileges for votaries of all the leading sects; and stores well stocked with every class of merchandise. Besides all this the people are glad to welcome new comers and to share freely with them the multiplied blessings they enjoy. There is no such thing as ostracism on account of religious or political creeds. The North Carolinians believe in free thought and free speech, in working for a living, and in maintaining social relations with all decent people, but they have no use for vagabonds or rogues. Many of the people of this section have gone there from New England since the war, or are descendants of those who emigrated earlier, and such hold in kind regard the States where their fathers and mothers were born. There is nothing of that false display in which those who have suddenly attained wealth too often indulge, but the richest people live without ostentation, while the majority belong to that middle class which is really the cream of American society. The evidences of quiet refinement to be seen at Raleigh, Durham, Greensboro and Charlotte, are characteristic of the people, and no one traveling among them for several months can conclude otherwise than that the ancient petition, "Give me neither poverty nor riches," has been generally offered and answered.

The leading industries of this section, outside of agriculture and horticulture, are the mining of iron and coal, manufacturing of woollen and cotton fabrics, merchandising, lumbering, getting out hubs, spokes, rims, shuttle-blocks and tool handles; cotton-seed oil mills; and the manufacture of all forms of tobacco from the very rich and valuable leaf which grows only in this State. Since the war several of these industries have risen at a rapid rate, and have poured steady streams of wealth among the people. Little crossroad villages have been transformed into large and prosperous boroughs, in which blocks of brick warehouses and stores, fine school-houses and churches, and numerous tasteful residences, have supplanted the few miserable shanties and their poverty stricken inmates that were to be seen in the same localities in 1865. The collection and shipment of dried fruits and of medicinal herbs are also important industries which bring into the state annually from one to two millions of dollars.

All these things are but the beginning of what may be.

Cattle, sheep, poultry, horses and mules, could be raised with large profit on many a tract of land long owned but never improved.

Manufacturers of farm wagons, of tinware, of boots and shoes, of agricultural implements, of cheap furniture are wanted. Good machine shops, well appointed and run by skilled workmen, would pay. But above all, there might be ten farmers and horticulturists for every one there is now, besides fruit and vegetable canners, and a host of others with some money and that experience which is better than money, to introduce and carry to success their respective trades.

One of the principal gold belts of the state runs through this section with many mines in operation. Those fond of this fascinating and uncertain pursuit can find no better place in which to prospect, and a few will make rich strikes as others have done before them, but the bright leaf tobacco of Granville and a dozen other counties will annually draw more gold from the sun and soil than all the mines in the state combined. Most of these mines of precious ores have required the expenditure of large sums of money for their development, but the farm lands of the state are more sure in the long run of paying handsome annual profits to their owners, and but a few hundred dollars are sufficient capital for an industrious beginner. In this section wild lands and old fields can be bought at from five dollars an acre upwards to $200, the price depending on the quality of the soil, the extent of improvements, and the nearness of railway stations and market towns. Some exceedingly desirable sites for settlements may be found in near proximity to the Western North Carolina road, between Salisbury and Henry's, the latter the last station before climbing the Blue Ridge over the most astonishing piece of railroad construction known to engineering science. The towns of Statesville, Hickory, Morganton and others that have sprung up by the side of the same road within a dozen years, are more like modern western than old time southern settlements in their rapid growth, extensive business, and the good taste, enterprise and public spirit of their citizens. Other roads, acting as feeders to this great and costly through line, are fast opening up counties between it and Virginia, where land may be obtained at lower prices, and where climate, soil and people have the same general characteristics that have already been noted. South of the Western North Carolina road and running to some point of intersection with it, several other roads are under construction that will eventually enter the mountains by one of the many gaps on the eastern and southern front of the Blue Ridge, while others are projected whose building is merely a question of time. The entire North Carolina frontage of the mountain range and the land between that and the imaginary line extending north and south from Raleigh, will repay examination, whether the visitor be a tourist "on pleasure bent," a capitalist looking out for profitable investments, or a farmer, grazier, manufacturer or artisan, seeking a suitable location for business and a home.

No man, and especially no native of the States north of the Potomac and Ohio rivers, or of

Europe or Canada, ought to decide upon a permanent location until he has visited that mountain division of North Carolina which lies between the two grand ranges of the vast Appalachian system. This magnificent section of the State is very thinly settled, except in a few widely remote localities, and much of it is in a condition of primeval nature. The capitals of the different counties are, with the exception of Asheville, small villages of a few hundred inhabitants, with a square brick court house in the centre, around which are the stores, churches, hotels, dwelling houses, schools, smithies, and other small shops, which supply the needs of the people. The Western North Carolina railroad, having climbed the mountains by way of Swanannoa Gap, descends easily to Asheville on the banks of the beautiful French Broad river, and thence runs northward to the celebrated Warm Springs, where connection is made with a branch line of the East Tennessee, Virginia, and Georgia system. The main line continues westwardly from Asheville, and runs daily trains from and to Pigeon River. Most of the grading has been done between there and Charleston, the capital of Swain County, and there is nothing of consequence to prevent the company from reaching that place before Christmas. Some miles west of Pigeon River station, the road strikes the Tuckaseege, a branch of the Tennessee, and follows the valley of that stream to its mouth, twelve miles west of Charleston. At that point the road will continue down the Tennessee, crossing the great Smoky Mountains at the State line, and thence, turning to the north, it will run to Marysville, thus completing a long projected connection with Knoxville and the west, by means of the railway already in operation between that city and Marysville. At the same time a grading force is at work on another important thoroughfare which is to connect the Knoxville extension with the famous Ducktown copper district of Tennessee; with the narrow gauge road rapidly nearing completion from Marietta, Georgia; and with the broad gauge that, starting at Athens, Georgia, carried thousands of passengers to Tallulah Falls last year, and will soon be pushed forward to Rabun Gap, and to the head waters of the Tennessee river, which stream it will follow to the mouth of the Tuckaseege, where it will effect a junction with the main western line as already described. Another road, starting from Spartanburg, South Carolina, has been in operation a number of years between that place and Hendersonville, the capital of Henderson County, which must at no distant day be finished either to some point near Pigeon river, or else to Asheville, in either case making a tolerably direct through route between Charleston and the great west, a matter of no mean importance to the mountaineers as well as to the people of South Carolina.

The natural resources of these mountains, if fully described, would require a large volume to do them even moderate justice. They may be divided into four distinct groups, under the head of forest, mineral, and vegetable products, and water powers. Of the first it is sufficient to say that nine-tenths of the entire region is covered with forests, in which are nearly all the varieties of trees needed for building, manufacturing, and ornamental purposes to be found in any State east of the Rocky Mountains. White pine, balsam, hemlock, hickory, ash, black walnut, chestnut, maple, birch, poplar, linn, locust, oaks of every kind, cherry of enormous size, spruce, cedar, gum, maples, laurel, butternut, persimmon, and dogwood (of which hundreds of thousands of shuttle blocks are sent north annually from the Piedmont district), and many other kinds. Since the Western North Carolina road has been in operation from Salisbury to Asheville and Pigeon river, a great impetus has been given to the black walnut trade, and hundreds of car-loads have been shipped both to the west and to the Atlantic coast, much of the latter having been ordered from France while the trees were still standing in their native forests. The poplar of this section is highly prized for many purposes, the trees often growing to an enormous size and admitting of three or four cuts of twelve feet each, below the branches. Within two years thousands of logs have been cut on the banks of the Tuckaseege, and floated down that stream and the Tennessee river, to be put into merchantable shape by the saw mills in the vicinity of Chattanooga, which are owned by some wealthy lumbermen from Michigan. For a number of years before the war some German cabinet makers had a factory at Asheville, and produced fine work from the native woods of that vicinity, which was carted hundreds of miles over the rough mountain roads and sold at a high profit to the wealthy inhabitants of North Carolina and Virginia. The civil war broke up that establishment, and the skilled artisans were employed at the large Confederate armory in Columbia, South Carolina, in making gun stocks. After peace was declared these men scattered, and the Asheville factory ceased to be. What was done by those Germans under the most unfavorable conditions could be repeated now without any of the disadvantages under which they labored, and there are hundreds of places in the mountains where all requisites for manufacturing either low-priced or expensive furniture may be had in close proximity to unfailing water powers and to railroad transportation.

The minerals of this mountain country are iron in all forms of the ore; copper, alone or in combination with other metals; gold in dust, coarse grains, and nuggets, in quartz, and in nearly all other forms; silver, which has been found with copper and galena, but not as yet in large quantities; manganese; lead; nickel; chrome ores; precious stones; asbestos; corundum (of which hundreds of tons are sent annually to Woburn, Massachusetts); marble, in every variety from pure white to that beautiful translucent pink which has been called "North Carolina onyx;" mica (which was known to the mound builders centuries before the white race effected a lodgment in North America); soapstone, from white to a bluish gray; talc; potter's clay, of every known quality; flexible sandstone (said to be the matrix of the diamond); ochres of many tints, and mineral paints; as also staurolites and many other of the curiosities of mineralogy which have no practical value. Two vast bodies of iron ores of remarkable purity have been traced for many continuous miles, and one of them in the northwestern corner of the State, near the Tennessee border, has recently been developed on an extensive scale. This, which is known as the Cranberry ore, has certain peculiarities which have made it famous among mineralogists and iron smelters all over the world. The other is a limonite ore of remarkable purity, which extends across the entire length of Cherokee (the southwestern county of the State,) and crops out at frequent intervals for thirty miles south of the Georgian border. Smelted and hammered into bars by the use of charcoal fires only, it is transformed into a pure steel of extraordinary strength and ductility. Although used by the whites ever since they began to settle the country, it has never been mined or manufactured on a large scale, because of its distance from market, and the expense of transportation. Within twelve months the Marietta and North Georgia railroad will run through the centre of a large part of this iron district, and a number of Northern gentlemen who have bought extensive tracts of this iron territory will soon build smelting furnaces and set bodies of miners at work. As soon as their operations are fairly started, there will be a grand chance for others in their immediate vicinity, such as plow, scythe and hoe manufacturers; shops for making all kinds and sizes of nuts and bolts, of nails, of hollow ware, of stoves, and of all such articles made from iron as are produced by machinery assisted mainly by unskilled labor.

The vegetable resources of this region cover an extensive range of subjects. Omitting the medicinal plants, roots, barks, berries and leaves, of which more than two thousand kinds are gathered annually for Wallace & Sons, of Statesville, who supply the greatest drug houses of America and Europe with these natural medicines, and the numerous barks and weeds bought for their excellence for either tanning or dyeing, there are others of greater value. The sweet herbs and succulent grasses of the mountains afford the best of pasturage for horses, cattle and sheep, for eight months of the year, while the mast of the countless oaks, beeches, chestnuts and chinquapins are equally abundant and nutritious for hogs and for domestic fowls. Many mountain farmers keep their stock on the range the year round, but there is no economy in that course, for the losses they experience in the long run are much greater than all that they save. Nature has made this a grand region for stock, which thus far has escaped the various epidemic diseases that afflict other cattle-breeding sections of the Union, and were one quarter the care bestowed upon them from the middle of December to the first of March that Ohio and Illinois farmers give to their stock, the North Carolina stock raisers' profits would be more than doubled. This is a matter of much greater importance than it used to be, for as railroads open the country and bring manufacturing industries in their train, a local demand for beef and mutton will be created, while the large cities of all the cotton-growing States will be constant customers. Besides the native grasses and succulent herbs already referred to, there are at least eight kinds of wild peas found in the mountains, which in both vine and fruit are excellent fattening food, of which hogs and all kinds of cattle are very fond. For human use there are wild plums of several kinds, grapes of many varieties from the little fox, that seems to be the same wherever found, to some large and luscious kinds as well worthy of propagation, as the Scuppernong or the

Catawba. One of these, which was found in the woods near Murphy by Professor William Beal, was transplanted, and after cultivation had proved its great merits, it was carefully propagated, and now there are many vines of it to be found festooning the cabins of the mountaineers, who call it "the Cherokee," the name given by its discoverer. Next to the grape in importance is the blackberry, of which there are three kinds, the white, the low bush, and the high vines. The fruit of the last, when cultivated at all, is equal in size to the Kittatiny and surpasses it in sweetness and flavor. It is an enormous bearer, and as it is easily and rapidly gathered and dried, tons of it are saved and bartered at the country stores for other merchandise.

The water powers of the mountain and Piedmont sections ought to have a chapter to themselves, but in this paper there is room for but a passing reference. In the former they are more numerous, in the latter, as a rule, they carry much greater power. It has been estimated by a careful scientist, that there are unemployed water powers in the State, the aggregate of which would represent a greater number of horse powers than all the locomotives and steam engines combined now running on this continent. This has at first sight the appearance of a Munchausenism, but after months of observation, this writer has been compelled to acknowledge that the eminent gentleman to whom that statement was imputed was entirely within bounds. In the mountains there are large and small falls that can be utilized for every manufacturing purpose, and in most cases without the need of costly dams to be constructed and kept in repair. Riding through the country one comes frequently upon a little log building called in the vernacular "a merchant mill," over whose large breast wheel a small stream of water, clear as crystal, is pouring, which has been diverted from its native brook by a narrow ditch, often not more than fifty yards long, only to join its parent waters again after doing its share of the miller's work. These little mills grind the wheat and corn of the neighborhood, and often are of so small capacity that twenty-five bushels is considered a good day's work. They are always picturesque, but never more so than when tended by the miller's daughter, usually a bright eyed, fair faced maiden, who looks shyly up from beneath her sun bonnet for a glance at the passing stranger, and then turns to the hopper again and attends to business. Another frequent sight in these mountains is that of a strapping bare-footed merry boy, whistling as he tramps along the road with his sack thrown over his shoulder, a half bushel of corn in each end " to keep the balance true." How many "matches are made in heaven," these mills being the portals thereto, who can tell? But besides these small branches with their frequent falls, there are many large creeks and rivers that can be made to do duty in the same way, and when railroads shall be finished, mines opened, furnaces built, and factories erected, the roaring cataracts whose eternal thunders fill the forest with their grand diapasons, will be tamed to man's use, and help to swell that sublime orchestra of trip-hammers and anvils, of saws, looms, and clattering machinery, that together make the music of modern civilization, and of science applied to the practical arts.

The mountaineers of North Carolina are a

sturdy race sprung from no ordinary stock. Among them, as in all communities, are some lazy and shiftless people, whose only care is to fill their bellies with the least possible outlay of labor and to build a new cabin close to the timber as soon as fire wood has to be hauled any distance. Then there are the "dog and gun men" that keep beyond the confines of that advancing population that drives the game from its fastnesses, and spoils their hunting. Mixed with these, but not of them, are a few outlaws from the circle of States around them, who may be wanted for some outrage, and, therefore, take up a residence in a well chosen spot from which in a day they can retreat to Tennessee, Georgia, or South Carolina, as prudence may at the time direct. Soon after the war these outlaws were numerous in the western counties, but the people made the country too hot for their habitation, and they have ceased to exist as a class. Desperadoes of this kind were numerous before the suppression of illicit distilling, but since that has been accomplished by the united efforts of the State authorities and the revenue officers, the local law has been sufficient to free the country to a great extent from these dangerous classes. As the mountain climate and soil was not suited to large plantations, very few negroes ever lived there, and the gregarious habits of that race, as well as the comparatively cool winters, have kept them from settling there in any considerable numbers since they became free. The mountaineers who constitute the majority of the population are a tall, handsome, athletic race, shrewd to a degree, fond of a joke, hospitable, proud, eager to have their country appreciated by strangers, and longing for the day when railroads and increased population shall give them more privileges, and a greater zest to their quiet lives. They especially long for northern men to settle among them and to start the various trades of which they have heard much, but know little. They are honest, religious after their fashion, can generally read and write, but have very little book learning, or that knowledge of the great outside world obtained from newspapers and periodicals. In the country towns there are neat frame houses, occasional gardens, and in some instances a few home adornments. There is usually an academy in which all are taught, from a. b. c. classes, to the youth pursuing classical studies. The farm houses are generally log cabins which tell the history of the family. One comparatively new will have a single room and a lean-to, in which all indoor life is transacted. That belongs to a young couple recently started together on life's journey. As children increase, (and the climate and soil dispose to fecundity) more room is required, and a second cabin is put beside the first, the space between being roofed over for the family loom. After a while one of the girls is married, and a third cabin is built next beyond the second, and a new family is started. Beyond this the mountaineer seldom gets, but his porch extends from the old cabin to the second and then to the third, so that all meet daily on a common platform. When a mountaineer lives on a road distant from taverns, he often arranges his domestic affairs so as to entertain strangers, and it is no unusual thing for several beds to be set up in one room, the man and his wife occupying the first, the children cuddled into the second, and the stranger in the third, but everything is managed with a homely delicacy that makes one unaccustomed to this style of living feel quite at ease.

The principal agricultural products are corn, wheat, rye, oats, cowpeas, beans, Irish potatoes, yams and sweet potatoes, sorghum syrup, cabbages (rarely onions and tomatoes, though both do well), butter, eggs and honey. Nearly every farm has peach and apple trees, the first generally yielding fair crops and the last never failing. During the summer, the drying of these and of blackberries takes nearly all the spare time of every member of the household, for these, with feathers, eggs, butter, honey in the comb, the medicinal herbs gathered, and the wool not carded for the family loom, are all taken to the store to be exchanged for sugar, coffee, snuff, and such few other things as they must buy. The wives of the mountaineers have a much harder life than their husbands, for in the absence of help they have all the ordinary work of the family to do, besides the carding, spinning, and weaving of the materials, and the making of all the family garments. They rise and, as a rule, go to bed with the sun. A trip to the county town once or twice a year, a camp meeting lasting a week, a birth, wedding, or funeral in the neighborhood, these are their recreations. In planting and harvest time they often help in the fields, in addition to the home drudgery and the care of their children. Yet as a whole they are as happy and contented a body of wives and mothers as can be found in the land, devoted to their husbands and children, and knowing no better life than that in which they but do as their mothers and grandmothers did before them. The usual food found in a mountain cabin at every meal is ashcake (a kind of corn bread wet up with water, moulded into an oblong loaf, and baked in the ashes), strong coffee without milk, fried eggs, fried bacon, stewed fruit, quick-raised wheat biscuits, sorghum syrup, honey in the comb, buttermilk, and often fried chicken. Occasionally, when one of the boys has caught a string of trout, or the old man has shot a wild turkey, these come in for variety, but such exceptions are rare as angel's visits. On the porch there is always a tin basin, a bucket of clear water, and a nice clean roller towel for the ablutions of a guest. The barn, the cowhouse, and the cornshed are all made of logs put up in cobhouse style, but with a tight roof over them. There are small coops for brooding hens and sheltered places for nests, but at night the fruit trees and outbuildings make their roosting places. The bees are hived in hollow logs, about thirty inches high, which stand in long rows in sunny places near the house, and are called "bee-gums." Eight months in the year flowers bloom in these mountains, and the "gums" are filled several times every season by these persevering little workers. It is delightful to stand under a wild plum, a sour wood, or a crab apple tree when in bloom, and hear the unceasing music of these busy insects as they load themselves with the sweets that are to be stored in their hives. Not content with what is gathered by the willing workers in his own "gums," many a farmer takes a day off now and then to engage in the exciting sport of hunting for bee trees. Equipped with his bait-box, his small tin can of wheat flour, his keen axe, and his bucket, he enters the forest, and selecting some sunny glade for his venture, he deposits his bait box on a stone, and sitting near he watches for the coming of his hoped-for prey. Ere many minutes pass two or three bees arrive and take the bait. Quickly he dusts them with flour, and when they rise he shades his eyes with his hand and notes the direction of their flight. Other bees have come meanwhile, whom he serves in the same fashion. If after a few minutes the first of his dusted guests return he knows their tree is not far distant, and removes his bait a few rods in that direction. Sometimes he is fortunate enough to find the right spot in a few hours; at others he will spend days in the quest, and finally discover the hive in a crevice of the rocks, or in some huge stump, surrounded by concealing sprouts. Usually it is in a tall tree, with a great hollow in its interior, which must be felled before he can get at its contents, the accumulation of many seasons' labors. If he gets twenty-five or thirty pounds of comb he feels well-paid for his sport, but when, as is now and then the case, he gets a hundred weight or more, he exults in his success, and is for the time being the great man of his township.

The pipe is the mountaineer's solace, and his inseparable companion; consequently nearly every farm has in summer its carefully tended tobacco patch, the leaf of which is cured and stored for daily use. Some three or four years ago a citizen of that part of the State which has long borne the name of "the golden belt," because of the valuable bright leaf tobacco raised there, cultivated a small patch of it in Buncombe County with such success that others took it up, and the result was to make Asheville an important tobacco market, and to distribute many hundred thousand dollars annually among the farmers of Buncombe and the adjacent counties. Experiments made in other counties between Buncombe and the Georgia line have demonstrated the practicability of the successful cultivation of this species of the weed in all of them, and the average returns to an acre are so large that many farmers have begun to raise this crop, without waiting for railroads to be completed to carry it to market. When transportation is as convenient for the Southwestern counties as it now is for those around Asheville, bright tobacco will be one of the staple products of that entire region.

After what has been written, it seems needless to add that the climate of the mountain counties is as healthful as can be found anywhere in the world. Malaria is a disease never seen there except in the person of some invalid from the lowlands, whose physician has prescribed the ozone of the mountains as a better remedy than all the drugs mentioned in the dispensatory. Besides the pure air, the equable climate, the crystal waters, and the resinous balsams of the highest mountains, there are innumerable medicinal springs of more than ordinary healing virtue. Most extraordinary of any yet discovered are the Warm Springs in the north-western corner of the State, six miles from the Tennessee line, to which a train of the North Carolina Western railroad runs daily from Salisbury, taking passengers from the Richmond and Danville at that place. The station bears the name of the springs, and has become a great resort for both pleasure seekers and invalids. Soon after the war a large hotel was built there, to which additions have been made nearly every season, not excepting the present. Situated in the midst of lovely scenery, and the centre of many unique natural curiosities, it would be a delightful summer resort, but with these springs as the central attraction, it will in time become a second Saratoga, drawing guests to its hotel from all parts of the continent, and from Europe. This place, with the beautiful scenery in its immediate vicinity, is but one of the numerous attractions of the mountains. Asheville has long been noted for the loveliness of its surroundings, and for the courtesy of its people to visitors. It has grown to be the seat of a large and lucrative trade with the people of surrounding counties, and in it are many elegant houses, the summer homes of families of wealth and refinement from both Northern and Southern States. There are few towns of its population in the Union which have a future as bright as that which has dawned upon this capital of Buncombe County.

Those who climb the tortuous track of the railroad to Swanannoa Gap, and go thence either to Asheville or to Pigeon River have no conception of the broad plateaus and wide beautiful valleys to be seen further westward. The first idea of these is obtained at Waynesville, the capital of Haywood County, which is said to be the highest town east of the Rocky Mountains. This town will be accessible by railroad by midsummer of this year and soon become a favorite resort for tourists and sportsmen. The creeks abound in speckled trout, and in the early fall there are plenty of quail. Here is a broad and beautiful valley, surrounded by rich rolling land, affording fine pasturage. Great crops of wheat, corn and oats reward the labors of the agriculturist, and on every hand are evidences of the prosperity of the people. A short distance from it is a fine white sulphur spring, near to which a commodious hotel has been built. A short distance from town are the saw mills and other buildings of the Mitchell Lumber Company, an Indiana corporation, which has purchased an immense number of black walnut trees and is now engaged in felling and hauling them to mill, in expectation of the speedy coming of the railroad. Jackson County, next west of Haywood, is another immense body of land, in which are a few lofty mountains, and great areas of farming and grazing land. In these two counties are many mines of copper and mica, and in the latter are extensive and well defined veins of nickel and chrome ores. In both apples, peaches, and grapes, are produced in perfection, and each is noted for the size and quality of the beef cattle fattened on its mountain ranges and hillside pastures. Webster, the capital of Jackson County, is a small and pretty village, built on the level summit of a high knoll, from which it overlooks the country in every direction. It is about four miles from the Western railroad, with which it will ultimately be connected by either a branch railway or a plank road. A large back country finds its market and obtains its goods there. In the southern part of this county, not far from the South Carolina border, is Casher's valley, a long and broad tract of well-watered land, noted far and near for its beauty, and for its adaptability to stock-raising and tillage. It will be some years yet before any railroad will pass through that part of the mountains, but Henderson does now and both Franklin and the new town of Highlands will ultimately afford all necessary transportation to the graziers, who have long been in the habit of driving their stock across the Blue Ridge into South Carolina.

Swain on the north and Macon on the south are the pair of counties next west of Haywood and Jackson. Through the former flows the Tennessee River in a northerly direction, passing by Franklin, the County seat, then making a sharp turn to the west, where it receives the waters of the Tuckaseege to its bosom, and from there to the Great Smoky Mountains it is the dividing line between Swain and Graham Counties. Macon is in some respects one of the most remarkable subdivisions of this mountain country. Girt on the south by the Blue Ridge Mountains, from whose crest much of South Carolina and a large section of Georgia may be seen with the unassisted eye; dotted with lofty peaks "*which proudly prop the skies*," and are covered with magnificent timber to their summits, all of these lofty peaks easy of ascent; watered by innumerable streams, some of which wind sinuously through verdant meadows, while others dash in grand cataracts down the steep cliffs and through bowers of laurels and rhododendrons; mountains rich in many valuable minerals which have scarcely been prospected at all; streams teeming with trout; woods and thickets, favorite haunts of deer, bears, wild turkeys, and lesser game; a soil that in many places never fails to reward the labor of the husbandman; the home of the vine, and of many a dainty fern and flower that would be prizes to northern florists; such is especially the southern end of this county, where is located the young and growing colony of Highlands, wherein more fine houses have been erected in the eight years of its existence than in any other place on these mountains, Asheville alone excepted. Further north is Franklin, the county seat, a flourishing village, with some handsome and many comfortable houses. The best public edifice in any of these western counties is the court house, a brick building that is a model in its way, and creditable to the taste and liberality of the people. Lieutenant-Governor Robinson has his residence in the village, and the yard in front of it, bright with flowers from spring to fall, gives evidence of the good taste of the ladies of his family. Franklin has long and deservedly had a reputation for the excellence of its schools and the attention paid to the education of its youth. One of these days the railroad from Athens will pass through the town and give to it renewed life and activity, for the fertile fields, the splendid pasture lands, the noble forests and the varied minerals of its mountains will all swell the tide of its business and quicken the energies of the people of Macon County. Seven miles distant is the little hamlet called Car-too-ge-chay, with its neat Episcopal church, whose white tapering spire shines like a finger of silver against the dark green back ground of mountain forests. This church was built partly by the offerings of the people, and in part by the liberality of the bishop of the diocese, and of southern and northern churchmen. It is as yet a missionary station, the people doing what they can, and the general mission fund making up all deficiencies. Some twenty miles west of Franklin, on the upper Nantehala, is Munday's, a place made famous by Christian Reid's beautiful sketch published some years ago by the Appletons, called "The Land of the Sky." That idyllic love story of a summer in the mountains painted this place in brilliant colors which were true to nature. Munday is a famous sportsman, who knows where the trout hide in the dancing river, and where among the laurels to start his hounds for the coverts of the deer. His house is always open to travelers, and his table never lacks the best of game from the woods and waters. A tour of the mountains without a short stay at this resort is something to be ever regretted. Following a northerly road from thence, Valleytown, in Cherokee County, is reached in time for dinner at the quaint home of a widow lady named Walker. Here again is a broad plateau, covered for the greater part with a grove of stately oaks. The house itself, a two story frame building, fronts upon a yard in which rows of box and some shrub evergreens are trimmed into square masses of rather solemn-looking borders. This good lady, whose husband died early in the civil war, has reared a large family of sons to man's estate, and they are now among the most respected and thrifty citizens of her own and the two adjacent counties. One of them is a merchant and occupies a well-stocked store on the opposite side of the road, where he does a considerable and profitable trade. Inside, the house is neat, homelike and sunny, and the table is always bountifully supplied with food well cooked and nicely served. From thence the road continues through an undulating country until it reaches the summit of Red Marble Gap in Macon County, not far from its northwestern line. This spot was recently the occasion of a lively litigation between two railway companies, but now all is peaceful between them, and it is expected that both the Western North Carolina and the Marietta and North Georgia road are ready to unite their efforts on terms mutually satisfactory. Following the rough trail (called road by courtesy), the traveler passes down through one of the most weird ravines to be found anywhere in these mountains, and he is glad at least to reach the narrow valley of the Nantehala which has been dashing over precipices, and through the darkness of dense forests ever since he lost sight of it a few miles north of Munday's. At the entrance of this valley is the farm of Nelson, a perfect type of the best kind of mountaineer farmers — a quiet, thoughtful, earnest man who cultivates his land thoroughly, looks after his stock, notes all the changes of the season, is a weather prophet that would put Vennor to shame, and is a good neighbor and an obliging host. Some four miles below his place is the property of the Jarrett estate, on which, besides valuable farm land, and several thousands of acres of grand timber, there is a high mountain of marble, white, black, gray, plaided, and the "North Carolina Onyx" so called. In the same vicinity is a very large vein of white Soapstone which was mined for some time in the interest of a Cincinnati firm engaged in the manufacture of lava tips for gas burners. This infant industry was destroyed by heavy importations from Germany, which were sold at a price much less than they could be made for here. At the closing session of the late Congress, Senator Vance presented a memorial from all the mountaineer legislators asking protection for this industry, and it is hoped that when Congress shall meet again next December, his efforts in that direction will be crowned with success. The beauty of this part of the valley cannot be portrayed in fitting words. The rushing river, the high mountains with scores of streams dashing down their precipitous sides, the forests of immense poplars and beeches, of black walnut and oak, of birch and maple, of hemlock and cedar, surpass all description, while the rocks are covered with mosses, tiny ferns, and multiform lichens, and the rich soil along the river's bank from spring to fall is a mass of blooms. About the middle of March the air is laden with the fragrance of arbutus, whose masses of white and pink blossoms fill all the crevices on the upper side of the highway. A bright pink phlox nods above them, while in the cavities where a little earth has lodged between the road and the river delicate lilies are opening their purple bells, and wax plants covered with spray shine like the work of the Frost King. Leaving this enchanted region and continuing down stream, the changed timber indicates a totally different soil. Instead of limestone it is a slaty formation; the timber is light, poor, and of little value, and there is a scarcity of vegetable life. Here the road runs high up the mountain side and is well kept for several miles, but in descending a new geological belt is entered, the timber improves, and wild grass and herbage are seen once more. Finally the road becomes a cut blasted out of a flinty rock, (a rough and unsafe place for any but sure-footed beasts,) close to the water's edge. Yet over this, heavily laden teams pass almost daily, carrying produce to market, and returning with store goods. Soon after passing this dangerous point, the traveler enters Swain County, still following the Nantehala whose mouth is not many miles ahead. As he nears it the mountains slope farther away, the valley widens, and a few settlers' cabins are seen. About three miles from the confluence with the Tennessee is the stockade, occupied by the seventy-five convicts who have commenced the work of grading the Western railroad up the river towards Red Marble Gap. These with their overseers, guards, cooks, and the hired skilled laborers, make quite a force, and as both powder and dynamite are used whenever needed, they will make rapid progress through this difficult territory.

The present method of reaching Charleston, the capital of Swain County, from the south or west, is by fording the river not far from the stockade, and climbing a mountain which has been settled by many good farmers during the last twenty years, the traveler having first forded the Tennessee River about two miles from the Nantehala. On this mountain can be seen the perfection agriculture has reached in this part of the world—orchards, corn fields, wheat lands, and sheep pastures are everywhere. As has been said by many travelers, it is in truth a second Switzerland, but without the denser population of that country. The houses also do not rise one above another, as though built on terraces, but usually occupy a cove, the common name for a level stretch of land scooped by nature in the side of the mountain, a warm sheltered nook, where cabins, out-buildings and fruit trees are protected from heavy winds and tempestuous storms. But a few miles from the northern base of this mountain is Charleston, a small village on the banks of the Tuckaseege, twelve miles from its mouth. On this side the valley is narrow for several miles up stream, but on the other it spreads out into broad meadows and magnificent stretches of high table land, the soil everywhere being exceedingly fertile. The contractors of the Western North Carolina road have promised to reach this town no later than next Christmas, and the people are naturally very happy. Swain County, and Graham, its next neighbor, are alike in many respects, but unlike in others. Both of them are rich in iron and copper ores, in the quantity and excellence of their timber, in their prospects of gold and silver (as yet they are prospects only) and in their fine lands for tillage and grazing. Swain, however, got the start of its neighbor in population, and having the advantage of being nearer to Asheville and equally near to Tennessee, it has gained upon the other rapidly in numbers and wealth. To these the railroad will contribute continually, and as from the natural formation it must follow the north side of the river into the adjoining State, population will increase in a much greater ratio than heretofore. Now the most western settler of that region lives near to Hazel Creek, a bold clear mountain stream about sixteen miles from the State line. The entire valley in Swain County, from six miles west of Charleston, seems to have been arranged by nature purposely for a railway, and from that point until within three miles of the dividing line, the estimated average cost of grading, bridging and laying down cross-ties does not exceed $6,000 a mile. One peculiarity of this part of the State is that while very little arable land is seen near the banks of the Tennessee, yet on crossing the high ridge that walls-in its course, or journeying up the valley of any one of the creeks that have cut channels through it to the river, the eye ranges over a vast region admirably adapted to every department of agriculture.

The last two counties at the extreme western end of the State are Clay and Cherokee. The first is a county of comparatively small area, but a large proportion of it is fertile and well watered. In it are mines of corundum and other minerals of value, and it is inhabited by a people noted for industry, energy and intelligence. It has plenty of timber, fine water powers, and raises large crops of grain and many fat cattle. Hayesville, its chief town, is built on a hillside, and has a superior academy, while in the suburbs are two new churches, one of them of an architectural design both novel and pleasing. Railroad or not, the citizens of that county are determined to thrive, and believing that a good education will be worth more to their children than bank stocks or railway shares, they are investing all their spare money to secure the best that can be had. Cherokee, though last, is any thing but least of the counties of western North Carolina, and in some respects she has advantages over all her sisters. Not to speak of her timbers, which are equal to any, her ores and nuggets of gold, her marbles and soapstone, she has in her immense beds of iron ores the sources of fabulous wealth in the hereafter that is fast coming. The broad, lengthy and rich valleys of the Valley River, the Hiwassee and the Notteley, will yield an indefinite store of corn and wheat every year when suitably cultivated, while the numerous tributary creeks and branches flow through land equally arable and fertile. If any one sub-division of North Carolina can fully verify the ancient promise to the Hebrews of a land flowing with milk and honey, Cherokee County is that favored place. Whether considered as a grazing, a farming, a horticultural, a market gardening, a dairy, or a manufacturing country, Cherokee can be either or all. Cornering in between Tennessee and Georgia, destined to be united with the railroad system of the former State before another year has come and gone, and with the great copper belt of Tennessee a little later on, she, first of all her sisters, will reach the great cities of the Cotton States with her products, and feed them from her teeming granaries and orchards. Then market gardening will pay, and the rearing of veal, lamb and mutton for the shambles. Winter apples, always worth more in the cities of the Cotton States than oranges, will no longer be left to waste, but the enormous surplus that the hogs have heretofore devoured will be carefully gathered and turned into gold. The Cherokee people are worthy of the blessings in store for them. They have waited patiently, worked faithfully, and sacrificed much to secure the end that will soon be attained, and in their early prosperity every citizen of the State will share, for whatever benefits even the least of the commonwealth is equally an advantage to the whole.

It so chanced that an assistant editor of a New England paper spent some time at Atlanta, Ga., in 1881, in attendance upon the International Cotton Exposition. The great number of inquiries addressed to him by New England people about the Piedmont and Mountain divisions of North Carolina, led him to make three extended trips, through the one by railroad, over the other in the saddle; and to the writing of more than two hundred letters to leading newspapers. The substance of those letters has been embodied in this publication, which has been carefully revised for the information of his fellow citizens.

Visitors, after examining the display of North Carolina at the New England Manufacturers' and Mechanics' Institute, will in many instances ask, where shall those go who wish to settle in that State, and how can they know that they have made a wise selection? These are pertinent questions, but easily answered.

First, make up your minds what business you wish to engage in if you can find a place adapted to it. Guided by what you have seen at this exhibition, confer freely with Hon. Montford McGehee, Commissioner of Agriculture, as to your wishes, and learn from him approximately the prices of land in that part of the State, the peculiarities of climate if any, and all other things you think you ought to know. After these things are settled to your satisfaction, go and see for yourself. If you expect to find a paradise you will be mistaken. If you hope to light upon a spot where you can sit with folded hands and enjoy ease while your wealth accumulates, you had better stay at home. But if you are willing to go to North Carolina (as tens of thousands have been going to the West year after year for half a century) "to grow up with the country," there is no place in all our grand American heritage that affords such splendid chances as are to be found in the Piedmont and Mountain divisions of North Carolina, and if you are young by all means select the latter.

From the Sea to the Ridge.

[Kerr's Special Report,* 1880.]

To present the resources of the belt of country adjacent to this line specifically and in somewhat of detail, let us set down the main features of *the route, its topography, climate, soils, minerals, forests, agricultural products, manufactures and water power.*

THE ROUTE.

By reference to the map, it will be seen that, at the point where this road crosses the Cape Fear, near the Gulf (to which slackwater navigation has been carried and can easily be restored), the Blue Ridge is within 150 miles of steam navigation to the seaboard—nearer than at any other point south of Richmond.

TOPOGRAPHY.

Below the terminus of the road at Fayetteville, the country rises gradually from the sea to an elevation of about 200 feet, and may be described as a nearly level and slightly undulating champaign, except where the rivers have channeled it out, and carved it, along their immediate courses, into hills and bluffs of very limited elevation.

The hill country gradually succeeds as we go

---

* Report by Dr. Kerr, Geologist in charge of the Southern Division of the U. S. Geological Survey, on the resources of the country along the line of the Cape Fear and Yadkin Valley Railroad, through the middle region of North Carolina, from the head of Navigation near the Atlantic Seaboard, to the Blue Ridge and the high plateau beyond, to the border of the great valley of Virginia and Tennessee.

inland, and above the Gulf it increases in the unevenness of its surface and its altitude, until, at Greensboro, it is 850 feet above the tide. This midland plateau rises along the watershed between the Yadkin and the Dan to 1,000 feet, and so passes into the mountainous Piedmont section that flanks the Blue Ridge in a breadth of fifteen to twenty miles, having an elevation of 1,000 to 1,500 feet. On entering this region, the road sends off a branch northward, by Mt. Airy, toward Fancy Gap and the New River Valley in Virginia, while the main road follows the Valley of the Yadkin, between the Brushy Mountains and the Blue Ridge, to Patterson, where it meets the narrow gauge road from Chester, S. C., at an elevation of nearly 1,300 feet. From this point is begun the ascent along the spurs of the Blue Ridge, which, in the course of some twenty miles, carries us over this escarpment, and on to a plateau of 3,000 feet altitude, drained by the New River, whose head waters descend from a plateau of a thousand feet greater elevation, around the flanks of the Grandfather Mountain. The descent of some 1,500 feet from this region, and the connection with the railroad systems of Tennessee and Virginia, is effected by the Cranberry and Johnson City road.

WATER POWER AND MANUFACTURES.

The water power developed in the region opened by this road, from Fayetteville to the State line, where the waters of New River and Watauga pass into Virginia and Tennessee, will aggregate more than a quarter of a million horse power, many times more than enough to turn all the cotton mills in Massachusetts. In fact, there are not more than a score of cotton factories in the region, but the number is increasing every year. And here is motive power for many other manufacturing industries, which will spring up with the development of the country, such as handle and shuttle factories (of which there are several already); wagon and furniture, and barrel and bucket factories, and others of like character, for which the rich and abounding forests furnish materials; woollen mills, the whole region being adapted to sheep husbandry; not to mention the numerous tanneries, flouring mills and tobacco factories, which are multiplying rapidly with the wide increase of tobacco culture.

SOILS.

As already stated, the distribution of the rock formations in zones parallel to the Blue Ridge, which are, therefore, traversed in succession, from the drift and alluvions of the latest age on one hand, to the oldest granites, gneisses, schists and limestones on the other, gives rise to the greatest possible variety of soils. About Fayetteville and coastward are the sandy soils, the sandy loams, clay loams and clays, and every variety of alluvial deposit, with a large aggregate of peaty, swamp soil of inexhaustible fertility. As the hill country is approached, the gray, gravelly soils and red and yellow and chocolate soils of the slate and gneissic and granite region supervene, with every variety of texture and composition and adaptation; and the northwestern terminus of the road will be directly connected with the limestone soils of the great Appalachian valley. Here, therefore, in this wide range of soil characters, is one important condition of a varied agriculture. The other and controlling condition is

CLIMATE.

It will bear restating and emphasizing that no other commercial route in this country, of the same length as this railway (with its navigable water connection to the seaboard), includes so wide a climatic range. A reference to the geological report of 1875 shows a range of mean annual temperature from 66° at the mouth of the Cape Fear to 45° on the Grandfather plateau ; and these are, also, the figures for southern Alabama, Mississippi and Texas on one hand, and Canada and Sascatchewan on the other; that is, the climatic range along this route, of less than 300 miles, direct line, *is continental in extent*, from subtropical to cold temperate. The annual rainfall, given in the same report for the middle region of the State, is nearly forty-six inches, which is distributed in nearly equal amounts through all the months of the year.

The above facts—the variety of soils, the wide range of temperature, and the abundant rainfall, have, of course, found expression in a correspondingly great range of natural products, the flora having a really continental breadth and variety, from the palmetto and live oak on the one hand, to the white pine and Canadian fir on the other ; so that what I have said in the geological report of the variety and richness of the forests of the entire State may be applied with scarce a modification to this tract, which includes both the extremes that gave its unique breadth of climatic and botanical characteristics to the whole. That is, there are about one hundred species of woods

—more than in all Europe; of twenty-two species of oaks in the United States (east of the Rocky Mountains) nineteen are found here; all (eight) of the pines; four out of five spruces; all (five) of the maples; both of the walnuts; three of the five birches; six of the eight hickories; and all (seven) of the magnolias; more species of oaks than in all the States north of us.

It goes without saying that here is a source of business, of freights and manufactures capable of immediate and indefinite expansion and development. Already the woodmen of England, Canada and the northern States are exploring and marking the vast tracts of white oak forest on the Cape Fear and its tributaries; and many attempts have been made to establish wagon and other factories along this belt in the interior, unsuccessfully for want of just the facilities which this railway will furnish. And the export of oak staves to Spain and other foreign countries carried on sporadically and in a very lame and limited way, only waits for the advantage which this line can offer, to widen into a large and permanent and profitable business. Attempts have also been made unprofitably to utilize the white pine, the walnut, cherry, birdseye maple, and other cabinet woods, which abound in different sections along this line, and to put them into the northern furniture market; they ought to be easily successful when this road is opened.

Of the twenty kinds of timber admitted to the shipyards of New York, nearly all are found here. The following is a partial catalogue of the commercial timbers common to one or another section along this tract:

Pine, six species; white pine; fir, three species;

hemlock, juniper, cypress, red cedar; oak, fourteen species; hickory, six do.; walnut, two do.; chestnut, beech, black locust; maple, three species; ash, four do.; elm, three do.; cherry, holly, dogwood; gum, two species; sassafras, palmetto, magnolia (cucumber tree), persimmon, poplar; birch, two species; sycamore, tulip tree (poplar), linn (basswood); sixty four species, valuable for their timber.

Among these a single species, the long leaf pine yields in timber and naval stores products of $3,000,000 value annually; and the long leaf pine belt is traversed by more than fifty miles of the C. F. & Y. V. R. R. There are many other trees and shrubs of less importance, or whose value consists less, or not at all, in their timber, but in their leaves or bark, as the sumac, sweet gum, cane, etc.; and in addition to these, several hundred species of medicinal plants are gathered for export to all parts of the world, (such as ginseng, hellebore, etc.,) amounting to many thousand tons a year, chiefly from the mountain section. Thus it will be seen, that in these indigenous forest products are found the means and materials for large businesses and freights for an indefinite time; and the value of these resources, and the demand for them, increases rapidly year by year, as the accessible forest regions of the continent are more and more rapidly suffering exhaustion. The shops of Pittsburg, with their annual consumption of 50,000,000 cubic feet of timber, having exhausted the forests of several States, are already turning this way for their future supply; and so of Cincinnati and of Chicago, as the forests of Michigan and Upper Wisconsin swiftly disappear.

AGRICULTUAL PRODUCTS.

The great range of climate and of soil of this region constitute, of course, the basis, and furnish the essential conditions of the most varied agricultural industries. In fact, the United States Census Agricultural Statistics show that in this State are found all the products of all the States from the Northern lakes to the Gulf, with the single exception of the orange, which, as has been seen, is equivalent to saying, that this variety of productions are found along this tract—the fig and sugar cane at one extreme, buckwheat and rye being characteristic products of the other, while between are the rice fields of the lower Cape Fear, a wide cotton belt of 150 miles, succeeded by the wheat and bright tobacco region from the Gulf to the Blue Ridge. One half, at least, of this region, also, is eminently adapted to silk culture, which has been successfully established at several points, and promises a large expansion; and jute has also been grown here equal to the best raised in India. The whole region is also adapted to sheep husbandry, which has been profitably pursued from the first settlement of the country, and still is so in the eastern section and in the mountains; and the access to the world's wool market, which the railway will furnish, as well as the impulse it will give to manufacturing, should give an immediate and large expansion to this industry. The exchange of products between the extreme sections of the region promises, in the near future, business enough for a railway; it is like bringing Canada and Mississippi or Texas within twenty-four hours of each other. In Watauga one readily imagines himself in Vermont or Ontario ; and among the rice fields and Palmettos of the lower Cape Fear one has the agricultural landscape of the Gulf Coast ; and this says nothing of the products of the great valley beyond the mountains, opened by the connections of the line northward and westward.

MINERALS.

As the widely variant conditions of climate and soil gave rise to a remarkably extensive flora, and a very great number of useful plants, and to a notably varied agriculture, so the underlying geological conditions already referred to give scope for a correspondingly great range of mineral wealth. In fact, North Carolina contains a far larger number of minerals than any other State in the Union. Among these, which number, as far as known, about 160, many of the most useful are found in abundance along the tract of country traversed by, or immediately connected with this railway. It is needful to mention here only a few, and such as are likely to furnish considerable amounts of freight ; and first the marls are worthy to head the list in this respect. These beds of native fertilizers abound on the waters of the Cape Fear for nearly 100 miles ; and as the little State of New Jersey, less than the region of North Carolina opened by this road, raises and transports more than 100,000 tons per annum from her marl pits to every corner of the State, to the great profit of the railways and of agriculture, so one of the great and permanent and most profitable sources of business for this road will be found in the transportation of this article of prime agricultural necessity to the whole region in question quite to the mountains.

Next in order as we go inland, is the coal of Deep River and Dan River, to be distributed both ways from each, and carried to the seaboard also. And associated with these beds and in the immediate neighborhood of them, are numerous and valuable deposits of iron ore, as well as between them, in the intermediate midland region, and in the mountains and beyond. The transportation of these ores, many of them of the highest grade, and in large demand for the Bessemer steel manufacture everywhere, to the coal beds of this State and of Tennessee, as well as to the steel furnaces of Pennsylvania, must give rise to a great freighting business for the whole line. The copper and gold mines will also contribute no mean item to the aggregate bulk of business. A single copper mine in Ashe County will transfer to it many thousand tons of freight, that are now wagoned fifty miles, at very heavy cost. And if to this list be added the millstones, grindstones, soapstones, porcelain clays and building stones of the Midland and Deep River section, and the limestone, plaster and salt beds of Southwest Virginia, which an advancing agriculture will require to be distributed along the whole line, and thence to the whole State, it will be seen that the possibilities of the development of business for the road are almost unlimited, except by the intelligence and skill of its management.

It may be satisfactory to add to the above summary statement, the following synopsis and statistics of the resources of the country traversed by and immediately connected with the Cape Fear and Yadkin Valley railroad, by sections:—

CAPE FEAR SECTION.

I have spoken of the marls sufficiently, which this region can furnish in indefinite quantities. Wilmington will contribute rice from the neighboring plantations, and groceries and tropical fruits from the West Indies and Florida. The merchants of the interior have long considered this a better market for the purchase of these articles than New York. And from the upper Cape Fear, above Fayetteville for 50 miles, will come large shipments of timber and naval stores, as heretofore. There are many hundreds of square miles of the long leaf pine forests in this section yet to be opened to commerce. It will be seen, by reference to the United States Census, that this trade amounts to more than three millions per annum, and a large part of it is concentrated along the Cape Fear. The returns for 1879 give the shipments of naval stores from Fayetteville as aggregating 96,000 barrels.

From this section, also, there is a considerable export of cotton, as well as from the

DEEP RIVER SECTION.

This part of the territory is near the northern margin of the *cotton* producing zone, but improved culture and the increasing use of fertilizers, has greatly extended this industry, and it increases and widens year by year. The re-opened navigation of the Deep River offers facilities for the concentration of this product from a large territory. The shipments from Fayetteville were 17,000 bales last year.

In this section the long leaf pine and *oak forests* meet. There are some fine bodies of the latter along the river bottoms and those of its tributaries, and all over the intervening ridges and hills, for a dozen miles above the Gulf; and with the various species of oak are found other valuable woods—walnut, hickory and dogwood, etc., in abundance. A company from Baltimore are making arrangements to ship large quantities of the two latter woods this season.

The *coal beds* of this section are too well known to require any detailed discussion. The " Geology of North Carolina," 1875, contains a description of their character, extent, accessibility and various uses. They have been opened at two points, Egypt and the Gulf; and at the latter, operations are now carried on. The following analysis, from the geological report referred to, will best indicate the character and adaptation of this coal:

Carbon	60.7	59.3	63.3	70.5
Volatile matter	32.7	30.5	25.7	21.9
Ash	5.3	10.2	10.1	6.5
Sulphur	1.3	....	1.3	1.0

The first and second (by Schæffer and Genth, respectively) represent the coal at Egypt; the third, by Johnson, that at Wilcox's, some eight or ten miles above the Gulf; and the fourth, by Genth, that at the Gulf. Admiral Wilkes, in his report to the Secretary of the Navy, says: "It is well adapted for fuel, coking, gas and oil. It is a shining, clear coal, resembling the best specimens of Cumberland. It ignites easily and burns with a bright, clear combustion, and leaves a very little purplish gray ash. It swells and agglutinates, making a hollow fire. It yields a shining and very porous coke, and is an excellent coal for making gas, or for burning."

The president of the Norfolk Gas Works, who had it tested, says: "Our superintendent thinks it about equal to the best Clover Hill coal, giving, of 16 candle gas, 3¾ cubic feet per pound;" and this from coal which had been mined three years. Testimonies from other sources are equally emphatic, as will be seen in the report above referred to. There are several seams of coal, but the only one large enough to be of economical importance at present, is 6 feet thick, or 7½, if a second seam be included, which is separated from the former by 1½ feet of shale and black band iron ore. It is evident, that such coals must make, at least, a considerable local market for themselves, when facilities for their transportation are provided.

With this coal are associated large deposits of black band and ball iron ore, for the analysis and discussion of which the same report, and Dr. Emmons's and Admiral Wilkes's reports also are referred to. And in addition to these, there are many other iron ore beds, both in the immediate vicinity and along the track of the railway for some 20 miles, and up and down the river for a still greater distance. The following analysis from the geological report will indicate the general character of them:

Sesquioxide of Iron	69.73	67.50	....	..
Protoxide of Iron	0.84	....	47.50	40.
Phosphoric Acid	.06	...	....	..
Sulphur	.09	....	3.39	..
Carbon	...	....	31.30	34.

These represent the limonites, ball ores and black band of common occurrence about Haywood, Sanford, Egypt and the Gulf. The Evans vein, of hematite, 6 miles above the Gulf, gives 96.4 per cent. of peroxide of iron, and is otherwise a very pure ore. It is six feet thick. Another "bed of reddish brown ore, 2½ feet thick, at the Tysor place," contains, according to Emmons, 61 per cent. of iron. And there are several other beds of magnetic ore in the neighborhood, undeveloped, as at Glass', Unthank's and Headen's.

But the most important ore bed of the region is found at Ore Hill. The ore is limonite, except one vein near the summit of the hill, of specular ore, like the Evans. Many of the veins have been opened and worked at various times. Several of them are large, 10, 15 and more feet in thickness. The ore is very cellular and porous, and easily smelted, and makes a tough iron. The following analyses of the ore from a shaft 90 feet deep will represent its character:

Silica.................................	1.42	3.79
Oxide of Iron.........................	82.02	83.80
Lime and Magnesia...................	1.80	....
Phosphorus...........................	.00	....
Sulphur...............................	.00	0.44
Iron..................................	57.41	58.67

These analyses are by Genth and Hanna, and the samples were selected by myself from a heap of several hundred tons. The purity of this ore is conspicuous, and its quantity seems to be very great.

There are other outcrops of *specular* and *magnetic* ore further up the river, in Randolph County, from which excellent iron was made during the war, one of the beds most used being reported as 3 feet thick.

The *red and gray sandstones and granites* of this section will come more and more into demand for building purposes as the country advances and facilities for their carriage improve. The sandstones will also be used for grindstones, as during the war.

There are several *millstone quarries*, also, in Moore County, from one of which a Baltimore company are now cutting 8 to 10 pairs of stones a month, and are turning out two complete portable mills per week, of a ton and a half weight each. These are shipped to all parts of the country and to distant States. And the business is enlarging continually. The stone is a conglomerate and is of excellent quality; it has been used all over the middle region of the State for a century. A considerable business also is done in the same line at another quarry of a different kind of stone found in the granite region on the upper waters of Little River.

The *Soapstone beds* near the borders of Moore and Chatham, have also been extensively worked before the war, and to some extent since, and have furnished a large amount of freight for the road, and no doubt will do so again, as there is always a large demand for this article for various purposes in New York and elsewhere. One shipper in Fayetteville has forwarded 9,000 barrels (of 300 lbs. each), and several hundred tons in mass; and this represents only a small part of the aggregate shipments.

The Gold Mines of Moore and Randolph as they are gradually reopened, with the accumulation of capital, will, as in the times before the war, give rise to a considerable business in the transport of machinery, ores and supplies.

The Cotton Mills of Deep River, of which

there are six in full operation, will require a continually increasing amount of freighting business. They aggregate already nearly 20,000 spindles and several hundred looms, consuming about 150 bales a week. I have estimated elsewhere the total water power of this stream alone at nearly one million of spindles, and of this and Cape Fear, above Fayetteville, at above 3,000,000, so that in this favoring climate, in the midst of the cotton fields, in a region which can produce its own food supplies, there must be a rapid and very great expansion of this manufacture, with a corresponding increase of all sorts of business.

This section also produces a surplus of *grain* to be transported to the Cape Fear and coast region.

MIDLAND SECTION.

This portion of the tract includes the upper part of Randolph and Chatham, a large part of Guilford and Forsyth, Stokes, Yadkin, Surry, Wilkes and Caldwell—a region of nearly as great extent, and of more varied and abundant resources, than some entire States. It contains wide stretches of the finest forests in their primeval state. They abound, in extraordinary richness along the streams in the southern part of Guilford and along many of the intervening ridges, and on the upper waters of Haw River in the western and northern portions of the county; and again on the head streams of the Dan, on the flanks of the Sauratown Mountains, and in the valleys of the Yadkin and its numerous tributaries that come down from the slopes of the Blue Ridge. These will furnish immense quantities of white oak, and other species of oak, hickory, walnut, poplar, while the uplands and ridges and the spurs of the mountains abound in hickory, dogwood, yellow pine, chestnut and black locust. And above Patterson there are large forests of white pine.

This section also contains some of the best *iron deposits* of the State. The extensive range of magnetic ores that stretches for 30 miles across the middle of Guilford County is crossed by this road. These ores are of the highest grade; they are now being shipped by rail to Pennsylvania. When they are brought within 75 miles of water transportation, there is no good reason why they should not supplant the African, Spanish, English and Irish ores in the Bessemer furnaces of Pittsburg and of the whole State of Pennsylvania.

The extraordinary purity of these ores will be evident from the following analyses, made by Genth:

Silica................	0.76	5.68	0.40	1.30	0.50
Titanic Acid............	13.52	11.67	11.95	1.27	12.27
Magnetic Oxide Iron.....	79.53	72.74	81.89	93.63	79.16
Mang. Oxide & Cobalt..	0.81	0.64	1.02	0.93	1.21
Oxide Chromium........	0.45	0.48	1.07	1.43	0.57
Alumina...............	1.68	5.08	1.06	0.55	3.64
Magnesia..............	2.79	2.61	1.99	0.75	2.04
Lime..................	0.45	0.56	0.24	0.14	0.03
Water.................	....	0.34	0.38	.00	.00
Iron.............	57.68	52.68	59.03	67.60	57.32

An average of 10 specimens, representing the whole range of 30 miles, gives iron 54.61, titanium 8.07.

None of these ores contains either sulphur or phosphorus. Their purity is absolute. And as to the titanium, its presence makes no difficulty under judicious furnace management. And as to their quantity, Dr. Lesley, State Geologist of Pennsylvania, from whom the above facts are obtained, says, "Centuries of heavy mining could not exhaust it."

Two other ranges of these high grade magnetites are found further on, one in Stokes County, near Danbury, and the other across the Yadkin, north and south, at the Great Bend, where the railway strikes it. Many analyses of these ores by Genth are given in the Geological Report, three of which will suffice:

Mag. Oxide, Iron....	86.39	70.61	79.75	93.47	85.09	79.71
Mang. Oxide......,....	trace	0.48	0.81	trace	trace	trace
Oxide Copper..........	0.09	0.15	0.13	.00	.00	0.00
Alumina...............	0.75	0.66	1.20	trace	0.70	2.27
Magnesia..............	0.77	0.90	0.90	0.20	0.11	0.17
Lime..................	5.70	1.34	0.86	0 13	0.29	0.31
Silica, etc..	10.83	24.28	14.46	7.20	13.76	15.66
Phosphorus	0,04	0.05	.04	.00	.00	.00
Sulphur...............	.00	.00	.00	.00	.00	.00

The first three represent the ore of the Great Bend, and about Pilot, and the others, three of the principal ore banks of Stokes, the Rogers, etc. These ores have been smelted for the local market for more than half a century and produce a metal of excellent quality.

The ores of Wilkes and of Caldwell, about Patterson and along the upper waters of the Yadkin to the summit of the Blue Ridge, are of equally high grade. An analysis of a beautiful martite schist which occurs at several points along this line gives sesquioxide of iron 96.14, sulphur 0, phosphorus, 0.07; iron, 67.32. This ore, in hand specimens, cannot be distinguished from the Marquette ore of Lake Superior.

The *coal* of Dan River outcrops near the line of the road on Town Fork. This is a semi-bituminous coal, a good fuel, and a good furnace coal. Lower down, near Leaksville, where it was mined during the war, it has a thickness of nearly three feet; it has not been opened elsewhere.

There is a large number of *cotton mills* in the upper part of this section and the number is increasing, and may be multiplied almost indefinitely. The power developed by the fall of the water of the upper Yadkin and its tributaries may be estimated at not less than 2,000,000 spindles, and not more than the one-hundredth part of this force is utilized.

All the counties named as belonging to this section of the tract, except the first two, belong to the *bright tobacco* belt, and the culture and manufacture of this product has extended with great rapidity during the last few years, so that here will soon be the the very centre of this profitable industry. This means enlargement of business activity in many directions.

A surplus of *small grain* and corn, and large quantities of fruit are produced throughout this section. The Brushy Mountains are noted as one of the best fruit regions of the continent. These products can be indefinitely increased with the increased facilities for transport.

There are also several mineral springs of considerable celebrity in the Piedmont, near the line of the road, to which summer travel will constitute no contemptible item of business.

MOUNTAIN SECTION.

We enter an entirely different sort of country; a country of cattle, horses and sheep, of hay, buckwheat, Canadian oats and rye, and of apples, cabbages and potatoes of superior excellence, and dairy products which can be exchanged readily, through this railway, for the products and merchandise of the east and the tropics.

Iron ore also abounds along this plateau, many of the beds of great extent and of the best quality—for the most part magnetites. Among these is the Cranberry ore bank, one of the most extensive and valuable deposits in the world. This bed alone can furnish hundreds of tons of freight a day for an indefinite period. The Cape Fear and Yadkin Valley Railroad will offer great advantages over all other routes for its rapid and cheap transport to the seaboard, and so to all the great iron manufacturing regions of the North, which now draw a considerable part of their supplies of these high grade ores from the other side of the Atlantic. An average of five analyses by Dr. Genth gives—iron 64.3, and barely a trace of sulphur and phosphorus. Many other ore beds of the same character and grade are found in different parts of the plateau, and have been worked in catalan forges in a small way, producing iron of the best quality. So that the supply of these ores may be set down as practically inexhaustible.

Copper ores are also found here in large workable veins. The Ore Knob Mine, in Ashe County, produces 800 tons annually; and its freights amount to about 100 tons a month, which will seek this outlet as soon as the road approaches the Blue Ridge, the wagon route of its present traffic being some 50 miles in length, and very expensive.

There are several other veins of this ore in this

section, of equal promise, which the access of the railway will speedily develop.

The *timber products* of this section are also of immense extent. The largest and finest cherry and walnut timber grows in these mountain coves, with curled maple and black birch (or mahogany). I have seen here forests of cherry, and have measured trees of more than three feet in diameter, and clear of limb for 75 feet. And almost unbroken forests of the heaviest oak timber; and chestnut, poplar, hemlock, white pine, linn, black locust and birch, mantle cove, ridge and mountain slope, to the highest summits.

The *water power* of this section is of course very great; here rise the Yadkin, both forks of the New River, Watauga, Elk, Doe, Toe and Linville Rivers, several of them descending more than a thousand feet within the limits of the plateau.

The summer climate of this remarkable plateau is unmatched for equability and salubrity, the noon temperature never passing 80°. There is no locality east of the Mississippi so inviting to the tourist from the plains of the south and east and southwest; the highlands of New York are not to be compared with it. This will be the summer resort of a dozen States, as soon as opened by the railroad, and the goal of an immense summer travel from all directions.

TRANSMONTANE SECTION.

Beyond the limits of the State this line of railway is brought into immediate communication with the great valley of East Tennessee and Virginia, by the Cranberry Narrow Gauge Road and by the road recently chartered by Virginia, down New River to the Virginia & East Tennessee Road.

These connections open to the business of the Cape Fear & Yadkin Valley Railway, the very heart of the continent, a region of the greatest and most undeveloped resources, destined to become, in the near future, the centre of the great iron industry of the continent, with a corresponding growth and power in many other directions.

Transmontane North Carolina.

The country west of the Blue Ridge Mountains and extending to the extreme southwestern corner, has many features common to the whole. It is a country of mountain, of valley, and of river; a country in which each mountain chain has its accompanying valley and its ever present river, and its numerous smaller streams, each bordered by its own pleasant little valley. A description of one part might serve for a description of the whole if general features were regarded. But in detail, there is endless variety of form and character, giving every feature of beauty or of value. There is no sameness or monotony in charm of scenery, while in material value there is remarkable uniformity.

The counties lying west of the Ridge are Mitchell, Yancey, Madison, Buncombe, Henderson, Transylvania, Haywood, Jackson, Macon, Clay, Cherokee, Graham and Swain.

MITCHELL COUNTY

lies between the Blue Ridge on the south and east, and the Smoky Mountains on the north, the west having a conventional boundary. The whole county is to a great degree mountainous, there being little valley formation except on the upper waters of the Toe River. The highest mountain is the Roan, which rises to the height of 6,306 feet. The North Toe River is the principal stream flowing out of the State under the name of the Nolechucky and one of the main affluents of the Holston River in Tennessee.

The soil of Mitchell is uniformly fertile, the timber of large size and of great variety. The cereals grow to great perfection. Apples, cherries and grapes are of great excellence, and much of the land proves well adapted to the production of very fine tobacco. The grasses flourish, and cattle are reared for market in considerable numbers.

The mineral products of this county are confined at present to mica and iron; copper and other metals have been found. The famous Cranberry Mines are in the northeastern corner of the county, and now extensively worked. They are connected by railroad with the Norfolk and Southern railroad at Johnson City, Tennessee.

The Mica Mines are the most extensive in the United States, and produce a large proportion of the mica put the on market. The most productive mines are those once worked by an aboriginal race.

The area of this county in square miles is 240 miles, and the population in 1880, 9,435. The county seat is Bakersville.

YANCEY COUNTY

lies on the west of Mitchell. It has an area of 400 square miles, and a population of 7,694. This county is pre-eminently mountainous. The Black

Mountains penetrate it from the southeast and extend to its centre near Burnsville, the county seat. There are twenty summits of this range in this county rising above 6,300 feet, the highest, Mitchell's High Peak, being 6,707 feet, the highest point in the United States east of the Rocky Mountains. The Smoky Mountains separate this county from Tennessee, the highest peak within its limits being the Bald Mountain, 5,550 feet in height. Numerous cross chains intersect the county in all directions, leaving very little valley land except along the margins of numerous small streams, with broader ones along the larger streams, Toe and Caney Rivers. But mountains are the characteristics of the county. These, without exception, are fertile to the very top, covered with deep, rich and friable soil, in their natural condition bearing trees of great size. The walnut often attains the diameter of eight feet, the wild cherry a height of sixty feet to the first limb, and with a diameter of four feet, the poplar with a diameter of ten feet, the black birch or mountain mahogany, the oak of several species, the hickory, maple and ash, the yellow locust and other trees, all of giant size. The quantity, magnitude and excellence of forest stores has attracted attention from abroad, and large supplies are now annually cut, sawed and shipped.

Brought into cultivation, the soil is very fertile, producing all the grains, grasses and fruits, the apples being of notable excellence. Tobacco of great excellence is produced, and the culture is rapidly extending. The mountain sides when cleared are finely adapted to all the grasses; large quantities of sheep are raised, and cattle in large numbers are annually driven off to the Virginia markets.

This county is rich in metals and minerals. Magnetic iron abounds but is not yet mined. Other ores of iron are abundant. Copper has been found. Asbestos, corundum and mica are abundant, one of the most prolific veins in the United States being worked near Burnsville.

BUNCOMBE COUNTY,

once so ample in its area as to receive, and almost merit, the title of the "State of Buncombe," is now much reduced in extent, and is no larger than many of the counties of which it is the parent. Its eastern boundary follows the line of the Blue Ridge, its crests forming the dividing line between McDowell and Buncombe. On the west the New Found range marks the separation from Haywood County. Madison on the north, and Henderson on the south have no natural boundaries, the lines of division being artificial.

The area of the county is 620 miles. The total population by the census of 1880 was 23,909; but since that date there has been noticeable increase. The acreage is 341,542, of which 99,602 acres were improved at the time of the same census. Nearly the whole surface is susceptible of improvement; for though the mountains predominate as natural features there are few without deep soil to the top, and much of the best pasture land, and a large portion of land now used for the culture of fine yellow tobacco is mountain side or mountain top.

Buncombe County is bisected by the French Broad River, which, rising in Transylvania, pursues a course nearly north, and passes out of the State into Tennessee at Paint Rock. It is a stream of considerable volume and of surprising width for a mountain stream. At Asheville it is 110 yards wide; and little less than that for twenty miles above. Below the character of the stream changes and the width varies. At Asheville the rapids begin; above that point the current is gentle, and there is natural navigation, with some obstructions which the National Government has partially removed up to Brevard in Transylvania, a distance by water of forty miles. The water power of the river has not been utilized. Above Asheville, there is none. Below the narrow interval between the river and the cliffs causes embarrassment in the location of mill sites. The Swannanoa is the only other river in the county of any importance; more noted for its beauty than for its usefulness. Numerous small streams prove much more useful in their applications to mills and machinery than the larger bodies of water.

The valleys of Buncombe County are narrow and limited in extent. The valley system of the French Broad may be said to cease at Fanning's bridge, 12 miles above Asheville, and thence, until it enters into Tennessee, the course of the river may be said to be in a narrow trough with occasional trivial expansions. The general surface of the country is hilly rather than mountainous, offering facilities for agricultural operations largely used: though mountains are sufficiently lofty and abundantly numerous to give a mountainous character to the landscape.

The soil of Buncombe is fairly fertile, but does not equal that of Haywood or Transylvania. But it is sufficiently productive in all the cereals, the grasses and fruits of the temperate zone. Wheat produces an average of ten bushels to the acre. Oats yields exuberantly, corn thrives and produces from 30 to 50 bushels to the acre; clover and all the grasses are so well favored by soil and climate as to appear indigenous. The fruits find a congenial home here, especially the apple, which, in size and flavor, and in abundant healthy yield, are seldom equaled. The Irish potato here finds a favoring soil and climate, the yield being great and of superior quality. All kinds of vegetables grow with luxuriance, and the cabbage is especially noticeable for size and good quality.

The timber of this county does not attain the size it reaches in some more favored counties. It includes, however, all the varieties known in the mountains. Oak, hickory, walnut, elm, beech, birch, sycamore, maple, locust, buckeye, pine, the hemlock, spruce, and others, with an undergrowth of chinquepin, dogwood, laurel, kalmia, azalea, and other shrubby trees.

Among the new products of the county is tobacco—the one which has most largely and most rapidly added to the profits of agriculture. It has been cultivated as a general crop only within the past six years, and the soil of the hills down the French Broad, and back a few miles from the river, seem better adapted to its culture than the southern portion of the county, where few planters have attempted it. The quality produced is almost altogether the bright yellow of a quality that commands prices equal to those obtained for the tobacco of the centre of North Carolina. The culture is increased under growing demand and convenient markets, and it has become the money crop of a greater part of the county.

Buncombe County is traversed by three railroads, or rather by three branches of the same road; the main stem of the Western North Carolina road entering the county from the mouth of the Swannanoa tunnel, and dividing at Asheville into the Paint Rock branch, which is 43 miles in length, and the Ducktown or Pigeon River branch, finished to a distance of 21 miles. The Asheville and Spartanburg road will be finished in the course of a few months, and will add to the stimulus already given to business enterprise, the effect of which is already felt in the increasing wealth, prosperity and population of the county.

There are three incorporated towns in the county—Asheville, the county seat, with a population of 4,000, with churches, schools, good hotels, with streets partially macadamized, with water works approaching completion, with a business of large dimensions, and with a character as a health and pleasure resort known and valued throughout the United States.

Weaverville, nine miles north of Asheville, is a hamlet, with an excellent, industrious and thrifty population, a good woollen mill and a large nursery seed garden; Arden, a small straggling village, ten miles south of Asheville, recently incorporated, better known from its proximity to the beautiful Arden Park, a pleasure resort, than from any other cause; and to these may be added Leicester, eleven miles northwest of Asheville, a thrifty little hamlet, with a population made up largely of industrious farmers.

In enumerating the products of this county it would make a sketch more complete if accurate information could be given of its mineral wealth.

Iron ores, magnetic and titaniferous, are known to exist; but there have been no works opened, and little is known of the extent or value of the deposits. Corundum has also been found; so has mica; but it cannot be said that the wealth of the county is in its minerals.

MADISON COUNTY.

This county lies north of Buncombe, which is its southern boundary. The Smoky Mountains separate it on the north from Tennessee, Yancey County bounds it on the east, and Haywood on the west.

The area of the county is 450 miles, with an acreage of 233,575 acres, of which 69,089 are improved. The population was 12,810 by the census of 1880.

The county is essentially a mountain territory. There is little or none of valley lands, the whole surface being traversed by ranges of mountains, ranging from 2,500 to 4,500 above sea level. None of them rise to the stupendous height they attain in the adjoining counties of Yancey and Haywood, the great Smoky range even being depressed below its average height. But though mountainous almost the whole soil is of surpassing fertility. In few counties does the timber attain such vast dimensions, and in some favored localities its size might appear fabulous. On the Laurel River walnut eight feet in diameter, poplar ten or twelve, wild cherry three or four, buckeye of the same, black birch of the same size and of proportionate height are the common growth of the county. And to them may be added other trees too many in variety to enumerate.

From such exuberance of soil much of agricultural prodigality of wealth might be expected. Nor is there disappointment in expectation, though from absence of the means of transportation agricultural effort was limited to the production of little more than the necessaries of life until the discovery that these mountainous hills had peculiar adaptation to the production of superior tobacco. For six years or more Madison County has been foremost in the production of very superior bright yellow tobacco. The impulse given by its culture has had marked effect upon the condition of the county. Land held at nominal prices has increased in value. Mountain sides and tops that seemed destined forever to wear their vesture and crown of forest have been brought into cultivation. Men that ten years ago scarcely knew the sight or name of money have become prosperous and relatively rich, and the county is now one most forward in improvement.

The soil is prolific in other products. All the grains are prolific in yield, and the grasses flourish in remarkable luxuriance, stock-raising being a very considerable source of revenue which might be indefinitely enlarged.

The mineral wealth of the county is known to be great, but undeveloped. Magnetic iron and other ores of the same metal are found in numerous localities. Corundum of good quality is found on Ivy River and tributaries. Barytes is mined to some extent below Marshall, and a company is organizing to prepare it for market. Lime exists in a vein of half a mile in breadth, exhibiting itself in lofty and picturesque cliffs a mile below the Warm Springs.

The French Broad River bisects the county, passing through it, a broad roaring torrent between precipitous hills, encroaching so closely upon the river as to leave little room for human habitation or enterprise. Laurel River and Ivy River both come in on the right bank, large bold streams, each cutting its way through the mountains, presenting characteristics similar to those of the French Broad and equally unavailable as water power.

Marshall, the county seat, is situated in a narrow strip of land between overtopping hills and the river, with a breadth of less than a hundred yards and a length of less than half a mile. It has a population of about 200, active and enterprising, and is the centre of a large tobacco business, there being here two tobacco sales warehouses.

Warm Springs, 16 miles below Marshall, is the most noted spot in the county, celebrated for its warm baths, its extensive hotel, and the beauty of its surroundings. Its importance is confined altogether to its character as a health and pleasure resort.

The population of the whole county by the census of 1880 was 12,840.

HENDERSON COUNTY

has an area of 360 square miles and a population of 10,281 by the census of 1880. This county is divided by the Blue Ridge into two unequal parts, a considerable portion of it lying on the south, on the South Carolina line, and on the east bounded by Polk County, being in the Piedmont section. The remainder, or mountain plateau, is bordered on the east and south by the same range, and intersected at wide intervals by low ranges of mountains extending toward the northwest, it is closed in by the Pisgah range, the peak of that name being the common centre for the county lines of Henderson, Transylvania, Buncombe and Haywood.

The county is intersected by numerous streams. Green River, at the foot of the Blue Ridge, flows eastward between that range and the Saluda Mountains, and is an affluent of the Broad River, flowing south into South Carolina. The French Broad flows through the north-western part of the county, and receiving the waters of Mills River, Mud Creek and other considerable streams, becomes a bold broad stream, which by appropriations from the Government has been made navigable for small steamboats.

A remarkable feature of this county is the apparent great depression of its surface, and the width of the valleys along the streams, assuming, as on Mud Creek, the character of wide swamps. The whole interior of the county presents the aspect of one valley into which project like elongated promontories small ranges of mountains. Looking north-west from Hendersonville the eye sweeps over a level expanse of thirty miles, closed at that distance by the Pisgah range.

The soil of this county is good, though not so fertile as other mountain counties, with the exception of the valleys, which are productive in grains and grass. Fruits are abundant and excellent. The mineral wealth of the county is not great. Limestone of excellent quality for the kiln is found on the west side of the French Broad, and is largely burned for the Asheville market.

Hendersonville, with a population of about one thousand, is the county seat.

TRANSYLVANIA

is a true mountain county, having on its whole southern border the Blue Ridge in its most massive and imposing form; and being the starting point for the Pisgah and Balsam ranges, which stretch through the county towards the north. The only exception to the rugged nature of the surface is presented by the valleys along Davidson's River, and along the French Broad and its tributaries, all of which flow through broad and fertile valleys, and all of these in cultivation and in a high state of improvement. These valleys are the foundation of the stock-raising which at present is the great source of revenue to the county; and great efforts by intelligent men are made to improve breeds, and still further develop this important industry. Much the largest portion of the county is in forest, covered with the usual timbers of the mountain, all of which attain enormous size from the great fertility of the soil.

The land reduced to tillage produces grasses, the cereals, tobacco and all the fruits of the temperate zone in great excellence.

There has been no development of mineral treasure; but there is enough known to predicate in the future a large exposure of mines of gold, silver, lead, nickel, copper, asbestos, corundum and mica, all of which are known to exist in the wilderness of the Balsam and Pisgah solitudes.

The area of the county is 330 square miles, with a population of 5,340. Brevard, a small village of 200 inhabitants, is the county seat.

HAYWOOD COUNTY.

This large and beautiful county is as remarkable for the long extent of its mountain ranges and the height of its numerous mountain peaks, as it is for the extent of its valley system and the fertility of its soil.

The Pisgah range skirts it partly on the east, culminating in the pyramidal cone of Pisgah Mountain rising to the height of 5,750 feet. This range, interrupted by a depression of several miles, is continued by the New Found range extended to the Tennessee line. A spur or range projects northward between the East and West Forks of Pigeon River, the highest peak of which is Cold Mountain, rising to the height of 6,063. Along the western border extends the massive line of the Balsam Mountains, in this county attaining their greatest elevation. Here are fifteen peaks of more than 6,000 feet in height. Richland Balsam is 6,425 feet high and Double Spring Balsam is 6,380.

The Western North Carolina Railroad, by the Murphy branch, crosses this range at Scott's Creek Gap at an elevation of 3,357 feet.

The valley system is no less remarkable than that of the mountains, and a just proportion has been observed between what must be given up to the undisputed sway of nature and what can be reduced to the use of man.

The most important of these valleys are those which lie along the Pigeon River, and on its two main tributaries, the East and West Forks. These extend to the headwaters of those streams, and are from a quarter of a mile to a half mile in width, of great beauty and surpassing fertility, producing abundantly wheat, corn, rye and oats, clover and all the grasses. They are held at a high value, the prices being from $75 to $100 per acre. After the junction of the East and West Forks the united streams flow northward through the same broad valley until it enters the Smoky Mountains, and is then contracted into a narrow gorge or canon, and passes out of the State of North Carolina a bold tumultuous stream. It is remarkable that this river has its whole course in North Carolina within the County of Haywood.

Richland Creek, a stream of considerable volume, affords another broad and fertile valley of about twelve miles in length. Jonathan's Creek, rising on the top of the Balsam Mountains, at the Soco Gap, flows eastwardly with a course of about fifteen miles through a valley constantly increasing in width, beauty and fertility, until it loses itself in Pigeon River. Along this valley are some of the most productive lands in Haywood County. Crabtree and Jones' Creek have each their valleys of less extent, but not of inferior value.

The mountain lands, except on the summits of the higher ranges, which are densely wooded with the balsam fir, are very fertile. The sides and summits of the lower ridges, when cleared, prove adapted by nature to the production of grasses in great luxuriance. Herds grass, timothy, red top and clover take readily to the soil. Within the last two years the *poa pratensis*, the genuine Kentucky blue grass, has appeared spontaneously, as did the *lespideza* or Japan clover, and will greatly add to the value of the mountain pastures. Stock raising is followed to considerable extent, and efforts are made to improve the value of the breeds. Sheep thrive, but are mostly of native breed, with little general effort at improvement. In the deeper mountain recesses their increase, and even their existence, is controlled by the presence of wolves, which are found in considerable numbers.

Fruits grow to great perfection, and the apples of Haywood are famous all over the mountain regions.

Tobacco, in portions of the county, has become an important article of industry, and the superiority of the product must tend to the increase of culture; the bright yellow tobacco proving little inferior to that of Granville, while the darker grades have characteristics in common with the famous Henry County tobacco of Virginia.

In mineral wealth there has been no development except in mica, which has been worked to considerable extent at Micadale, near Waynesville. Gold, copper, iron, lead, asbestos, and other minerals are known to exist, but no mines are worked.

Haywood County has an area of 740 square miles, with a population of 10,271. Waynesville is the county seat, with a population of about 800. Near it are the White Sulphur Springs, remarkable for the surpassing beauty of their surrounding scenery, and with some repute as curative waters.

JACKSON COUNTY

has an area of 920 square miles and had a population of 7,343 by the census of 1880. It extends from South Carolina on the south nearly across the State, being separated by the narrow county of Swain from the State of Tennessee. The general form is one broad valley lying between the Balsam Mountains on the east and the Cowee Mountains on the west. But the term valley would convey an erroneous idea, since the space between these two dominant ranges is filled with numerous cross chains, making the mountain character predominant, while the valleys are exceptional. These are confined to the borders of the Tuckaseege River, a stream attaining before it passes out of the county a considerable volume and an average width of two hundred feet; and to its tributaries the East and West Forks and Caney River, and to the smaller streams, such as Cullowhee, Savannah Creek, Barker's Creek, Soco and Scott's Creek, all of which flow through vales of surpassing beauty and fertility. These valleys are the present seat of culture. Little encroachment has yet been made on the massive forests which clothe the hills and mountains. Nowhere in the mountain country is the timber more varied in kind or more majestic in size. The buckeye attains the height of one hundred and twenty feet with a diameter of four feet. The poplar and chestnut are of enormous growth. Oaks of several species, cherry, linn or basswood, hickory, walnut, maple, ash, all are abundant and of great size. With the exception of the high plateau at the south end of the county where Casher's Valley is situated, and where the soil is light and somewhat thin, the soil is of great fertility, remarkable for the high percentage of productive arable lands.

The usual crops and fruits of the mountain section thrive luxuriantly. Tobacco is found to be well adapted to both soil and climate, and its culture is increasing.

This county is very rich in minerals though there has been little development of quantity or value. Several copper veins of ascertained richness have been opened. Chromic iron is found in large quantities near Webster. Nickel ores or Genthites are found in the same locality. Other ores of iron are abundant. Mica, asbestos, corundum are also abundant.

In the northern part of the county along the Tuckaseege River, and along the waters of Soco Creek, is an Indian reservation inhabited by the families of Cherokees, who are also distributed through the adjacent counties of Swain and Graham. The whole number in these counties is nearly fifteen hundred. They have adopted the habits of the white men, and are engaged in agricultural pursuits. They have their schools and churches, and are under the guardianship of their Chief, W. J. Smith, an educated and intelligent native.

The county seat of Jackson County is Webster with a population of about two hundred.

MACON COUNTY

Extends from the South Carolina and Georgia lines on the south northward to the southern boundary of Swain County. It lies between the Cowee range on the east and the Nantahala Mountains on the west; while along the southern border stretches the Blue Ridge here assuming its boldest, most precipitous and picturesque forms, the precipices of Whitesides, Black Rock, Fodder Stack, Satvola and Scaly breaking down towards the south with perpendicular faces of a depth of from 1000 to 1500 feet. The highest peak in the Cowee range is the Yellow Mountain, 5,133 feet high. The Nantahala Mountains are a majestic range, beginning with Pickens Nose 4,926 feet high, thence extending northward with a uniform general height of about 5000 feet, the highest point being the Wayah, near where the State crosses the Gap at a height of 4,138 feet, that mountain being 5,494 feet in height. Between the Tennessee river and its tributary the Cullasagee, a range extends northward from the Blue Ridge terminating near the confluence of these streams; the highest point of which is the Fish Hawk 4,749 feet in height. Numerous shorter spurs project at right angles from the main chains of the Cowee and the Nantahala between which are streams of ten or twelve miles in length flowing through broad and fertile valleys. The chief of these are Cartoogajay, Wayah, Cowee and Ellijay.

The Tennessee river is the principal stream, rising in Georgia near Rabun Gap and flowing northward through a fine valley of great fertility, until it unites with the Tuckaseege. The current of this stream is more gentle than any found among the mountains, and the fall is so gradual that it is selected as a railroad route, the grade not exceeding 47 feet to the mile through the whole length of Macon County. The whole valley of the Tennessee is in cultivation, the whole being very fertile.

The next largest stream is the Cullasagee or Sugar Fork of the Tennessee. This stream in its whole length has a tumultuous course, rising on the high plateau of the Highlands, 4,000 feet above sea level, and cutting its way down to the level of the Tennessee through the opposing mountains in a series of rapids, cascades and cataracts, adding greatly to picturesque effect, but except as water power, adding nothing of economical value. The Nantahala is a beautiful mountain stream, having its bed in a trough on almost the top of the Nantahala Mountains, the depression between that range and the Valley River or Tusquittah Mountains being very small.

The area of open land, assimilating in character to the features of the Piedmont country is greater than in any other western county. Farms are more numerous and more continuous and population more dense; the soil is productive.

Minerals are abundant, but no mines are worked except those of corundum and mica. The former near the Cullasagee are worked extensively, the product being about thirty tons a month. Mica is mined extensively in several localities.

The area of the county is 650 square miles, with a population of about 10,000.

Franklin is the county seat, with a population of about 500.

Highlands is a new village established by northern settlers as a Sanitarium on the crest of the Blue Ridge on a broad plateau, at an elevation of 3,750 feet above the sea. It is thriving, and has a population of about 500, representing 31 States and territories. It is proposed to connect the village with the general railroad system at Rabun Gap.

J. D. C.

THE SOUTHWESTERN COUNTIES.

The counties of Cherokee, Clay, Graham, Macon, Swain, Jackson and Haywood occupy the extreme southwestern portion of the State and abound in the finest scenery as well as the best water powers and manufacturing opportunities offered by any portion of the country. The area of this section is estimated rather lowly at 3,910 square miles, of which a little more than 305 square miles is under cultivation, divided into 6,100 farms, with a population of 43,295, and a production amounting annually to $1,056,005, according to the Census report of 1880.

The resources of this section are as yet almost entirely undeveloped, but the Western North Carolina Railroad and the Marietta, N. Georgia & Murphy Railroad are now fast pushing their iron tracks into its interior, and already the prospector is abroad looking for profitable locations to invest capital in manufactures, mining and agricultural pursuits.

The timbered land amounts to at least twelve-thirteenths of the entire area and is covered generally with a heavy growth of almost all the varieties of the oak except the live oak, interspersed with white and scaly bark hickory; tulip or (poplar) of two varieties, cucumber and wahoo, white ash, wild cherry, (black and bird cherry) black and white walnut, black and sweet gum, red, white, mountain and ash-leaved maples, persimmon, dogwood, chestnut and chinquapin, red, yellow and black birch, sassafras, white, yellow and black pines, hemlock (or spruce pine), linn or lime, snowdrop tree, black, yellow and honey locust, yellow wood (virgilia lutea), crab apple, service, hornbeam and ironwood, sycamore etc. Portions of Cherokee, Graham, Swain and Macon Counties contain very large quantities of chestnut oak as well as hemlock, and can thus furnish the materials for the largest tanning operations, as the climate and waters are so mild and pure as to offer great inducements in this line as soon as the Railroads are completed to this section.

The agricultural products embrace all the cereals cultivated in the temperate zone. Wheat, oats, rye, barley, buckwheat, corn, etc., grow extremely well and yield large crops of very fine grain. Grasses also, such as red and white clover, timothy, orchard grass, herdsgrass, millet, etc., do well and yield good and remunerative crops, and I have a sample of orchard grass cut from a field which has been seeded twelve years and cut twice each season, which measures five feet in length. The Italian rye-grass bids fair to be one of the best grasses for the mountains, as it is finer in quality than the orchard grass, grows quickly after it is cut and bears cutting well and grows very thick on the ground.

The bright leaf tobacco has just been introduced here and

bids fair to be a great success as it does well, and samples have been shown valued at a dollar a pound, and whole crops have been sold as high as thirty cents a pound. The dairy has as yet received but little attention, but the quality of the butter made here where the cattle feed on our natural grasses and wild pea vines is not excelled in any section. Fruits of all kinds grow readily, such as apples, pears, plums, peaches, grapes, and all the small fruits, and it would be hard to find any section which will excel this in this respect. Grapes seldom fail in making a good crop; peaches are uncertain in some localities, but the other fruits succeed well and large quantities of them are shipped regularly to market both as green fruit and dried.

There is a large amount of balsam timber in parts of Jackson, Swain and Haywood Counties which offer inducements to establish the manufacture of chewing gum, as it is of a very superior character and at present is not utilized, although one of our sister states annually sends abroad $100,000 worth of spruce chewing gum.

The minerals of this section are abundant and quite varied. Gold is found in Cherokee, Clay and Macon Counties and has been worked quite extensively by ordinary placer mining with the use of hydraulic power in a few places. Vein or quartz mining is carried on only on a small scale. Silver is found in small quantities in connection with galena, but there has been but little work done on this line. Iron is found in large quantities in Cherokee of the very purest varieties of limonites. Magnetic ore is found in Macon and Haywood Counties, but has not been worked much although some of it is of very fine quality. Corundum is found in Clay, Macon, Jackson and Haywood Counties in very large quantities, also mica; and those minerals have brought in a large amount of money and are yet destined to yield a large amount of wealth to the citizens.

Marble of almost every shade of color is found in Cherokee,

Macon and Swain Counties, also soapstone; and the Western North Carolina Railroad will soon run through this entire belt in such close proximity to the marble and soapstone as to enable parties to load it directly from the quarries into the cars. The soapstone has heretofore brought much money into the country and with the aid of R. R. transportation we may look for the amount to be spent for it to be much increased.

Manganese is found in Cherokee and Macon Counties of fine quality but has not as yet been utilized, although it can be furnished in large quantities.

Nickel is found in Jackson and probably in Macon and Clay Counties, also chromic iron; which are much sought after at this time by parties wishing to purchase, but there is no work done of importance in developing the mines.

I have given you the facts in regard to this country so that you may arrange them to suit yourself. I will, however, give you a few dimensions of timber which you can use if you wish. A black walnut in Graham County is 76 inches in diameter 12 feet from the stump. A wild grape vine grew on the farm of James Farmer, 2 miles below Murphy on Hiwassee River, 15 inches in diameter. I have measured an apparently sound tulip tree 36 feet in circumference. I have just cut a wild cherry four feet in diameter at the stump, 47 feet of beautiful sound body to the fork where it is fully three feet in diameter. Sassafras grows to be four feet in diameter on Snowbird. Peruvian bark does not grow here; the so-called tree is a variety of wild cherry.

I notice that the yellowwood you mention in "*Woods and Timbers*" is a very different plant from our yellowwood which grows sometimes to be a tree two feet in diameter, wood very hard and strong, takes a fine polish and is one of the finest timbers to make nice canes. It is classed by Gray as Cladeastis tinctoria and by Michaux as Virgilia lutea.

The people are kind and hospitable and are desirous to have colonists come among them and aid them in utilizing the immense resources of the county, and by this means make this section one of the most desirable in the world for beauty, healthfulness, and everything necessary to make mankind comfortable and happy. W. B.

ALLEGHANY COUNTY

Was formed out of a portion of Ashe in 1859. But owing to the war and its results did not get fairly under way as a county until 1870.

The territory composing the county, while belonging to the county of Ashe, being remotely situated from any centre of trade, had made slow progress in development. The lands being cheap, were principally held by a few men whose other capital was not sufficient to put them in a proper state of cultivation. The consequence was that farming was carried on in a rude state. The forests of heavy timber required an amount of labor to remove them so great that the then land owners, when they had succeeded in removing the forest from a spot of land, would continuously cultivate it in corn, oats, rye, buckwheat, etc., as long as it would return a sufficient yield of grain to repay them for their labor of cultivation. Scattered over the county, however, one would occasionally find a community of more enterprising men who had made more progress in developing the splendid lands of which it is composed.

Nature has evidently formed this county for one grand purpose, to wit: Grazing, and as a consequence, stock raising and dairy farming. After the war, a younger and more active class of men came to the front, and seeing as they did for what nature had formed the county, they went to work to put it in a condition to carry out the original purpose of its formation, and for a backwoods county as remotely situated as it is the progress has been wonderful. Where but a few short years ago roamed the wolf and the bear, and others of their kind, now upon thousands of acres of the same soil the luxuriant timothy, clover, blue grass, orchard grass, and in fact all the grasses may be seen upon which the improved breeds of cattle and sheep, with the best grades of horses and mules, annually feed preparatory for market.

While this improvement is so marked in the last few years, it is not the only evidence of the improvement of the county. Roads have been constructed in every direction. Churches and school-houses dot many of the hills. Lumber and planing mills have gone up in many sections, while many more are under and in contemplation. In the principal portion of the county land has advanced from about an average of $2 to about $12 per acre, and is still going up. Farming in all its branches has greatly improved; the reaper and mower have displaced the old sickle and scythe. The yield of wheat will now average about 15 bushels to the acre of unimproved lands, where a few short years ago it was not grown at all. Corn and other grains return a much larger yield than before from unimproved lands, the result of improved system of farming, while from the improved lands the return of course is much greater.

While this is so in the greater portion of the county, still there are yet large bodies of land, notably one section of the county, the southeastern, in which may be found as much as four or five thousand acres of unbroken forest, in a body of timber upon lands that when reclaimed will furnish as fine grazing as any lands in the world, that even now may be purchased for $4 to $5 per acre, the timber of which upon any railroad line in the United States would bring ten times the price of the lands, besides paying for its removal.

While the county is truly a mountain county, it is not so rough as some of the neighboring counties in Virginia and North Carolina. The country is rolling, but has none of the high mountains covered with rock that is common to the mountain counties. There are not within the borders of the county 2,000 acres all told not susceptible of profitable cultivation.

As a further evidence of the thrift and prosperity of the county, two large and well patronized institutions of learning of high grade have sprung up in the county—the Alleghany Collegiate Institute at Sparta, and Laurel Springs Academy at Laurel Springs. Then the increase of population from 1870 to 1880 was about 50 per cent., and has been more rapid since that time. As a further evidence, not $50 of taxes has been collected by distraint in five years, nor has $100 worth of property been sold under execution during that time.

Of minerals there are numerous beds of iron in many sections of the county, with valuable deposits of copper in some sections, notably the Peach Bottom copper mines now being worked by a company of Baltimore gentlemen.

The forests are covered with all classes of the oaks, poplar, hickory, walnut, buckeye, cherry, beach, ash, chestnut, with pine, both white and yellow, in some small sections.

The soil is well adapted to the growth of all the cereals as well as tobacco, but until there are more convenient markets for shipment of the product of the soil it is evident that stock raising is the most profitable to the farmer.

The religious societies are principally Methodist and Baptist.

The county site, Sparta, is a thriving little village in the centre of the county, which is now showing substantial evidence of rapid growth.

As a fruit growing region the county is unsurpassed.

The county is traversed by New River, the fountain of the Kanawha, which with its tributaries furnishes an amount of water power far beyond what will be utilized for generations to come.

The probability of the Cape Fear and Y. V. R. R. penetrating the county at no distant day has given a stimulus to the country and he who sees the county penetrated by any R. R. line will find it one of the most desirable spots on the continent. E. L. V.

ASHE COUNTY

Lies in the extreme northwestern corner of the State, and is bounded on the north and west by other states. It is about 30 or 32 miles in length from east to west, and about 29 in breadth from north to south. It contains about 600 square miles of territory. The Blue Ridge separates Ashe from Wilkes. The Stone Mountain is the line between it and Tennessee.

It is watered by the North and the South Forks of New River, and has perhaps the greatest water power of any county in the State on account of the large creeks and streams that flow down into the river with such rapidity from the mountains.

The country is hilly and mountainous. Of course there are valleys of level land. Its altitude is on an average about 3,000 feet above the sea. About one-fourth of the land is cleared and in grass or other crops; but grass is the staple, though wheat, rye, corn, buckwheat, Irish potatoes, etc., are raised plentifully.

The timber is oak of various kinds, chestnut, hickory, walnut, ash, beech, birch, white pine. spruce pine, with hundreds of others down to the ivy and rhododendron, which is being sought after so much. All kinds of fruit of this latitude grow finely here. apples, peaches, pears, plums, cranberries, etc.

The population was 14,437 in 1880, and are agricultural in their pursuits generally ; Methodist and Baptist in their religion, democratic and republican in their politics, pretty equally divided. Jefferson is its county town, with Court House and about 300 people.

Several copper mines are in operation in the county. Mica is mined here and some magnetic iron is now made from the very large fields of that ore in this county.

There are curious places here. Long-Hope Creek falls 1,000 feet in about a mile. The Bluff, the Bald, the Phœnix and Three Top Mountains are grand. J. W. T.

WATAUGA COUNTY.

Watauga is one of the best of the mountain counties of North Carolina, less developed than most of them, but behind none in its natural resources as a grain, grass, live stock, dairy, fruit, wine and lumber region. It abounds in undeveloped mineral wealth, one of the many copper mines in and around Elk Knob being the only one which has as yet been actively worked, and extensive operations on it have only very recently commenced. The scenery and summer climate of Watauga will soon advertise the county and insure that it will be much resorted to in summer. The Railroad to Cranberry near the Watauga line makes Watauga accessible now from the west, northwest and southwest. On the east and south the nearest railroad stations as yet are Hickory, Icard and Morganton; with the best road from Hickory by way of Lenoir. W. W. L.

MITCHELL COUNTY.

The population of Mitchell County is now 12,000 or 13,000 (about 3 1-2 per cent. colored). The land is hilly and mountainous, but very productive even to the tops of the highest mountains.

The principal crops of grain raised are wheat, corn, rye,

oats, and buckwheat. The production per acre on land without manure is from 20 to 40 bushels of corn; 15 to 20 bushels of wheat; 20 to 30 bushels of oats; 20 to 25 bushels of rye; and buckwheat, 30 to 40 bushels. Vegetables of all kinds grow well. We raise from 50 to 200 bushels of Irish potatoes per acre, and cabbage, turnips, beets, parsnips, etc., do equally well. Some very fine tobacco is raised in this county. All of the grasses, especially timothy and clover grow well. Timothy will grow as high as a man's head on the hills and mountain sides without manuring. This is without doubt one of the best counties in the State for stock raising. Land can be bought at from $2 to $10 per acre.

A narrow gauge railroad runs from Johnson City, Tenn., to Cranberry Forge in the N.E. part of the county, but Marion, N. C., and Johnson City, Tenn., are the nearest R. R. stations to Bakersville, the latter being 38, and the former 35 miles.

Our people are quiet and law abiding, and for the most part industrious, but we have few good farmers, the most of them following the old ways.

This is a good fruit county, especially for apples.

The county is rich in iron ore and mica. Mica is found in almost every section, and new discoveries are made almost every week.

The county abounds in timber such as cherry, poplar, white oak, ash, maple, linn, cucumber, etc. Black walnut is not so plentiful as it has been, owing to the great quantity shipped within the last two or three years.

Our people are, perhaps, nearer on an equality than in any other place. We have no wealthy people and but few very poor, a very large majority of the heads of families being land owners and very few who do not own land.

The water power is all that could be desired. Mountain trout abound in the head waters of most of the streams.

Some deer and wild turkeys are still to be found and smaller game is abundant.

The health of this county is as good as can be found any where. We have no extreme heat nor cold—the mean temperature in summer is about 71°, and in winter about 36° above zero. The water is pure freestone.

The population of Bakersville, the county seat, is about 500 or 600.

Roan Mountain, the highest in the State, except the Black, is in this county and within two hours' ride of Bakersville.

Baptist and Methodist are the principal religious denominations, though there are some Episcopalians and Presbyterians here.   -   J. H. G.

HENDERSON COUNTY.

This county was formed in 1838, is situated in the southwestern part of the State of North Carolina, and forms a part of its western division. Its county seat is Hendersonville, one of the most beautiful villages in the State, on the S. & A. R. R., containing a population of about 800. It is situated on the southern dip of the Blue Ridge Mountains, overlooking the Ochlawaha valley and a wide expanse of country unsurpassed in grandeur and beauty.

The county has a population of 13,500, and contains very nearly as much bottom or meadow lands as all the other counties west of the Blue Ridge. It is traversed by the French Broad River, Mills River, Green River, and Broad River, besides Clear Creek, Hooper's Creek, Crab Creek, Shaw's Creek, and the Ochlawaha,—tributaries of the French Broad.

Its soil is peculiarly adapted to the cultivation of the grasses, and it is considered one of the best stock raising counties in the State. The forest lands are covered with all woods peculiar to the mountains of western North Carolina, containing all kinds of oak, with pine, chestnut, walnut, poplar, ash, birch, linden, hickory, locust, etc. The products of the county are tobacco, corn, wheat, oats, rye, grass and live stock, fruits and vegetables. Improved meadow lands sell from $10 to $30 per acre, owing to location, and other lands can be bought in quantities from 50 cents to $15 per acre.

There are 49 public schools in this county—38 of which are for white children, and 11 for colored children; besides private schools kept up at individual expense.

Hendersonville is the principal point of shipment, from which are shipped in large quantities cattle, hogs, sheep, corn, fruits, vegetables, poultry and lumber.

This county is a summer resort for people from all parts of the South and Northwest. It is celebrated for its beautiful residences, and its climate (Winter and Summer) cannot be surpassed in the world. Great attention is being paid to agriculture and improved stock. Lime is found in great abundance. This county, bordering on the State of South Carolina, and connected by railroads with the cotton fields of the south, is destined at an early day to be of great importance as a manufacturing locality. It contains some of the finest water powers in the South, capable of turning millions of spindles. The people, owing to their extraordinary educational facilities, are intelligent and hospitable. They are anxious for immigration. W. W. J.

Wilkes County.

Wilkes is one of the older counties of the State, and was originally a county embracing a very large territory. But the policy of carving new counties out of portions of old ones, some years since so popular, stripped her of much of her best land, as well as most desirable portions of her population. Much of the territory of Alexander, Caldwell and Watauga Counties, I think, was taken from Wilkes. She is, however, still a county of a very considerable territory, containing a population of about twenty thousand inhabitants. A good many historical incidents might be introduced that would be interesting to the general reader, but not pertinent to the purpose of this sketch. Suffice it to say on this point, that she has furnished one Governor for the State and other individuals favorably known throughout the State, as well as being of influence at home. General Gordon, Col. Stokes, Major Carmichael, and Col. W. M. Barber, whose lives were sacrificed in the late war, were all residents of this county ; the first three were natives.

This county lies mainly between the highest ridges of the Blue Ridge, on the northwest, and those of the Brushy Mountains, on the southeast. The slopes of these two mountain ranges furnish the water sheds which meet in the Yadkin River. These water sheds abound in streams of much beauty, furnishing at the same time, by means of their many waterfalls and shoals, very abundant water power ; while along their banks there is very fertile and beautiful land for farming purposes. Beginning on the west side of the Yadkin River, next to the Caldwell line, and going northeast, we encounter the Elk, Stony Fork, Lewis Forks (north and south prongs coming together near the Yadkin), Reddie's River, dividing into three prongs as we approach the Blue Ridge, Mulberry, Rock Creek, Buggaboo and Roaring River. The latter, some eight miles above its mouth, divides into three prongs, each one of which is sufficient to carry a considerable amount of machinery. Much might be said in behalf of the water power furnished by each of these streams, separately, but being better acquainted with Roaring River and Reddie's River throughout their whole length than with any of the others, and believing them to differ little from the others in natural features, I will say a few words about these two only.

Such are the shoals and general fall of these two streams that one might safely say factories could be established at intervals of one mile throughout their whole course. The beauty of this water power lies in the cheapness of dams. A dam four feet high, with a canal two hundred yards long, in many cases, will afford a head of water, at the pier head, of twenty feet. I know of one such case, and believe many others could be found. When a dam is made the water is backed for so short a distance that there is no danger of injuring low lands or sowing the seeds of local diseases. Take for instance Dr. Hackett's mill. His dam is at the lower end of a shoal. It is not less than ten or twelve feet high, and yet there is a rapid current within a few hundred yards above it.

When we begin at the Caldwell line on the opposite side of the Yadkin, we encounter Beaver, Warrior, Moravian, Fishing, Brier and Swan Creeks. These also furnish great facilities for running machinery. They are, however, neither so large, so long. nor so abundant in shoals as those on the opposite side of the Yadkin. Moravian Creek furnishes one site of great beauty and attractiveness, as well as of usefulness. It is known as the Moravian Falls. Here the stream, after tumbling over shoal after shoal for a considerable distance, finally leaps down a precipice of some thirty or forty feet. These shoals are peculiar, from the fact that the shoals and precipice are one solid rock, many yards in width and perhaps several hundred yards in length. The only expense incurred to utilize this water power is a few sticks of timber, so placed as to conduct the water into a fore bay, from which it is poured on to an overshot wheel. The other streams on this side of the river are not wanting in facilities for water power, though nothing striking or peculiar pertains to any of them.

Besides the streams mentioned as flowing into the Yadkin there is Hunting Creek, which rises in the Brushy Mountains, and flowing an easterly direction through Iredell empties into the South Yadkin, Davie County, about four or five miles from Mocksville. This stream has many fine falls which are utilized for propelling machinery. Towards its source, however, it is chiefly noted for the fine corn lands afforded by its bottoms. It may be said of all these streams, as well as of the Yadkin, that the fertility of their low lands renders Wilkes a very abundant corn country. The Yadkin River flows through the county from the southwest towards the northeast, a distance of about forty miles, and on both sides there are low lands of considerable extent and great fertility. It runs through the county in such a way as to have eight townships on its south side and ten on its north. The low lands on the river are peculiarly adapted to corn ; but, with proper culture, grow wheat, rye and oats very well. There are lands on this river that are said to have had corn on them for nearly a century without any rotation, and still their fertility is seemingly unimpaired. They receive recruits from time to time from overflows. These overflows are not attended with so much disaster to growing crops as in many other places, because of the shortness of time during which these lands are covered. They are rarely covered longer than ten or twelve hours by any one freshet. There is very little attention paid to the cultivation of the grasses, though doubtless they might be profitably raised. The greatest discouragement the farmers have in this line is the liability of their meadows to be overrun by sedge.

The ridges and mountain slopes are peculiarly well adapted to the raising of the various fruits. The fruit crop is here much more certain and of a better quality than on the low lands. One gentleman has told me that he had a peach orchard which had not failed in a course of twenty years to produce an abundance of peaches. The Brushy Mountain apples, wherever known, are celebrated for their fine quality. The late Bishop Atkinson frequently had apples from this region sent to him to Wilmington, and I have heard him say that, both in his own estimation, and that of his friends, they were superior to those obtained from any other source whatever.

Between the Yadkin River and the foot of the Blue Ridge there is a large extent of rolling land that can be purchased at a low price. This land is very poorly suited for raising corn, and though its occupants insist most perseveringly on its doing so, it utterly fails, especially in dry seasons to reward their toils. Wheat and rye, however, can be profitably raised. By the aid of fertilizers also tobacco of the finest quality can be produced. The tobacco which took the premium at the Vienna fair, shipped by Samuel McDowell Tate, was raised in Wilkes County. So much also are these slopes exposed to the sun, that I have often thought that by the same appliances cotton might be profitably raised. The expense of transportation here would be a hindrance.

Within the past few years considerable attention has been paid to the cultivation of the vine; and the most sanguine expectations of those engaged in it have been fully realized. These enterprises are confined to the Yadkin, while it is evident that the mountains and ridges are just as superior to the river section for the grape, as for any other fruits.

As to the mineral wealth of this county no important developments have, as yet, been made. While gold may be found in almost every part of the county, it is so diffused as to prevent the collection of it ever being profitable.

There are mineral springs of the same character as those found in various parts of the Piedmont section of the State. And as to the healthfulness of the climate there can be no question. There are but two practicing physicians in the county, and they may be found at home the most of the time.

The timbers of the forests are the various species of oaks, pines, the chestnut, walnut, hickory, ash, etc. Walnut Grove township abounds in walnut trees of great heights, and will furnish logs of considerable diameter.

The elevation of Wilkesboro above the sea-level is about eleven hundred feet. Poor's Knob, a mountain nine miles distant, is about sixteen hundred feet above Wilkesboro.

For the first fifteen miles below Wilkesboro the Yadkin falls forty-six feet.

As in all other mountainous sections there have always been very few colored people in this county, and since emancipation I think the tendency to emigrate, on the part of this race has been such as to prevent any increase; while the voting population of the white race is perhaps twenty-five hundred, that of the colored race does not exceed five hundred.

I neglected to mention at the proper time that there is a great deal of very rich cove land along the slopes of the Blue Ridge and Brushy Mountains, which may be obtained on easy terms. These sections rarely suffer from drought. They are so much depressed from the level of the land about them as to prevent the soil from becoming very dry; and besides in the dryest seasons there are always partial showers which water these coves. R. W. B.

Caldwell County.

Lies in nearly the centre of a tier of counties, known as the "Piedmont Section" of North Carolina. The word *Piedmont* is fitly applied—it meaning at the "foot of the mountain." This belt of country, lying to the eastward and southward of the great high wall of the Blue Ridge crossing the State diagonally here, is protected by this natural barrier from the extreme cold winds and storms that prevail in the regions beyond, and embraces what, in many respects, is some of the most desirable territory in the whole United States. Caldwell lies about equally distant from Virginia on the north, and South Carolina on the south. It has some claims over all the sister counties lying to the right and left. In fact, in some of its physical features, I know of no country on earth that can compare with it.

First, it offers to the fruit grower and agriculturist a greater variety of altitudes, in similar latitudes, than any section of the world. The lowest elevation in this county is about one thousand feet above sea-level, and the highest is nearly six thousand,—at the summit of the Grandfather Mountain. We exhibit here, as the growth of this county, both Canadian and tropical productions. We have figs, grapes and nectarines. The fir balsam is indigenous here also. The renowned "Frostless Belt" of the South runs through this county, and a total failure of the fruit crop has never been known. The fact is, this is one of the most reliable sections for fruit in America. Thousands of bushels are annually shipped from this county, selling in markets elsewhere. The apples grown are remarkable for the keeping qualities. It is no uncommon thing for the farmers to keep them the whole year round. At this writing (June 5th) I have luscious apples grown in 1882, while on my table are cherries and strawberries of this year's growth. We have also on hand an abundance of sweet and Irish potatoes of last year's growth. I kept on exhibition here some time ago an apple that had been picked eighteen months. It was a seedling, and grown by the late Wm. A. Tuttle. The late Bishop Atkinson used to say that he considered grapes grown in the vicinity of Lenoir of finer flavor than those he had eaten in Italy.

But it is not only as a fruit-growing region that this county can boast of excellence. The agriculturist here finds the very best of corn and wheat lands. A fact worthy of note is the productiveness of the soil here under the influence of manures. Our clay lands improve with exceeding rapidity. Some few years ago a gentleman bought a "worn-out" place here, and in two seasons of fertilization with stable manures he made over twenty bushels of wheat to the acre on his crop. As we have the great variety of elevation, so we have a great variety of soils. Our light gray sandy lands produce the very finest of yellow tobaccos. The tobacco which received the highest award at Vienna in 1874 was grown by a citizen of Caldwell County.

This County is beginning to grow cotton also. With the aid of commercial fertilizers on all the best lands of the southern portion of the County, very liberal and encouraging crops of this staple were grown during the past two years; and the acreage for 1883 is largely in excess of the plant for previous seasons. This has encouraged capitalists to utilize valuable waterpower in the cotton-growing section, and a large spinning mill has just been completed on Gunpowder Creek, twelve miles south of Lenoir, the County site, and near the projected C. & L. N. G. R. R. One of the most successful cotton and woollen factories in the South has been in operation in this county for many years, on the Yadkin River at the village of Patterson, eight miles north of Lenoir. There are few handsomer manufacturing towns in the South than can be found at this place—Patterson. They have in operation there a large cotton-spinning and weaving mill, a mill for spinning and weaving wool, flouring mills and a large wood-sawing establishment which turns out considerable quantities of finest walnut lumber, also hickory spokes, rims, etc., while pine lumber is also sawn and shipped North at these mills.

The shipment of hickory and other hard-wood lumber has become a very important item in the industries of the County, and numerous steam and water mills have recently been erected. Our timbers have been attracting the attention of lumber men ever since the Philadelphia Centennial, where the Western North Carolina Land Co. had on exhibition a large and interesting collection of the native woods of Caldwell County. No County can boast a greater variety of useful and ornamental trees.

Nor can any County show a better exhibit of agricultural products. It has been stated time and again that the productions of this county fill every column in the last U. S. Census Reports (Agricultural Department) with perhaps only one or two exceptions—West India molasses being one of the exceptions. In lieu of this we produce the sorghum syrup in finest and largest yields known.

The mineral exhibit from Caldwell County is almost as remarkable as its vegetable productions. Several of the more valuable metals are found in abundance in our mountains. Iron of superior quality is found in many places here. Gold-mining has been an important industry for many years, but all as yet on a small scale. Much attention has been attracted to our mines during the past twelve months. To illustrate how this industry manifests itself, I will give one instance coming under my own observation not long ago, A gentleman having a small country store in the mining region of the County, sold one day in Lenoir six hundred pennyweights of gold dust—the result of a few weeks bartering for the precious metal. In addition to this he reserved (as he told me) about 100 pwts. of finest nuggets. Asbestos is found also in this County in great abundance and of superior quality. Several other minerals have been discovered here, all of which will attract more attention on completion of railroad facilities into this County.

The Chester and Lenoir Narrow Gauge Railroad has been graded to Lenoir through the County, and contract has been made to have cars running to Lenoir—through, from Chester, S. C.,—by 1st July, 1884. On the completion of this railway a new impetus will be given to the industries of this county. Real estate is already advancing in price, and we have so many advantages here to offer to persons seeking desirable homes, it is confidently predicted that an era of great prosperity is soon to dawn upon us.

Among the other advantages this county offers is that of climate ; for, situated as we are under the protecting shelter of the Blue Ridge, we are not subjected to the great extremes of heat and cold. We do not have the long and rigorous winters that reign in the western counties. While their summers are, perhaps, a trifle cooler than ours, our springs come earlier and are not subject to the violent changes often known there. We have early fruits and vegetables from four to six weeks sooner than counties lying west of the Ridge. Our fall seasons are longer and more enjoyable than theirs. We rarely have more than one or two "cold spells" during the winter, these about Christmas or early in January. We have occasionally some "raw weather," but the climate generally is dry and not so oppressive to consumptives or persons troubled with either bronchial, lung, or rheumatic disorders. Physicians report this as one of the healthiest counties in the whole United States.

The surface of this county presents a great diversity of feature. One-third may be considered mountainous ; one-third valley land, and the remainder rolling uplands and hills. The valleys are remarkably fertile, producing grains and fruits. The uplands yield well in tobacco, cotton and wheat, especially with fertilization. The county is traversed by four mountain ranges, running parallel, Blue Ridge, the Rip Shin, Green, and Brushy Mountains; these lying nearly east and west. The Pine or Lick and Globe Mountains are north and south.

As we have great variety in soil and elevation, so we have great range in prices—figures running from fifty cents to one hundred dollars per acre for farming lands. Good lands can be bought at from five to twenty dollars per acre.

Lenoir, the capital town of Caldwell County, is considered one of the handsomest villages in the State. It is noted for its fine society, its schools, and churches. The Presbyterian, Episcopal and Methodist churches are all near the public square. The Baptist church is two miles away. The population of the town and suburbs is over five hundred, and the registers of the various denominations show about the same number in membership.

The town has an important geographical location. It is about fifty or sixty miles from the Virginia line on the north, the same distance from the South Carolina on the South, and same from Tennessee on the west. It is directly on an air line from Washington City to Atlanta, Ga.; on an air line from Cincinnati to Charleston; and an air line from Louisville, Ky., to Wilmington. Hence there is a probability of Lenoir, at some period of the future, becoming a railway centre of great importance. Surveys have already been made in the direction of Cumberland and Round Gaps in Kentucky, with a view to extending the narrow-gauge system of railroad coming from South Carolina into the mineral sections of East Tennessee. West Virginia and Kentucky, as their nearest outlets to the ocean are through this place.

While Caldwell County presents but few objects of interest to the mere tourist or pleasure seeker, its mountains and water courses afford the student of nature a peculiar study. Although this county is small in comparison with others, it has four large streams running to the four points of the compass. The Yadkin River, rising on the summit of Blue Ridge, flows from the village of Patterson through the county in an almost easterly direction. John's River, rising also in the Blue Ridge, flows in an almost unbroken southerly current. The Catawba River, running due east also washes the southern base of the county. Lower Creek, a large stream rising near the Wilkes line, flows almost due westwardly; while King's Creek, an important tributary of the Yadkin River runs nearly due north. The valleys of Lower Creek and Yadkin are separated by the Green Mountains. The hunter on the summit of these mountains sees the peculiar spectacle of two large streams, one on his right flowing west, while the one on his left runs east, and far to his front runs the King's Creek at right angles to the others. Near Lenoir is the famous "Hibriten" Mountain, from the summit of which a good view can be had of territory in four states. Far better views can be obtained from the summit of the Grandfather Mountain which is partly in this county.

Referring again to the water courses of this county, it is said, with much truth, that there is not a farm in the county but has a running stream upon it; and that nearly every farmer in the county has a good spring somewhere on his place. Very few wells are used in the county, excepting in the villages. The water power of this county is among the best in North Carolina.

The county contains several villages, in addition to the county town Lenoir. The most important is Patterson, the manufacturing village owned by the company, Gwyn, Harper & Co. The manufacturing village of Granite is owned by another company operating cotton mills,—Shuford, Gwyn & Co. Collettsville, 10 miles from Lenoir, north-west, is a prosperous place, having two stores, one tobacco factory, a flouring mill and two churches. Hartland has two stores and a wagon factory; a large church near by. Lovelady has one store, two churches, a steam saw mill and a resident physician. Horse Ford has a toll-bridge, one of the most popular flouring mills in the county and a large mill for wood working. The flouring mills of this county have a reputation extending far into South Carolina. L. C. Hope's brand always commands high prices. The village of Gainesville has a steam saw mill and one store, and a large new camp ground near by. Petra Mills is also a considerable place of business.

The churches of this county deserve especial mention, as they speak well for the religious influences here. Since the war some sixteen new houses of worship besides the large Marvin camp ground buildings, have been erected by our people, besides repairs and improvements upon older buildings. On none of those houses is there any *debt*—so far as my information extends. In fact our people and our county as a whole are not burdened with any excessive debt or taxation. The public treasurer pays all the dues of the county in cash on demand, and our county scrip has been at par for several years; we have no outstanding bonds or public liabilities, and our jail is empty nearly all the while. It is a rare occurrence to find lands here sold for taxes. But few bankruptcies have ever occurred in the county, and business is conducted here on probably as small a credit basis as anywhere in the South. These facts may all be accounted for in the high moral tone of the people of this community. Our people generally are liberal, generous, and have a ready welcome for all new comers into this county. Society already is somewhat cosmopolitan, and various states and nationalities are represented in the trades, professions and industries of the county.

M. V. M.

Burke County.

Was organized in 1778, including the territory lying west and north of Rowan and Tryon. Its boundary has from time to time since been curtailed by the erection of new counties as the settlement of the country required, until its present limits are confined to what may be called the Catawba Valley, embracing, however, the greater part of Linville Mountain, Jonas' Ridge and Brown Mountain on its western and northern border and the Brushy or South Mountains on the south and east. Being thus almost entirely surrounded by high mountains, the body of the county is an undulating plain of about twenty miles in width, traversed by the Catawba River from west to east, which, by reason of its numerous affluents, pouring in on either side, becomes on the eastern side or end of the county, the Great Catawba, requiring bridges or ferries to effect a crossing. These tributaries, on the left, with their sources in the great mountains of the north and west, are clear limpid streams furnishing almost limitless water powers, with large bodies of rich alluvial "bottoms" as they approach the parent stream, while those of the south or right side are corrupted by the gold washings or red lands of the wheat grower till they partake in color of the lands through which they pass.

The plain lands are covered with original forest growth of pine and the hard woods in great variety, and the mountains have, in addition, the white pine, hemlock, locust, chestnut, cherry, walnut, etc. Iron, copper, lead, zinc, asbestos, mica, etc., are abundant in the mountains, and in the hills and valleys gold has been worked for more than fifty years with satisfactory returns. Roofing slate and building stone, indeed all kinds of building material are abundant and cheap. Twelve millions of brick, made within a mile of Morganton for the Lunatic Asylum, are admitted by Samuel Sloan, architect, to be of the best clay and finest unpressed finish in the South.

Pulmonary diseases do not originate here—indeed it is a sanitarium for such. The general level of the plain is about 1150 feet above tide, while the Grandfather, Hawk's Bill, Table Rock, etc., reach an altitude of 6,000 feet and the Black 6,711—all on the north and west ; the southern range is about 2,500 feet. Owing to the conformation of the surrounding heights, tornados are impossible and storms insignificant, the great blasts passing high over head. The general elevation of the valley is sufficient to secure fine breezes from the mountains and cool refreshing nights for sleep in the midst of the summer heats, while the severe rigors of winter are unknown. Laborers can work out of doors every day in the year, if not raining. No malaria or local cause of sickness.

With a climate unsurpassed, if equaled, and a soil that yields generously to cultivation, it is not surprising that this region was early settled and that those who came remained. Added to these advantages was the picturesque beauty of the landscape views. Professor Mitchell, who was authority in such matters, as Gov. Swain was in history, in North Carolina at least, used to say that Morganton afforded the finest mountain scenery of any point in his knowledge. We read that,

> " Distance lends enchantment to the view
> And clothes the mountain in its azure hue,"

and I am disposed to accept that as a fact, for certainly I would rather look at the Black, 35 miles away, standing more than a mile above me, than attempt to realize its enormous proportions by " tackling " its rugged sides. The writer once ascended the steep slopes of Table Rock, 5,000 feet above tide, on a sunny day in July with a fat miss. He "made it," miss and all, but to this day, though 40 years ago, he has never felt compensated for the effort.

The early settlement of this valley was by Scotch Irish Presbyterians, either direct from the north of Ireland, or by the way of Pennsylvania and Virginia. Of course there were pioneers and others who were neither Scotch-Irish nor Presbyterians, and some of the Scotch-Irish were not particularly distinguished for religious belief, but the leading elements were such. The first church built in Morganton was of brick, and for their use. That building, remodeled, is now the place of worship for the followers of John Knox, the same yesterday, to-day and forever. The Methodists are now the most numerous, the Baptists next, while the Episcopalians, though few in number, are, generally, highly intelligent and wealthy. The present population are the offspring of the early settlers, *there not being a dozen foreigners in the county.* The old stock were a sturdy people as well as intelligent, and they were enterprising too. The books and papers of ye olden time have recorded all here given to their credit. It is a singular fact that the first cotton ever sent abroad was raised in Burke County. John Rutherford, Sen., who had learned the hatters' trade in the old country, raised the cotton as an experiment, picked and packed it in bags, and carried the crop to Charleston, S. C., in his wagon, and sent it to England to test its value as a fibre compared with flax, for making cloth ! Though far removed from the large colleges the old folks appreciated the value of education, and, when able, sent their children off to school ; but if there was not means to send all, the boys must needs give way to the girls, who, whatever happened, must get their "finishing touches" abroad; and with a gallantry for which they have ever been distinguished, the boys never questioned the superior claim. Hence it is, I suppose, that Governor Vance has said, " Burke has the finest women and the sorriest men in the State." This is rather a biting jest, but it is true that the women are more cultivated *and ambitious* than the men. They are remarkable for all the graces that make the sex lovely, and with it all have the pride of Lucifer himself. This led strangers to regard Morganton as the "seat and centre of civilization and refinement in Western North Carolina."

The young men are a lively, dashing set, who would prefer to do "head work" and let the negro do the digging—many would rather charge a battery than plough an acre, but as they mature, are singularly level-headed and conservative in their views. They would ride a day to oblige a stranger, or drop any business to discuss politics. The average Burke voter can resist more temptation or absorb more Federal patronage and still vote the Democratic ticket than any man in America!

This people have an immense deal of family pride and it is dangerous, where each thinks his or her family a little better than all the rest of the world, to mention names. But at the risk of bullets let it be said, that since the day Waightstill Avery signed the Mecklenburg Declaration of Independence and Charles and Joe McDowell assembled the neighbors of this valley at their plantation, Quaker Meadows, forming the nucleus of the little army which stormed the heights of King's Mountain and made good that Declaration, the men of Burke have stood in the forefront.

Burke is a good and pleasant county for *white folk* to move to, but carpet-baggers and dead-beats "need not apply."

Cleveland County

Borders on South Carolina, and its northern extremity is the top of the South Mountain Chain, in which rise, 1st., Broad River, running through the county, also Knob, Buffalo, Sandy Run and Brushy Creeks—all good sized streams, with abundant falls and fine water-power. Scarcely any county has more good shoals, though some have falls of greater power. Our lands vary. The northern half being very rolling (extreme northern mountains). The southern portion is somewhat rolling, but generally lies fine for farming for a western county.

Timbers are abundant and very fine. The various oaks common to Western North Carolina, hickory and yellow pine are abundant, chestnut in the mountains; also some wild locust and black walnut, though the latter is not abundant. We also have some ash, poplar, maple (white), dogwood, etc. As soon as virgin forests are destroyed the lands spontaneously produce "*old field pine*" in abundance. It grows rapidly and in fifteen years makes good lumber and fuel. Fruit grows finely—all kinds common to North Carolina.

We produce corn, cotton, oats, wheat, generally; some tobacco which grows finely, but farmers prefer cotton as being as profitable, and less risk and trouble. The health of this county *cannot be surpassed.* No local cause for disease, right under the mountains. We have an abundance of fine, bold, cold, freestone springs, as clear and pure as an icicle. Our atmosphere is perfectly pure and bracing, and we seldom have a drought. Clouds form in the mountains north and west of us, and in a few hours we have the showers. We have many mineral springs, principally sulphur and chalybeate. Among them the celebrated Wilson, or as now called, Cleveland Springs.

Our town, Shelby, is the terminus of the Carolina Central Railroad, and is one of the prettiest, healthiest and most thriving towns in the State. In it is located the Shelby Female College, recently started and prospering. We also have two fine flourishing high schools—Shelby and King's Mountain. Names locate them. The C. & A. Airline Road runs through the southern end of the county, and King's Mountain (called from its proximity to the battle-ground) and Whitaker give a fine market to the southern, while Shelby gives an elegant market to all other points of the county. We have two small cotton mills, two foundries, three tobacco factories recently started, and a warehouse soon to be erected,

Our farmers are of the most progressive kind and are making money, and have in ten years improved more rapidly in farming than we did in 50 years prior to 1860. We will soon raise enough grain to supply us, and from 8,000 to 10,000 bags of cotton. Large quantities of improved farm implements are bought every year. All mountain vegetables flourish here, and the world can't beat Cleveland County for good living. A man is as rich here on $5,000 as in many places on ten times that amount, and can have more of the real luxuries of life.

Fine stock is being imported and every year our progress can plainly be noticed. We owe a remnant of debt made by taking $50,000 worth of railroad stock, which will be paid out entirely next year, if not this. Lands are rapidly advancing in price. Scarcely any lands, outside of mountain lands, can be bought for less than $6 per acre, and in choice locations improved farms of upland bring $10 to $12, and where the lands are of good quality, $15 per acre. We welcome emigrants, need them and want them. Here *where they have access to two great railroads* is the backwoods of North Carolina so accessible, healthy, and affording such a fine field for investment. Our timbers in upper Cleveland are a mine in themselves. Large tracts near the mountains can be bought at $3 to $4 per acre, heavily timbered with yellow pine which, if put into lumber or shingles, would make fortunes to the purchaser. The factories buy their cotton at their doors. Good churches are abundant all over the county, Baptist, Methodist, Presbyterian, Lutheran, Episcopal, etc., the two former predominating. H. F. S.

Lincoln County.

This county is traversed by Carolina Central and Chester and Lenoir Narrow Gauge Railroads.

MINERALS.—*Iron.*—A vein of magnetite runs through a portion of Ironton township. It is the same vein that is upon the High Shoal property, in Gaston County, and disappears at the South Fork River, and coming out at Big Ore Bank in Lincoln County, runs thence into Catawba, disappearing near Sherrill's Ford on Catawba River.

The Big Ore Bank has been worked since 1792, and the quantity of ore seems inexhaustible. One shaft is down 125 feet and several 50 to 75. The Brevard Bank adjoins this, and has been worked since 1800. The vein appears continuously in Lincoln and Catawba Counties for ten miles or more. This iron has no superior for strength, and is well suited for the manufacture of ordnance, and cables, wires, etc. This ore smelts *without aid of lime or any other flux*—fluxes itself. Vesuvius, Rehoboth, Madison and Stonewall Furnaces and several forges are on this belt. There are several beds of brown hematite near Lincolnton and in North Brooks Township.

Limestone and Marble.—There are two quarries in Iron township—Keener and Finger.

Manganese.—There is a bed of oxide on lands of V. A. McBee, in Lincolnton township, and a vein of silicate crosses Catawba Springs and Ironton.

Gold.—There are several mines. Burton, Morrison, Barneth, Lowe, Hoke, Sharpe and Dalton. Some of these have been remuneratively worked.

Copper.—The Graham mine shows gold at the rate of $60 per ton in first five feet, but at twelve feet, changes to

Copper	$60.00
Gold	30.00
	$90.00

with indications of becoming a copper mine of remarkable richness.

Sulphur-Darby Mine. Amethysts at Rendleman's. Beryl at A. E. Horney's. Lazulite at D. F. Abernethy's on Chubb's Mountain.

Timbers and Woods.—Oaks, white, post, red, black and Spanish are all over the county, with willow oak in occasional places. Hickory, dogwood and maple in great abundance; ash, beech, birch, poplar (both yellow and white), cherry, persimmon, gum, (both black and sweet,) linden, sassafras, elms, (three varieties,) pine, (yellow), honey locust, chestnut, (but are dying out,) willow and sycamore.

Manufactures.—There are several shoals on Catawba and South Fork Rivers, some of which have been utilized. The creeks in the county afford a great many shoals, many of which have been utilized for furnaces, forges, flouring, grist and saw mills and carding machines.

Phifer and Allison have a cotton mill at Lincolnton, on Clarke's Creek, with 2,016 spindles and 75 looms, which pays well.

Phifer and Sumner have a wool carding machine at Lincolnton. J. H. Marsh has a chair and furniture factory.

As good flour is made by a number of mills in this county as can be found anywhere.

Agricultural Products.—Wheat, oats, corn and cotton are the principal market crops. Some tobacco and grass are also raised. A large portion of the county is admirably suited to the growth of fine yellow tobacco, and it will become one of the chief industries. Fruit of all kinds flourishes—though sometimes destroyed by late frosts. Clover, orchard and blue grass flourish. W. A. G.

Gaston County.

MINERALS.—*Iron.*—Magnetite, on High Shoal lands, in large quantities, suitable for making Bessemer Steel, also car wheels, etc., has been worked for sixty years. Brown hematite—several beds in Cherryville township.

Gold.—There are several mines in the belt of Huronian slate, which crosses this county. Some of which have been extensively worked.

Building Stone.—Several quarries of excellent granite, also soapstone and gneiss.

Timber.—Same as Lincoln County.

Manufactures.—This bids fair to surpass all other counties in number and power of its factories. The Catawba River and South Fork furnish many excellent shoals—the Mt. Island on Catawba and High and Spring Shoals on the South Fork being the finest in the State. The "Bend" in the Catawba River occurs in this county near Rozzell's, where by a canal of two miles in length, a fall of sixty feet in the Catawba River can be obtained, which would afford an immense amount of power. There are now in operation the following cotton mills: Mt. Island on Catawba River; Woodlawn, Linebarger, Wilson and McAden (at Spring Shoal) on South Fork, and Mt. Holly, on Dutchman Creek. There are a large number of flour, grist and saw mills on the rivers and creeks of the county, and several run by steam.

Agricultural Products.—Same as Lincoln.

The Charlotte and Atlanta, and Carolina Central Railroad, and Chester and Lenoir Narrow Gauge, traverse the county. W. A. G.

Catawba County.

Is located in the Piedmont section of Western North Carolina, nearly midway between Virginia and South Carolina. The general altitude of the county is from ten to twelve hundred feet above sea level. It has been settled more than a century, but about two-thirds of it remains in original forest. The Western North Carolina Railroad runs through the northern part of this county. On this road are located Newton, the county seat, a town of six hundred inhabitants, Hickory, with a population of fifteen hundred, and Conover, with one hundred and fifty inhabitants. The northern portion of the county abounds in yellow pine timber, which makes good lumber and shingles for building purposes. Saw and shingle mills are numerous along the line of the Western North Carolina Railroad.

The county was colonized by immigrants from the German Settlements of Pennsylvania, and the frequent recurrence of German names indicates a large infusion of that people.

The Lutheran, Reformed, Methodist, Baptist, Presbyterian, Episcopal and Catholic Churches are all represented, but the four first mentioned are the most numerous of these denominations.

Schools.—At Newton there is a male and female school of high grade, under the charge of Revs. G. C. Clapp and I. A. Foil, assisted by other competent instructors. At Hickory there are three schools of high grade, two for females and one for males. Claremont College (female) is under the charge of Rev. A. S. Vaughn, who employs five assistant lady teachers. The Sisters of Mercy have charge of a Catholic female school located there, and Professor H. C. Dixon conducts a good elementary and classical school for boys.

Hickory is a new place which has grown up within the last ten years, and is already an important trading point. It has seven churches, two tobacco warehouses, five tobacco factories, two hotels, three tanneries, three livery stables, twenty stores, a large wagon manufactory, two weekly newspapers, and a number of other industrial establishments.

The Crops best suited to this section are wheat, of which Catawba County exports a large surplus, Indian corn, oats, tobacco, cotton, apples, peaches, cherries, pears, small fruits, clover and the grasses. The soils vary from the thin gravelly uplands, well adapted to the production of fine tobacco, to the dark soils, better adapted to grain crops. The ridges possess a fine porous red clay subsoil, which enables them to resist drought, when deeply ploughed. They are susceptible of the highest cultivation.

By the Census of 1880 the total population of Catawba County was 14,946, of which 12,469 were whites and 2,477 were colored. In 1870 the population of the county was 10,984, showing an increase of nearly four thousand, or about 36 per cent. in ten years.

The county is entirely out of debt, and taxes as low perhaps as in any county of the State. Newton the county seat is 183 miles west of Raleigh. Hickory is ten miles west of Newton.

The Piedmont country of North Carolina possesses an admirable climate, being mild in winter and temperate in summer. The air is free from malaria, the drinking waters pure and cold. The soils are good and adapted to a wide range of productions. Building material consisting of timber of excellent quality, clay suitable for brick, and rock is abundant and cheap. Society is orderly, railroad facilities good in the central part, and improving in other parts. I regard it as the most promising part of the State. R. K. B.

Iredell County.

This county was formerly a part of Rowan. It was during the revolutionary period the scene of many stirring events and is rich in historical interest. It was settled principally by the Scotch-Irish, and in its population this sturdy race yet predominates. It is singular in the uniformity of the distribution of property among its people. There are no extremes of poverty and riches. The people are thoroughly well off, and to their material prosperity add a large general intelligence. Extending about forty-five miles north and south, and about twenty-five east and west, it embraces in its territory a great variety of geographical formation and an equal variety of soil. The southern part of the county, for example, is strikingly level, running to rolling lands in the central section and reaching to the mountains in the north where it joins to Wilkes and Yadkin. Red clay lands predominate, but they are well interspersed with gray gravel and loamy soil. It is therefore a boast of the people that anything that can be grown anywhere can be grown in Iredell.

Up to twenty-five years ago the agricultural population

was almost wholly given over to the growing of corn, wheat and oats, in the production of which these lands excel. Later, however, with the more general introduction of commercial manures, the growing of cotton and tobacco has been largely gone into. The success that has been realized with these crops has been very great. This is particularly true with regard to cotton in the southern portion of the county where it is grown to perfection, but not only there—its culture has been pushed to the very foot of the mountains, where a quarter of a century ago it was not supposed it would grow at all. The adaptability of the gravelly lands to the growth of tobacco is a recent discovery. Now the county is known as the centre of the bright tobacco district. This product is grown with great success and at fine profit, the quality of the Iredell leaf being such as to cause it to be eagerly sought after in distant markets. These advances of the past few years have resulted in the establishment of considerable cotton markets at Statesville, Mooresville, Troutmans, Elmwood, and Mt. Mourne, and a very prosperous tobacco market at Statesville, the county seat, where there are now two large tobacco warehouses and four factories.

Fruit of every variety grows luxuriantly, while the mountain counties scarcely surpass these lands in the production of the different grasses.

The Western North Carolina Railroad crosses the county from east to west, while the Atlantic, Tennessee and Ohio Railroad from Charlotte, pierces it from the south to Statesville, the centre. Thus the capital has railroads running in three different directions, while an extension of the Atlantic, Tennessee and Ohio Railroad from Statesville to Taylorsville, Alexander County, is projected, as also an extension of the Virginia Midland Railroad from Danville, Va., to Mooresville.

Iredell is a well-watered county. The Catawba river is

its southern boundary; the South Fork of the Yadkin River crosses it from northwest to southeast, and it has numerous large creeks, which turn quantities of machinery and furnish the county a full area of bottom lands. There are three cotton factories on these creeks, and about fifteen tobacco factories in the county.

Rutile and corundum are found in this county in considerable abundance and of excellent quality.

The forests of the county present a great variety of timber, and so abundant and of such excellence is it as to have attracted here, within the past eighteen months, two factories for the working of it.

Different religious denominations are represented by Methodist, Baptist, Presbyterian, Lutheran, and Episcopal churches.

The finances of the county are in excellent condition. It owes no floating debt. Its bonds outstanding and not yet due cannot be bought at par.

ALEXANDER COUNTY.

Is a daughter of Iredell, and lies just to her west. Never having had any railroad facilities, her advancement has not been as rapid as it would otherwise have been. A subscription of $22,000 has, however, recently been voted to a proposed railroad to Taylorsville, the county seat. The lands are largely ridge, and the chief products are wheat, oats and corn. Fruits and all other necessary farm products are raised and the people live largely within themselves. They are intelligent and as progressive as their pent-up condition will admit of. They produce considerable cotton, though under the shadow of the mountains, and as much of this as is not marketed at Statesville is consumed by the two mills within the county. The water power is abundant and turns a number of grist and flouring mills, saw mills, etc.

Alexander County is chiefly distinguished for her mineral wealth. Within her borders are found rutile, corundum, garnets, emeralds, and, within the past few years a new and beautiful gem, to which the name Hiddenite has been given. This is the only locality in the United States where this gem has been found. It is one of rare beauty and great value, and is being very diligently worked by Prof. W. E. Hidden, of Newark, N. J., the representative at the mines of the Emerald and Hiddenite Mining Company, which was organized last year in New York for the purpose of developing this property.

The general surface of this county is elevated and rolling. It has a fine forest growth of timber of many different kinds.

Baptist, Methodist and Presbyterian churches are found in different portions of the county.

YADKIN COUNTY.

Like Alexander, Yadkin is without railroads and without the hope of any except such as is held out by the Cape Fear and Yadkin Valley road. It has been noted for years for the excellence of its vineyards and the superior quality of its whisky. In these it is unrivaled in the State. It abounds in water courses, and the bottoms adjacent to these are highly productive, particularly of corn, which is the county's great staple. The lands are generally rolling, to the north mountainous. Tobacco is cultivated to a considerable extent in the southern and western sections, but cotton can scarcely be said to have gotten a foothold. The county has a number of tobacco factories, but cotton or other forms of manufacturing have not been much established.

There is a strata of iron ore running across the county, but it has never been developed. Many years ago iron was mined and worked on a small scale in Yadkin with some success, but owing, probably, to lack of capital and of facilities for doing such a business in so remote a region, it was abandoned. There are also believed to be deposits of coal in the county.

SURRY COUNTY.

Formerly Surry and Yadkin were one, with Rockford as the county seat. They are divided now by the Yadkin River, which waters both. The topographical features of the two counties are not essentially different. Surry is more mountainous. Their products are likewise much the same, and any sketch of one would very nearly cover the other. Surry is necessarily behind some of her sister counties by reason of the fact that she has never been developed by railroad, but she is fortunate in that a good deal of manufacturing enterprise has been exhibited by her citizens. For a number of years cotton manufacturing has been conducted on a large scale and with profit at Mt. Airy, which is the site also of tobacco warehouses and factories, which make it a point of more consequence than Dobson, the county seat. At Elkin, on the Yadkin, large manufacturing interests are carried on. The Elkin Manufacturing Company work up a considerable amount of cotton, while the Elkin Valley Woollen Mills do a large and increasing business. Its indirect benefits are neither few nor small, for it is stimulating sheep husbandry not only in Surry but in adjacent counties.

Surry is more prominent on account of her manufacturing interests than aught else, though her agriculture does not languish. In point of mineral wealth she has not developed much, though there are deposits of both iron and coal in her borders. Doubtless with the building of a railroad this hidden wealth would be unearthed and there are reasons to hope that this aid to development will not be much longer lacking. J. P. C.

Stokes County

Is situated in the north-western portion of the State, bounded on the east by Rockingham, on the south by Forsyth, on the west by Surry, and on the north by the Virginia State Line. Danbury, a picturesque little village situated on a spur of the Saura Mountains, near the head waters of the river Dan, is the county-seat. Its area is 500 square miles. Of this, 57,393 acres of land are improved, and 168,780 unimproved.

The north-western portion of the county is in some places very rough, although nearly all of it, except the mountains, can easily be cultivated. Upon the uplands the soil is generally of a light gray color, in every way adapted to the cultivation of very fine tobacco, and it is no uncommon occurrence for farmers to obtain forty and forty-five cents a pound for their tobacco. Here we also find every variety of garden vegetables raised, and were transportation better, this would be of incalculable benefit to the farmers and people generally.

The soil upon the lowlands is a rich sandy loam, where very good corn, wheat and other grain crops are produced. The following are the principal productions in 1882:—Corn, 338,781 bushels; Rye, 5,023 bushels; Oats, 72,391 bushels; Wheat, 55,284 bushels; Tobacco, 2,131,161 lbs.

The timber is superb, mile after mile of forest, consisting of such wood as walnut, oak, maple, hickory, poplar, gum, ash and many other varieties, that have never known an axe. The timber is so easy of access that many large sawmills are springing up over the county. The land is well watered by the Dan River, and such large creeks as Town Fork and Belew Creek. A few miles above Hairston's Ford on Dan River is one of the finest of water-powers. Cattle and sheep raising is quite extensively carried on in portions of the county. The mountainous district seems peculiarly adapted to the raising of sheep.

Along the base of the Saura Mountains large quantities of iron are found. The vein at Danbury is eight feet thick and was successfully worked by the Confederate Government during the war. Lime and coal have also been discovered in large quantities, although no decided efforts have as yet been made to develop these important minerals.

At present there is no railroad completed into Stokes, although the Cape Fear & Yadkin Valley R. R. has been graded to Walnut Cove, eight miles from Danbury, and will be in running operation within a year. The Virginia Midland R. R. Co. has also located its North Carolina extension through this county, and as there is no other way for them to go, even if they wished, there is every reason to believe it will soon be built.

Near Danbury are the Piedmont Springs, noted for their mineral qualities, and much frequented by parties in pursuit of health and pleasure. They are situated within the heart of the Saura Mountains, where one may inhale the purest of mountain air and almost bow in adoration to the magnificent scenery on all sides.

The population of Stokes County in 1880 was 15,353. The character of the people is all any one could desire—kind towards strangers, generous to a fault and free from all political and religious contention. The majority are poor, although many hospitable mansions belonging to the rich are scattered over the county. E. T. B. G.

Forsyth County.

This county is located in the north-western portion of the State, about 100 miles north-west of Raleigh, and 25 miles west of Greensboro, on the line of the N. C. R. R. It was formed from Stokes County in the year 1849.

Its population is about 20,000—five-sixths white.

The assessed value of property is about $4,000,000.

The general surface is comparatively level, only sufficiently broken to afford good drainage ; none too broken to cultivate.

The County is bounded on the west by the Yadkin River, and is watered in all portions by Muddy, Belew's, Abbott's, Old Field, South Fork, and many smaller creeks, which afford an abundant supply of good fresh water for stock, besides power for mill purposes in all seasons. Drinking water is easily obtained from numerous springs and wells, from 25 to 60 feet deep, all of pure cold free-stone water.

The principal crops are corn, wheat, rye, oats, hay, potatoes, and tobacco ; some cotton.

About one-half of the County is gray soil well adapted to the growth of fine yellow tobacco, frequently producing from one to two hundred dollars per acre a single crop. The red lands of the County, comprising the other half perhaps, are admirably adapted to the growth of wheat and the grasses ; averaging in some instances the present season thirty bushels of wheat to one sown on an entire farm. These lands when well prepared will produce five tons of hay per acre an ordinary season.

Apples, peaches, pears, plums, apricots, cherries, strawberries and grapes, of many varieties are grown in large quantities. More dried fruit is annually shipped from the depot at Winston than from any other point in the State.

About one-half of the County is covered by original forests of white oak and other species of oak, poplar, hickory, persimmon, dogwood, with some cedar, locust, walnut, elm, and birch.

There are extensive granite and lime quarries in this County.

Winston, the county town, has grown from a small village of three or four hundred inhabitants in 1873 when the railroad was completed to this place, with one or two stores, to a small city of 6000, two national banks, with 48 stores, 24 tobacco factories manufacturing several million pounds of leaf per annum, 4 large warehouses for the sale of leaf tobacco, 2 sash and blind factories, with saw and planing mills and steam grist mill ; all giving employment to at least three thousand laborers.

Salem, separated from Winston by a street (the two forming in fact but one town), is an old Moravian town settled originally by Germans. Its present population is principally of German descent, numbering about two thousand ; a thrifty, industrious, go-ahead people. The Salem Female Academy, noted throughout many of the Southern States, is located here ; is under most excellent management and in a most flourishing condition. Salem does a good mercantile business, has extensive cotton and woollen mills, planing and sash and blind factories, one large and extensive manufactory of agricultural implements, and saw mills and other manufacturing establishments. While an old town it has on new clothes and is keeping pace with its twin-sister in her march of progress.

Kernersville, Bethania, and Waughtown are all thriving towns in the County. The two first named are engaged in tobacco manufacturing extensively, and the last named is noted for its wagon factories, which sell their work as far south as Florida. The first and last named have doubled their population within five years.

The climate of the County is healthful, the air dry and salubrious, the people long-lived. The County is thickly dotted with churches. The principal denominations are Methodist, Baptist, Presbyterian, Episcopal, Christian, Moravian and Dunker. Free public schools are taught in each school district (white and colored separate but equally provided for), for a term of from four to six months in the year. Winston has established a graded school, and is now erecting a free school building for the purpose at a cost of $10,000.

The rate of taxation is about 68 cents on the one hundred dollar valuation of property.

The County is on the high road of prosperity, has fully recovered from the results of the war, and is to-day far beyond the point she occupied in 1861, and stands holding out her hands inviting labor, capital and brains to come among her people, guaranteeing welcome and protection to all who come to share in her prosperity.   C. B. W.

Davidson County

Is one of the largest and finest counties in the State. It was established in 1822, from Rowan, and was "named in compliment of Gen. William Davidson, who fell at the passage of the Catawba River at Cowan's Ford during the Revolutionary War, 1st of February, 1781."

It is situated in the central portion of the State, in the Piedmont section. Whether viewed from its eastern and western or from its southern and northern boundaries, it is nearly in the centre of the State, although Lexington, its county site, is one hundred and seventeen miles west of Raleigh. It is bounded on the north by Forsyth, east by Guilford and Randolph, south by the Yadkin River, which separates it from Stanly and Rowan, and on the west by the same river, separates it from Rowan and Davie.

Lexington is its capital, a most flourishing and beautiful village.

The population of the county, by the census of 1880, is 20,333—an increase of about 3,000 during the last decade. Of this 16,341 are white and 3,992 colored. The county is out of debt, with a small surplus in the treasury. In 1879 it produced 549,906 bushels of Indian corn, which quantity was exceeded by only four other counties ; oats, 122,063 bushels, being exceeded only by five counties ; wheat, 174,671 bushels, which is 36,393 bushels more than was produced by any other county. It is the eighth county in the production of tobacco, and the second in the value of orchard products ; first in the production of hay—8,667 tons ; first in Irish potatoes—26,108 bushels.

It has numerous mines of gold, silver, copper and lead. A large number are now being worked with handsome profit. The most noted are the Silver Hill, Silver Valley, Conrad Hill, the Lalor, the Ward, the Welborn, the Hoover and the Emmons.

The North Carolina Railroad runs through the centre of the county, entering on the east at the Guilford line and running to Thomasville, Lexington, Linwood and to the Yadkin River, where it enters Rowan.

It has six villages besides Lexington, to wit : Linwood, Jackson Hill, Teaguetown, Clemmonsville, Yadkin College and Thomasville. The first three are small, with but few inhabitants ; the fourth and fifth are somewhat larger, but the sixth—Thomasville—has some five or six hundred inhabitants, with several stores, a large number of shoe shops, and is one of the prettiest villages in the State. Lexington and its suburbs have about 1,200 inhabitants, twenty stores of various kinds, among them a drug store and hardware store, a steam grist and flour mill, cotton press, two foundries, two steam saw mills, and agricultural implement shops, three tobacco factories, two warehouses, six churches, two beautiful blocks of stores and quite a large number of dwellings and business houses are now being built and repaired ; a fine male school and several private female schools.

Davidson has two fine colleges, one male and the other female. Yadkin College is ten miles west of Lexington, at Yadkin College village, and the Thomasville Female College is at Thomasville, ten miles east of Lexington, on the N. C. R. R.

There are other colleges close by, though not in Davidson County, viz.: Trinity College, seventeen miles distant, Salem Female College, the old and celebrated German school, twenty-one miles ; Greensboro Female College, thirty-five miles—all within a day's ride.

The Yadkin River and other streams that traverse the county afford some of the finest and most productive lowlands or bottoms to be found any where. About two-thirds of the county, embracing the western, northern and a part of the eastern portion, is of the very finest kind of tobacco land, and when well cultivated and the tobacco well cured large prices are obtained by the farmers and heavy profits realized. Some farmers are known to have made $900, $1,000 and $1,100 on one acre of land by raising fine tobacco.

About one-fifth of the county, known as the Jersey Settlement, in the southern part of the county, is the cotton producing section, where nearly 1,600 bales were raised in 1879. These lands are rich and fertile. And while cotton and tobacco are raised to perfection in the sections named, the whole county is emphatically a great grain producing section of the country, as is shown by the figures above given.

The climate is pleasant and salubrious, not being subject

to the extremes of heat and cold. The numerous springs and wells afford the purest, clearest and coldest drinking water to be found in any State. The celebrated Healing Spring, a pleasant summer resort, is fifteen miles south-east of Lexington.

Taken all together—the water, climate, soil, educational advantages and accessibility to market, Davidson County is a most pleasant and desirable place to live in.

M. H. P.

Davie County,

Bounded on the East by the Yadkin and on the South by the South Yadkin River, is a very fertile and prosperous county belonging to the middle section. It is principally a grain growing and tobacco county and is especially noted for its fine tobacco. The stock law prevails in the entire county. Its surface is hilly and undulating; its soil rich and loamy. The minerals are iron and copper. The principal products, wheat, corn, oats, rye, tobacco and cotton. Fruits: grapes, apples and peaches. It has an area of 240 square miles (153,506 acres) and its population is 11,096; white, 7,770; colored 3,326. Value of real estate $1,000,000, and of personal property, $500,000.

Schools are kept up from three to four months in each school district.

Mocksville is the county seat with a population of 600.

It is a finely timbered county, the principal timbers being hickory, oak, ash, gum, pine and poplar. A very fine quality of wine is made in this county. The principal manufactures are tobacco and whisky. This is one of the few counties that makes its own bacon. The people are sober, industrious and hospitable. Flourishing schools are in

operation at Farmington, Fulton, Smith Grove and Mocksville.
L. S. O.

Rowan County.

This County, situated near the centre of what is known as the Middle Section of the State, bounded on the East by the Yadkin and on the North by the South Yadkin river, is one of the most fertile and prosperous counties in the State. Eight large creeks, from five to eight miles apart, intersect the County, making it rich in bottom and meadow lands. Surface hilly and undulating. Soil rich and loamy. Principal products: oats, wheat, corn, rye, cotton, tobacco, sugar cane, hay, peas and potatoes.

Fruits: Apples, peaches, pears and grapes.

Timbers: Hickory, oak, ash, maple, dogwood, poplar and pine.

Minerals: Gold, copper, silver and iron.

This is perhaps the finest grain-growing County in the State; more oats in 1880 and, with one exception, more corn and wheat having been raised here than in any other County. More hay beyond any comparison is shipped annually from this point; 1,400,000 lbs. having been shipped in 1881. From eight to ten thousand bales of cotton are produced annually; and tobacco in certain portions of the County is raised with great profit and in abundance. There are twenty-five flouring mills in the County, all run by water.

For the present year two dollars per capita for each child over six years of age has been appropriated for school purposes, which will give a four months' school in each district.

The stock law prevails in the entire county with exception of one township.

Salisbury, the county seat, an enterprising town of 3,000

inhabitants, is the eastern terminus of the Western North Carolina Railroad, and is on the direct line of the Richmond & Danville or Piedmont & Air Line Railroad which runs through the County dividing it in twain. It possesses the most ample railroad facilities, being in direct connection with the great cities of the North and South; and lately through connection has been given over the Western North Carolina Railroad with Louisville, Cincinnati and the great West. Within the last year a fine tobacco market has sprung up here and already two large tobacco warehouses and three factories are in active operation.

It contains a magnificent public school building handsomely equipped and a flourishing graded school is conducted.

It has six handsome churches for the whites and four for the colored representing the Methodist, Baptist, Lutheran, Presbyterian, Episcopal and Roman Catholic denominations.

That portion of the County lying East of the R. & D. Railroad, is in the great mineral belt of the State. And over fifty gold and copper mines have been opened, some fifteen of which have been equipped and are at work or are ready to be operated. In this County are situated the celebrated Gold Hill mines out of which over $2,000,000 in gold has been taken. They are now extensively worked by English capitalists.

Population of the County, 19,965; whites, 13,621; colored, 6,344; area, 485 square miles (310,453 acres); value of real estate, $3,000,000, and value of personal property, $1,200,000.

The County is out of debt and has several thousand dollars surplus money in the Treasury.

The people are sober, industrious, moral and hospitable.

L. S. O.

Cabarrus County

Is located, 750 feet above sea level, in the south-western part of the State, midway between the Yadkin and Catawba Rivers. The tier of counties between these two rivers is unsurpassed in their excellent characteristics of climate, soil and general aspects of nature.

County Seat.—Concord, the county seat, is 40 miles north of the South Carolina line and 20 miles north-east of Charlotte, North Carolina. It is a town of 1,500 inhabitants, upon the North Carolina Railroad, very near the exact geopraphical centre of the County, and is the main shipping and freight receiving depot of the County.

From this depot are shipped annually 12 to 15,000 bales of cotton, raised in Cabarrus and adjoining counties. The mercantile trade of the town, in all lines, aggregates much more than half a million of dollars annually and is increasing yearly.

Railroad.—The North Carolina Railroad runs entirely through the County from north to south-west and is a part of the *Main Line* of the *Richmond and Danville Railroad* system, which carries the through mails from Boston and New York to New Orleans.

Area and Population.—The area of the County is 350 square miles.

Population in 1870	11,954
" " 1880	14,964
White Population in 1880	9,849
Colored " " "	5,115
Foreign-born Population in 1880	37

Debt, Values, Taxes, etc.—There is no County debt whatever.

Assessed value of Real Estate 1883,	$1,600,000
Assessed " " Personal Property 1883,	800,000

OF NORTH CAROLINA.

Average yearly State and County tax on $100 worth of property, *in cents*, 66⅔. This,—66⅔ cents—is the *Constitutional* limit for State and County taxes in North Carolina.

Valuation of farms, including lands, fences and buildings, according to census of 1880,	$2,205,643
Valuation farming implements and machinery—census 1880,	$90,364
Value live stock 1880,	296,697
Value of all farm products 1879,	764,084
Number of farms 1880,	1,729
Improved lands 1880, (in acres),	90,514
Number of horses 1880,	2,167
Mules and asses "	1,583
Working oxen "	37
Milch cows "	2,547
Other cattle "	3,575
Sheep "	3,551
Swine "	12,284
Pounds of wool "	7,663
Pounds of butter "	127,927
Pounds of cheese "	325
Farm Products.—Bushels Indian corn 1880	381,321
Bushels oats 1880	54,514
" wheat "	84,656
" rye "	355
" Irish potatoes "	7,062
" Sweet " "	11,241
Bales of cotton "	7,467
Tons of hay "	3,496
Pounds of tobacco "	3,239

Soil.—The soil of Cabarrus is noted for its great fertility, easy cultivation and general adaptability to the production of cotton, corn, wheat, rye, oats, clover, grasses, peas, potatoes and tobacco, the latter not yet much cultivated. The general character of the soil is that of a sandy loam and a clay loam, both underlaid with a red clay sub-soil, and is possessed of great vitality and energy unexhausted by cultivation for a century in some instances.

In the eastern half of the county the land is undulating, somewhat "broken" by hills—the western half is rather level and plateau-like.

Water.—Natural springs are in great abundance in all parts of the county, and good well-water is easily obtained at depths ranging from 20 to 40 feet. The lands of the county are well watered by Rocky River and several creeks and small streams, *all perennial*, with an average annual rain-fall of 48.2 inches.

Trees and Timber.—Fruit trees, of almost every variety, flourish and grow in abundance on nearly every farm, and the county is well timbered with virgin oak, pine and hickory, and later growth of the same. Black walnut is also found in considerable quantity. Much experience has proven that many varieties of grape can be successfully grown in this county.

Climate.—The climate is that of a *warm Temperate Zone*, and is admirably attempered to human comfort, physical health, and exercise. The hottest month in the year is July, of which the mean temperature is 79°; the coldest month is January, with a mean temperature of 38°.

The People of Cabarrus are exceptionally intelligent, law-abiding, moral and thrifty. The eastern portion of the county is inhabited, in the main, by people of German descent, and the western part by those of Scotch-Irish extraction.

Fences.—Farm fences do not exist in Cabarrus. Under a State law, which had its origin in this county, and now applies to several counties in North Carolina, every owner of live stock and cattle of every description is required to fence up such stock and cattle upon his own premises: and thus the great expense of farm-fencing, and the consequent immense destruction of timber for that purpose is avoided. The law works admirably and gives entire satisfaction to all classes wherever it has been tested, and is known, after much experience, to be of incalculable benefit to the county generally, and especially to the farming interest.

Churches for the White Population.—There are in the county the following churches:—Five Presbyterian, with an aggregate membership of 1,000. Two of these churches, —Rocky River and Poplar Tent,—are historic, antedating in their organization the American Revolution: that at Rocky River being established in 1754. The churches at Concord, Rocky River and Poplar Tent are handsome brick edifices, the two latter having each an Academy connected with them, thus keeping religion and education hand in hand. These three churches have each a neat and comfortable parsonage for their pastors. This denomination occupies a very prominent position in the county.

Fifteen Methodist, with a membership of 1,500. The Methodist have good buildings for all their congregations —that at Concord they are now making very handsome— and are in a flourishing condition, commanding by the number and character of their membership great respect.

Fourteen Lutheran, with a membership of 1,500. The Lutheran Church was established in the eastern part of the county several years prior to 1776. The German Reform and Lutherans before 1771 worshipped in the same building, known as the Dutch Buffaloe Church. In 1771 the Lutherans, at the suggestion of Capt. John Paul Barringer, and chiefly with the means furnished by him, built their own church, now known as St. John's. The new Lutheran Church at Concord is the largest, most beautiful and attractive church building in Cabarrus. This denomination has a College, non-sectarian in its instruction, with large and handsome buildings, at Mt. Pleasant, and wields a great and good influence in the county.

Two German Reform, with a good membership in number and quality, and one handsome brick church at Mt. Gilead; and one Episcopal, at Concord, of recent establishment, with a neat and well furnished brick church and a small but very intelligent and influential membership. All these denominations have connected with each of their churches a regular and well-attended Sunday School.

For Colored Population.—Four Presbyterian, with a large membership. The Africo-Presbyterian Church at Concord, founded and built by Northern generosity, is a very beautiful brick building. Twenty-two Methodist, and two Baptist.

Schools for White Population.

Common schools,	64
Total attendance per year,	1495
Average attendance at each school,	23
Average length of school term, in weeks,	8

For Colored Population.

Common schools,	39
Total attendance per year,	1052
Average attendance at each school,	27
Average length of school term, in weeks,	9

These common schools are maintained by taxation under the State School Law. By the *State Constitution* the schools for whites and blacks are forever "*separate*," without discrimination in favor, or to the prejudice of either race. And each and every school is located in the various townships with a view of justice to the school population.

Besides these *Common Schools* and the two Academies mentioned before there are several schools in Concord with capable and efficient teachers, chief among which are:

The Concord Male Academy.—Located in Concord, supported and patronized by members of the Presbyterian, Methodist and Lutheran churches and others and under the management and instruction of Prof. R. S. Arrowood, a fine scholar and teacher.

The Concord Union School.—Established and sustained by "The Ladies Board of Missions of the Presbyterian Church of New York," aided, originally, by funds of private citizens of Concord.

This school was founded to promote and aid the education of those white children unable to pay tuition. It is well conducted and the instruction good.

White Hall Seminary.—A limited boarding and day school, for white children, within three miles of Concord. This school, taught and managed by several well educated and accomplished ladies from the North, was established and is supported by "The Ladies Board of Missions of the Presbyterian Church of New York," and is doing a great and good work in the cause of education.

Scotia Seminary.—A school for colored girls located in Concord, instituted and sustained by "The Freedman's Board of the Northern Presbyterian Church." The building, situated in beautiful and capacious grounds, is a magnificent and costly brick structure. There were present during the session just ended 225 scholars; 165 of whom were boarders. The course of instruction is full and thorough. The institution is presided over with eminent and practical ability by Rev. Luke Dorland and his wife, aided in their work by a corps of well educated and proficient instructors all of whom, with Mr. Dorland and his wife, are Northerners. This school is a great blessing to the colored race, and is doing very much for its advancement in furnishing well trained teachers for the colored schools in this and other States, and in educating and refining its women.

The last three mentioned schools, so useful and beneficial,

are splendid monuments to Northern generosity and charity.

Mineral Interests.—The chief mineral, in the county, of intrinsic value is *gold*, found in the abundant gold-bearing quartz veins, which occur mostly in the metamorphic slates, bordering upon the granites.

Placer-mining is only limited, because the general plateau character of the county does not admit of a concentration of the *detritus* containing the free gold. Still, for a great many years, placer mining has been and is yet carried on here and there with some remunerative success. But the universal distribution of free gold over a very large area of the county led to the discovery of its source—the veins. And a very large number of highly remunerative, true fissure veins have been found and are worked to-day.

These gold-bearing quartz-leads generally conform to the inclination of the country rock, and the direction of their outcrop, which is northeast, southwest. And east and west as well as due north and south veins have also been discovered. The gold found in these veins has been, from their apex down to the water level, in a free state but below the water level the ores become sulphurets; baffling the free gold miner so that he gave up in despair, knowing at the same time that the ores were rich in the precious metal. And many enterprises were deserted in consequence. And in going over Cabarrus County the traveler will see the deserted places in great number where the free-gold miner had to abandon the rich sulphurets. But in recent years the eminently successful working of these sulphuretted gold ores by the chlorination process has overcome all obstacles; a daily proof of which is seen in the results at the Phœnix and Tucker Mines.

The Phœnix, at which there has been expended over $100,000, in a complete plant for the reduction of these ores by the Mears chlorination process, has been explored to a depth of 300 feet by 2,100 feet in length; showing a continuation of splendid ore downwards as well as laterally. At present the Phœnix Company has a three years supply of ore in sight averaging, in value, *not less* than $25 per ton. This property is now highly renumerative to its owners. The Tucker Mine has been for some time working under the Plattner process of chlorination, but is changing now to the Mears process of chlorination. At this mine there has been a development to the depth of 100 feet and about 500 feet laterally showing, in all its workings, very rich sulpheretted veins with a heavy iron pyritic ore, carrying 1 to 2 per cent. of copper. At the Tucker there are many tons of ore on the surface. There are on the property four well defined veins rich enough in gold to pay handsome dividends to the owners with a process that can be depended on to work the ores within 5 per cent. of the assay value, at a reasonable expense.

Besides these there are the Cullen, Furnace, Quaker City, Faggart, Barnhardt, Newell and other properties which, from full prospecting, have given proof that they are very valuable.

In a word, while the gold-mining interest of Cabarrus is still in its infancy, it can be truthfully said that enough is *known* to insure this interest to be of immense value and a most profitable investment for the capitalist, whose coming many rich properties are awaiting.

Factories and Mills.—There are three cotton factories in Cabarrus. One, known as *The Rocky River Factory*, is located 8 miles from Concord on Rocky River and is run by water. At present not in operation. The others are known as the factories of

The Odell Manufacturing Company.—This Company own two mills, run by steam and located in the town of Concord.

Mill No. 1 was established in 1840 ; the horse power of mill No. 1 is 80 ; the number of spindles 2,000 ; the number of plaid looms, 74 ; the number of bag looms, 12. Mill No. 2 was established in 1882 ; the horse power of mill No. 2 is 175 ; the number of spindles, 4,000 ; the number of plaid looms, 138 ; bag, 20. Capital stock of company, $130,000; operatives employed in both mills, 275. The products of these mills are sold in the south, west and southwest. The two mills together use 2000 bales of cotton and consume 2,000 cords of wood per annum. The profits to the Company are large.

Each township and neighborhood in the county is well supplied with flour, corn and saw-mills, run both by steam and water. P. B. M.

Mecklenburg County

Is located in the southwestern portion of North Carolina, north of the 35th parallel of latitude, about two hundred miles from the Atlantic coast, and one hundred miles east of the Appalachian range of mountains, and is bounded on the south by the State of South Carolina, and on the west by the Catawba River. According to the observations of the Government signal station at Charlotte, its mean annual temperature for the four years past was 60 9-10° Fahrenheit, with a mean annual rainfall for the same period of 49 77-100 inches, while its mean elevation above tide water is 770 feet. These conditions contribute to give it a delightful and healthful climate. Its area comprises about 313,000 acres. According to the census of 1880, its population numbered 34,299, and of this number the whites have a decided majority, and control in all departments of the county government. Of the entire population only 277 are of foreign birth. The county was originally largely settled by Scotch, with Irish, Germans, and English, intermingled. By the census of 1880, the value of farms in 1879 was, $3,382,544, and the estimated value of farm productions was $1,451,470. The appraised value of property for taxation in the county for 1881 was $6,354,327. For the year 1882 it was over $6,500,000. These assessments are much below the actual values. The real value of the personal and real estate is estimated to be over $12,000,000. But two other counties in the state show greater value of farms and of annual productions. The natural soil is very fertile, consisting of a loam from 2 to 8 inches deep on the uplands, with a much greater depth on the branch, creek, and river bottoms. The subsoil is clay and is capable of the highest degree of improvement, being less liable to wash, and more retentive and absorbent of fertilizers given to it than other earths. The surface is undulating and in places hilly, but rarely ever too steep for the use of the plough even on the hill-sides. Half a dozen creeks with their clear streams run through the county, emptying into the Catawba and Yadkin Rivers, and giving much rich and productive land to its riparian owners. These streams furnish the power for many mills, located upon them, for sawing lumber, grinding wheat and corn, and for other purposes. The Catawba River alone, 12 miles from Charlotte, has a fall of 35 feet in one mile, and is capable of running millions of spindles in sight of the growing fields of cotton.

The chief productions of the county are corn, wheat, cotton, oats, rye, clover, lucerne, orchard grass, turnips, beets, cabbage, potatoes (sweet and Irish), apples, peaches, pears, cherries, strawberries, peas, beans, and almost every variety of grain, grasses, fruits, and vegetables, grown in the temperate zone. Of the leading grasses, clover, lucerne, orchard grass, etc., will with the same culture here yield far more abundantly than in any state north of the Potomac river. No better grape region is to be found this side of California than this section extending west up to the range of the Alleghany mountains. Many varieties of native grapes are indigenous to this section, including the Catawba, while nearly all the cultivated grapes of other countries as far as tried, grow luxuriantly and yield abundantly, and are less liable to curcullia, and diseases incident to other localities. The latitude, mild and genial climate, give longer seasons for the growth and perfect maturity of cereals, grasses, grapes, and other fruits than the conditions of higher latitudes, a killing frost rarely occurring before November. Farmers are giving more attention than ever before to the culture of such products, and it may not be long before their wine may vie with the best vintage of France and Germany.

The country is well adapted to raising horses, mules, cattle, hogs and sheep. The abundant yield of grains and grasses, with the short and mild winters, greatly facilitate their raising. It is not unusual for agriculturists to produce from thirty to forty bushels of wheat per acre, and one hundred bushels of rust-proof, or black oats, on well cultivated lands. With the present loose methods of cultivation these results are much above the average, yet with the *intensive* system of farming they are destined to become near the average in the not distant future. The agricultural development and capabilities of this county are not fully realized or appreciated by even its own intelligent population. Improved breeds of horses, cows, hogs, and sheep are rapidly supplying the places of the old stocks. This is particularly the case since the enactment of the law requiring all stock to be fenced-in instead of inclosing the cultivated fields. Lands sell at from $7 to $20 per acre—good farms with dwelling and necessary out-buildings at from $15 to $30 per acre.

The forest growth comprises all varieties of the oak white, black, post, red, etc., and hickory, dogwood, ash, maple, walnut, pine, cedar, gum, elm, cherry, etc., etc.

Many of these are valuable on account of the lumber of commerce manufactured from them. After the clay the principal rocks are granite, silicon, slate, quartz, trap and *copardite*. These are not in sufficient quantities to interfere with proper tillage except in very rare instances. The principal minerals are gold, copper, soapstone and barytes. For over fifty years the gold mines have been famous for their yield of rich ores. After descending below water-level, twenty to forty feet the ores of the veins are converted into sulphurets, and no complete process has yet been introduced and established by which the gold, silver, lead and copper can be eliminated. A perfect process for separating the valuable metals from the earthy substances would prove invaluable, and develop many of the richest mines of the continent.

A large capital is now invested in these mines, some of which are being successfully worked.

Manufacturing is rapidly increasing; grist, flour, and saw mills exist on the creeks and rivers. In addition, steam mills are being erected near the forests. One cotton factory is in operation and others contemplated.

The system of agriculture is improving, the mower, reaper, drill, new ploughs and other implements, have been successfully introduced. While cotton is still the leading production of the farms, labor is finding other and greater variety of employments. The mechanical arts are inviting fields for skilled labor, more of which is required to supply the hundreds of agricultural, mechanical and domestic tools and implements, made of iron and wood, now imported from other States, with the woods and iron ores in profusion around us. The freight saved on those manufactured here would be a good profit, with the raw material in close proximity to the factory. Inexhaustible beds of iron ore are within thirty miles, and coal within one hundred and fifty miles.

This county contains four towns.—Davidson College, Pineville, Huntersville and Matthews, besides the city of Charlotte, the county seat, all showing commercial life and activity and affording markets for the country. Charlotte, called after Princess Charlotte of Mecklenburg, has a population of over 8,000, and does a large commercial and manufacturing business, and is noted for its schools and churches, as is also the county generally. Four railroads terminate at Charlotte, and one passes through, making six lines that radiate in different directions from the centre, leading directly to Washington City, Richmond, Norfolk, Wilmington, Charleston, Augusta, Atlanta and East Tennessee. The free school system is in operation, offering education to all, the white and colored being separate, while many high schools and academies are in the country and towns, with two graded schools in Charlotte containing an average of over one thousand scholars. The people have ever been distinguished for their love of liberty, law and order, education and refinement. Queen's College existed in Charlotte long before the Revolutionary war, and Davidson College, now so flourishing, is an institution that the lovers of learning very justly admire wherever its thorough curriculum and able faculty are known. Perhaps no county in the South is more devoted to the cause of education and religion. The Presbyterians, Methodists, Baptists, Seceders, Episcopalians, Roman Catholics, and Lutherans, all have their churches, and worship God according to the dictates of their own consciences.

The early settlers of Mecklenburg County were exiles from civil and religious tyranny. Impressed with the harshness of monarchies, and deeply imbued with the principles of civil and religious liberty they transmitted them to their descendants. These principles were also developed in the Declaration of Independence for the county, proclaimed to a large assemblage in Charlotte on the 20th of May, 1775, and in the first Republican form of government adopted by the people for the county on the 31st of the same month.

This section is located hundreds of miles in a southwestern direction from the Atlantic coast, with extended forests intervening, and is sheltered from the north and west by an elevated mountain range. One may visit many portions of this continent, and when he considers all the conditions existing here calculated to make life agreeable and happy, the almost entire exemption from great and sudden meteorological changes, storms, hurricanes, cyclones, the complete exemption from cholera and yellow fever, and nearly so from pulmonary diseases, equable and mild climate, pure spring and well water, fertile soil, mineral resources, water-power and varieties of timber, grains, grasses, fruits, and flowers, intelligent and moral population, school and church facilities, he will find no country more inviting than old Mecklenburg to the intelligent and industrious emigrant, who will at all times be cordially welcomed and generously received by her people. W. J.

MANUFACTURES AND MINING.

Within a radius of 30 miles of Charlotte, all of them tributary to Mecklenburg's trade, there are 10 cotton factories:

1. The Mountain Island Mills, 12 miles from Charlotte; 5,000 spindles; makes osnaburgs, plaids, sheetings, yarns and warps; lights with gas of its own manufacture; sells its products in Philadelphia, St. Louis and Chicago, and at Charlotte, N. C.

2. The Woodlawn Mills, 16 miles; employs 200 hands; 75 looms and 2,500 spindles; manufactures osnaburgs, plaids, sheeting, yarn and warps, plain, colored and knitting yarns, and sells all its productions from this market. One mile from Lowell. Water power for sale or lease.

3. The Lawrence Mills, 16 miles; 5,500 spindles, capacity

25,000 ; makes warps and yarns ; ¼ mile from Woodlawn Mills. At Lowell, Gaston County, distant one mile, is depot. Water power for sale or lease.

4. Mount Holly Mills, 12 miles, 2,000 spindles ; makes warps. By survey there is here 12,000 horse-power of water developed, only 200 in use. Sells North ; is increasing.

5. Gastonia Mills, 17 miles ; 4,000 spindles, makes warps and yarns, and sells North.

6. Stowesville Factory, 16 miles ; 2,000 spindles, 24 looms ; makes yarns and shirtings for home markets ; is increasing.

7. Odell & Co. Mills, 18 miles ; runs 2,000 spindles and 50 looms ; makes yarns and sheetings for home market.

8. Phifer & Allison's, 35 miles ; 1,500 spindles and 30 looms ; makes shirting and yarns for home market.

9. Rocky River Mills, 20 miles ; 1,000 spindles, 15 looms ; yarns and sheetings for home market.

10. McAden Mills, 8,500 spindles, capacity 50,000. Manufactures warps and yarns, uses electric light. Water power for sale or lease ; 10,000 horse power developed, 200 in use. Located at Lowell, N. C.

The Lawrence Mills, mentioned above, are entirely new, having commenced operations in June 1879.

Charlotte can show better opportunities for various manufacturing enterprises than any other city in the South. It has a start and cannot retrograde.

All in all persons locating in and about here will find a greater blending of all the requisites which produce business ease and home luxury, at less cost and with lighter effort than can be found elsewhere.

There are nine gold mines in this County. Its mining developments are mainly auriferous, but with the gold which has been found there, has nearly always been a small per cent. of silver. Most of the mines yield at times some copper ore, and a few mines show a tendency to ore of that character nearly exclusively. Lead in the form of galena, or sulphuret of lead, has been found in the Moore and Smart mines, on the borders of Union County.

Numerous surface indications of iron are found in the western portion of the County, notably in Steel Creek township. The scarcity of iron in the South during the late war between the States, and the necessity for a good supply of that important "sinew of war," stimulated an active search for the iron deposits which were thought to be indicated by the surface specimens, found in several parts of the County, but the search was not rewarded with such success as to lead to the developing any iron mines of importance, and there is now little hope that any mineral wealth of that character will ever be found in the County. Just over the line, however, in Lincoln and Catawba Counties, iron mines of great value have been worked, some of them for a century at least, and recently the owners of the High Shoals mines have been shipping the iron ore to Pittsburg, Pa., at a good profit.

The gold mining industry of Mecklenburg County, like that of this metal everywhere, has been an eventful one; now in vigorous work, then almost dead. Not less than fifty-five localities, within the area of the County, have been explored for gold. At present the following are worked:

THE HOPEWELL MINE is nine miles northwest of Charlotte. It has been worked down for about 100 feet, with good results. The ore, which has a considerable per cent. of copper, is said to assay only moderately well for gold.

THE MCGINN MINE is five miles northwest of Charlotte, has three well defined veins, two carrying the gold ores usually found in this section, and a third having rich copper as well as gold ore. The latter is the only ore prospected now. The depth reached is 165 feet, from which a drift has been lately run nearly to the vein. The more prominent of the two gold veins has been penetrated to a depth of 150 feet, and worked .with some success as deep as the machinery could control the in-flowing water. Different assays of the ores have been made which range in value from $4.37 to $137.93 per ton. The gold vein above alluded to runs on the south into the adjacent

CAPP'S MINING PROPERTY, where it is joined by another prominent vein. The system has been worked to a depth of 200 feet, but work at present is not carried on lower than 150 feet. At last reports several hundreds of tons of good ore were on the dump, and the work of development is to be continued. It has been worked for many years, by different owners, and how much gold it has produced is a matter of conjecture, though it is credited in the neighborhood with over $2,000,000. Different assays made at long intervals have been per ton as follows: $7.10, $56.35, $96.37, $133.00 and $133.76.

THE ARLINGTON GUARANTEE MINE, five miles west of Charlotte, has been worked to a depth of about 100 feet, and a large amount of brown ore is at command. The milling machinery at present in use is a modified form of the old Carolina gold mill, and the prospective outlook is favorable.

THE CLARK MINE, two and a half miles west of Charlotte, has been worked to a depth of seventy feet only, and nearly always with good results. Its ores have assayed from $8.34 to $164.44 per ton.

THE RUDISILL MINE, located one mile southwest of Charlotte, has been worked down to a depth of 300 feet, and its product is thought to have been very remunerative to its owners. No one now knows when it was first worked, or how much gold it has produced, though it is popularly credited with $2,000,000, and it has proven so far the most valuable gold mine in the county, possibly because it has been more largely developed. Being almost in the suburbs of Charlotte, it has always had a larger share of attention, and a larger capital has been employed in its development than any other mine in the county. The title to it has repeatedly been in litigation, but it is now finally settled and the title perfect, and this fact has prevented the development which should have taken place. The ores are very rich, but the gold is found in sulphurets, which, until the establishment of reduction works in the neighborhood, have proven very refractory. It is equipped with a ten stamp mill, and other necessary machinery for keeping out the water, and also for elevating the ores. The highest assay of its ore, made at the branch mint in Charlotte, was $130.22 per ton. It is in full operation now, and is paying handsomely.

THE ST. CATHERINE MINE is in the near vicinity of the Rudisill, on the same vein probably, and is only one-half mile west of Charlotte. Two shafts have been sunk to a depth of about 100 feet, and a considerable dump of good ore has been accumulated, from a vein from three to four feet wide. The highest assay of ore from this mine was $147.50 per ton.

THE SMITH AND PALMER MINE, one and a half miles west of Charlotte, is probably on the same vein with the Rudisill and the St. Catherine mines. A shaft has been sunk to a depth of 100 feet, and developments so far indicate good results. The highest reported assay is $149.59.

THE BALTIMORE AND NORTH CAROLINA MINE is situated nine miles east of Charlotte, near the Carolina Central Railroad. It is equipped with first-class machinery and has been successfully worked for some years. It has five veins on its property, three only of which are worked. The mine is entered by five shafts, the deepest being 120 feet. The ores are heavy sulphurets containing some copper, with some brown ores. The vein is from one to four feet wide, the total length of which is said to be some four miles. The ores have always assayed well, and the plant is thought to be very valuable.

THE FERRIS MINE lies six miles north east of Charlotte, and is regarded as a prominent mining property, with at least three veins. It is not now operated. Assays of ores from this mine have shown a value of $512.94 per ton, though of course this was from an extra good specimen of ore.

THE SIMPSON MINE, in the same neighborhood, yields quartz ores with little sulphurets. Assays of ores from this mine show it to be valuable.

THE STEPHEN WILSON MINE, nine miles west of Charlotte, has ten well defined veins, on its 310 acres of ground. Assays of ores taken from this mine have reached as high as $355.96 per ton.

THE BLACK MINE has a small, but very rich vein of the finest kind of brown ore, which at different times have assayed as follows: $50.16, $56.86, $62.00, $488.12. A Chilian mill is used for reduction purposes, and large lots of the ore have milled more than $50.00 per ton.

These thirteen mines comprise the principal mines in the County, but besides these gold, silver and copper, and sometimes all three have been found at other points.

The Carson, Sam. Taylor and Icyhour, south-west from Charlotte.

The Wilson and McDonald, one and a half miles to the south-east.

The Davidson Mines, one mile west.

The Trotter, three miles south-west, cut through by the Air Line R. R.

The Dunn Mine, nine miles west, with three veins, one with copper.

The Frasier, Hipp and Todd, are near by.

The Henderson and the Chapman are to the north-west.

The Hunter Mine, at Huntersville, sixteen miles north of Charlotte, has been explored to a depth of 23 feet, with promising exposure.

The Crosby, Rogers and Pioneer Mills Mines, are 12 to 17 miles north-east of Charlotte. They all carry copper pyrites in considerable quantity. The Newell and Pharr mines are near by.

The Johnston, Stinson, Maxwell and Rea Mines are 7 to 9 miles east of Charlotte.

The Tredennick Mine is 7 miles east.

The Alexander is 5½ miles east.

The Caldwell is 6 miles north-east.

The Harris Mine is ten miles nearly east of Charlotte. The stretch of mining property upon which this mine is situated is thought to have some rich gravel. Surface Hill, one of these localities, is famous for its rich nuggets, and occasional pockets of ore are found of extreme richness.

The farm of the Elliott Brothers, five miles south of Charlotte, is thought to contain several veins of gold ore and the Nolan, Jordan, Means, Bennett, Cathey, G. C. Cathey, Sloan, Gibson and the McCorkle Mines are all within easy reach of Charlotte.

It may be safely asserted that the *outlook* for the development of the mining interests of Mecklenburg County is very favorable.

The discovery and development of the gold mines of this county has exhibited the same phases as in other parts o the country where gold has been found. It is a tradition that the Oliver Mine, in Gaston County, near the Mecklenburg line, was worked prior to the Revolutionary War by a German miner, and a similar tradition attributes similar work to a mine near Rock Hill, S. C. A more reliable tradition indicates considerable underground work in the "Aborigines' Tunnel," at the Brown Mine, in South Carolina.

The first recorded discovery of gold in this section of the South was at the Reed mine in Cabarrus County, at that time a part of Mecklenburg County. Conrad Reed, son of the owner, in 1799 found a piece of native gold "as large as a smoothing-iron," which is correct as the traditional "piece of chalk." Its value was not even guessed and it is asserted that for several years it was used to hold the door of Mr. Reed's cabin in position. Its remarkable weight together with continued abrasions of its surface finally led to an inquiry as to its value, and finally Mr. Reed took it to Fayetteville where a jeweler paid him three dollars and fifty cents ($3.50) for it—which was perhaps not more than one fiftieth of its real value. The same locality was for many years prolific of large masses, the largest indeed known, until the gold discoveries of California and Australia. Col. Jno. H. Wheeler in his "Sketches of North Carolina" gives a list of fourteen nuggets found mainly in this section, which aggregated weighed 115 pounds avoirdupois. The active work at the Reed mine must have been considerably later than the beginning of the present century, and the substantial rewards received for this regular work, led to a very general hunt for the precious metal along the entire Appalachian slope as early as 1820, and in numerous localities a general harvest was reaped.

At first only placers were worked, but the exhaustion of these led the miners to hunt up the veins which were the source of the supply, and it is certain that many of the mines mentioned in this catalogue were opened as early as 1825. At the outset the veins proved no less remunerative than the placer mining had done, for the ore was easily and cheaply mined, and the ores were quickly "reduced". The point was reached then, however, when the easily treated ores became refractory from the presence of unaltered sulphurets, and the occurrence of large bodies of water below the permanent water line (40 to 60 feet) made expensive pumping apparatus a necessity, so increasing the cost of mining that work in the mines was seriously retarded, and many of the veins were abandoned. As a rule the ores now mined in this section are the refractory sulphurets, which need a smelting or chemical treatment.

The production of gold in this part of North Carolina had become so general by the year 1830 that grave inconvenience was experienced in its conversion into coin. The merchants charged a large commission for handling it and four months were generally necessary for returns from the Philadelphia Mint. At length, in 1830, a commission was appointed by the State Legislature to investigate and report upon the subject, and this report and subsequent agitation led to the establishment of the Branch Mint at Charlotte by the act of the Federal Congress of March 3, 1835. The mint was opened for business Dec. 4, 1837, but it was burned down in July 1844. It was re-erected in 1845–47, and did business regularly until the beginning of the civil war in 1861. It was revived in 1867, but only as an assay office.

The entire amount of gold bullion deposited at the Charlotte mint from its opening to June 30, 1882, was $5,473,765.[46] The entire amount of gold bullion deposited at *all* the offices of the United States up to June 30, 1882, from North Carolina was $10,786,316.[09] In addition to this large amount it may be safely said that the amount actually produced was at least twice this amount, since it is well known that for forty years the beauty of our native gold led to the consumption of large quantities for jewelry, which never passed through the government offices.

The ores of the County, as has already been stated, are mostly refractory sulphurets. To treat these three "Reduction Works" have recently been erected in the County. The "New York and North Carolina", the "Adams'" and "Designoll's". The two former are not in operation now, but the latter is said to be doing a fine business.

In Charlotte there are several large foundry and machine shops, and a large cotton seed oil mill is in course of erection. It will be in operation this fall. C. R. J.

Anson County

Is situated in the southeastern part of Middle North Carolina. It was established in 1749, and comprehended all the western portion of the State from New Hanover and Bladen on the east as far as the limits of the State extended on the west. It derives its name from Admiral Anson who obtained a victory over the French Fleet off Cape Finisterre a short time before the county was erected. It is bounded on the east by Richmond County,—the Great Pee Dee River, the name by which the Yadkin River is known after its confluence with the Uwharrie, runs the entire length of their common boundary; on the south by Chesterfield County in South Carolina, on the north by Stanly County, Rocky River being the line of divide, and on the west by Union County. It is on the 35th parallel of latitude and 3rd meridian of longitude. Its height above these a level is from 550 to 700 feet. The surface of the county is hilly and its area is about 500 square miles.

There are a number of creeks in the county which give it a fair proportion of good bottom lands. Lane's Creek in the northern part, Big Brown Creek about seven miles from it, with the same general direction in the course of the two, that is from the west— northwest to east—Little Brown Creek, Goulas Fork and Culpepper, all of these are north of the Capital Town of the county, Wadesboro; originally Newtown, changed to its present name after Col. Thomas Wade, who achieved reputation in the war of 1776. It is 125 miles by rail from Raleigh, 135 miles by rail from Wilmington, 51 miles by rail from Charlotte, 160 miles by rail from Charleston, South Carolina, and 65 miles from Salisbury. It is located about the geographical centre of the county, which is nearly square in shape. South of the Capital Town, the most important of the streams is Jones

Creek. Dead Fall is in the western part of the county. and Savannah, Cedar, Smith, and other creeks rise and empty in the eastern part of the county. The southern part of the county has a good deal of long leaf pine. The streams, including the two rivers, afford water power amounting to hundreds of thousands horse power, and their banks are in many places covered with choice shell bark hickory, common hickory, white oak, water and other oaks

The two geological formations, that is the flat low country bordering the ocean and extending thence one hundred or more miles, and that common in the more elevated part of the State, meet and overlap each other about the Pee Dee River. There are many beds of the finest building stone in Anson County. Red, pale and gray sandstone, blue and gray granite, abound; indeed the quantity is such that the necessities of several cities as large as Richmond, Virginia, and Charleston S. C. would not exhaust it in many years.

Cotton, corn and the small grains are the staple crops of the county; cotton is the leading crop, and the staple grown here is the best upland cotton grown north of Mobile, Alabama. It is said that many of the fleecy woollen blankets made in the United States are manufactured of Anson County cotton. The granite grit immediately north and south of Jones Creek is specially noted for the superior staple produced on it. The late Dr. Mitchell of Chapel Hill, who lost his life in the interest of science, pronounced the gray granite grit of the Jones Creek section the best for cotton he had seen. It is confidently believed this part of the county would produce as good tobacco as is grown in the United States. Blackberries, strawberries and raspberries grow spontaneously and yield most bountifully when cultivated. Vegetables of all kinds grow to perfection and mature as early as at any other place in the State as far from the Gulf Stream as this. The grape is an unfailing crop, free from disease, and the fruit of excellent quality.

Since the late war the system of farming has been greatly improved in Anson County and the yield of cotton per acre has been increased 100 per cent. This has been wrought by judicious attention applied to farming, showing itself in improved seeds and tools, better manipulated fertilizers, increased home made manure, more thorough preparation of the land, and fuller and more accurate knowledge of the cotton plant. It is believed that a system of rotation of crops, such as has been tried and approved by leading intelligent farmers of the Atlantic cotton belt, will become the settled policy of our farmers at an early day and that the results will far surpass the most sanguine calculation of to-day.

Every man who owns cattle, hogs, sheep, goats or horses, in Anson County is now compelled to pasture them on his own land. None are allowed to run at large on the range. This system came into effect in our county about two years ago, and so much is it esteemed already that a return to the old style of fencing the crops against the incursions of stock is next to impossible. This is regarded as the most important single step taken in this county in the last twenty years. Its beneficent influence is apparent in the great appreciation of our cattle. If people have to keep a cow up and feed her they will be sure to have a good cow to begin with or improve the strain at the earliest convenience. Very little virgin growth will be felled in future. Clearings will extend only to lands once cleared and tilled, then turned out and now covered with old field pines, perhaps the best friends owners of worn out Southern fields have in the way of recuperators of the soil. Now the hedge rows are cultivated, brier beds have been cleaned and turned into smiling plats. Flats have been invaded and made to yield of their opulence. This no-fence system in a county like Anson, which has been long cultivated and much of the original growth destroyed by our fathers, and all of the present labor to hire and pay for, is a solid blessing. If the solid and sure progress thus far accomplished were supplemented with well made roads, Anson County would be as desirable a spot as there is on earth.

Our educational advantages are good. Choice schools at Ansonville, Polkton, Lilesville, Wadesboro and other points afford abundant opportunities for those who wish high academic training. Our public school system is intelligently administered.

The health of our citizens in unsurpassed in this division of the State. We are entirely free from contagious diseases.

Our public debt bearing interest is about $15,000 ; our floating debt is cashed at sight. The officers who control public affairs are honorable and just, and there are but few petty jealousies in the county. We have a population largely composed of honorable and brave men, accomplished and virtuous women. R. T. B.

Montgomery County.

Is the second from the southern boundary of the State. Area, 575 square miles. Population : white, 6,857 ; colored, 2,517 ; total, 9,374. Assessed value of taxable property in 1883, $1,151,057.

The general surface is undulating and a large proportion is susceptible of profitable cultivation.

The best farming lands are smooth, level and near the creeks and rivers, and are of a dark loam and very productive ; characterized by uniformity of crops, principally grain. A still larger proportion is a light gray loam and sandy soil, fairly productive. The county is about one-third of the latter class.

It is estimated by the census returns that there is in the county 150,000 acres of thickly wooded long leafed pine, averaging 60 pines per acre of 500 feet each, board measure, of merchantable lumber.

There is also 50,000 acres covered by a variety of other timbers, such as short leafed pine, oaks of the several kinds, hickory, ash, elm, gum and dogwood, of which oaks, hickory, pine, gum and dogwood are most abundant.

The principal streams are the Pee Dee, Yadkin, Uwharrie and Little Rivers, and Cheek's Mountain, Downing, Clark's Island, Barnes, Hamer, Dinson, Rocky and Beaver Dam Creeks. The Yadkin and Pee Dee is the dividing line between Montgomery and Stanly Counties. The first named is noted for its falls and narrows just above its junction with the Uwharrie, making the Pee Dee.

Ten miles above the mouth of the Uwharrie the Yadkin is a fraction over 600 yards wide and at three miles above the mouth of the Uwharrie is the Narrows, where the stream rushes between its banks only sixty feet apart, falling thirty-five feet in one-quarter of a mile, and just below the Narrows is the falls, where the stream makes another rapid fall about half that of the Narrows, and it is estimated that the falls in the Yadkin River for eight miles aggregate over 100 feet, furnishing numerous sites for mills where its waters now rush wasting by. Uwharrie and Little Rivers as well as the creeks furnish water for mills. Numerous springs of pure water abound, and some are resorted to for their healing properties, the most noted being the Sulphur in the eastern part of the county.

The soils are adapted to a diversity of crops. Corn, wheat, cotton, oats, rye, barley, potatoes, Irish and sweet, and sorghum grow well and return a large yield. Peaches, plums, apples, pears and grapes are successfully grown, and a large portion of the county—being the eastern and middle—is wonderfully adapted to the growth of grapes, which ripen perfectly, yielding the finest wines, and we have native grapes of the finest variety. Vegetables of all kinds grow well.

Unimproved lands suitable for farms can be bought from $2 to $10 per acre, while improved lands can be bought in proportion to the value of improvements. Lands under cultivation can be rented from $1 to $5 per acre.

Native grasses in the timber furnish good pasturage most of the year and the mast of oak and pine one year in three is sufficient to fatten hogs for the market and generally sufficient to keep stock entirely; and many are found wild in the woods, never having been fed. Domestic fowls are easily raised. In parts of the county there is much game, deer, turkey and other smaller varieties. We have fish in all our streams, but shad are most highly prized.

There is a great number of saw and flouring mills run both by water and steam. Pine lumber is worth from $5 to $6 per thousand at the mill.

Troy, the county seat, in the centre of the county, is a pleasant place, noted for its good water, healthy location and quiet citizenship. There is an excellent school all the while and two churches, Methodist and Baptist.

The Methodist, Baptist, Presbyterian and Christian denominations have church organizations and many excellent houses of worship.

There are 70 public free schools for a scholastic population of 3,276. There are also five high grade private schools.

One other fact but little known to the public is the vast amount of territory in the county yielding gold and other minerals undeveloped, both of vein and placer diggings. The developments so far are of a crude and unsystematic character. These belts of mineral lands run through the county in parallel lines, about north 40° east, and vary from 4 to 6 miles apart. The most eastern runs about central through the county, embracing the Sam Christian, a placer mine, and the Carter and Reynolds Vein Mines. From the former nuggets have been taken weighing four pounds and eight and a quarter pounds avoirdupois. The next belt is northwest about four miles; about the same in length as the first (16 miles), embraces the Wood Run Mine—placer—at the southwest, and the Moore Mines northwest, the latter a vein lately discovered and but little worked, the ore yielding from $10 to $40 per ton by actual mill test. The next belt, about six miles further northwest, is chiefly placer diggings, and running nearly parallel with the Uwharrie River and about one mile distant, embracing the Island Creek Mines, Worth Mine, Bunnell Mountain and Dry Hollow. Of these the Worth, Bunnell Mountain and Dry Hollow have yielded large amounts of gold, but to be successfully worked requires water to be brought from the Uwharrie River, which has never been done. The largest nuggets from these mines weighed from one to four pounds, the largest being from Dry Hollow. The next line is about four miles northwest of the last named, and embraces the Hearne Mine, Steele Mine and Rigins' Hill, all vein mines; the Steele being regarded as the best and is still very rich, and is owned by the Baltimore & Montgomery Mining Company. The next line embraces the Peebles Gold Mine and others of recent discovery, known as the Davis or Dutton Mine, all vein mines, the latter reputed rich. The next line embraces the Beaver Dam Mines, the Davis Mine and Harris Mine, chiefly of a placer character, except the latter, which has both vein and placer diggings, considered good but only partially developed. Some very fine nuggets have been found along this line, and from the Beaver Dam in one year, worked in the old crude way,' $20,000 was taken out.

The iron of the county is without a test so far, except to ascertain that it is a good quality. At two or more points immense quantities are found in hills or masses. Galena is found at two points, one on each side of the Uwharrie River—one near El Dorado P. O., and the other near Uwharrie P. O.

The sandstone of the county is on a line about twelve miles southeast of the first gold belt mentioned. The whetstone quarries and grindstone quarries are between these belts.

In this county is a fine field for enterprising miners, manufacturers and others, and those wishing to visit the county to reach the Court House at the nearest railroad point will get off at Lilesville, on the Carolina Central Railroad, or at Manly, on the Air-line Railroad. A daily mail runs from Troy to Lilesville. C. C. W.

Randolph County.

The geographical position of Randolph County is a little west of the centre of the State. It contains 728 square miles. Its population in 1880 was 20,836; in 1870, 17,551. Its farms in 1880 are stated in the census to number 2,923, of 100,888 acres of improved land, at $2,197,516 value; and their products at $633,167. Its corn crop was 477,168 bushels; wheat, 137,104 bushels; hay, 4,951 tons. Its manufactures are valued at $894,462—nearly 1-20th of the State's productions reported in the census.

The county is intersected by two principal streams and their tributaries. Deep River, a component of the Cape Fear, runs in a tortuous course from near the northwestern to the southeastern corner of the county. Its bottoms are narrow, the hills often rising abruptly on either side from the water's edge. Although the bottoms are too small for extensive crops, the adjacent hills within the range of evaporation from the river are productive.

The Uwharrie River, a tributary of the Pee Dee, runs across the western border of the county, from north to south, within a few miles of the Davidson line. The bottom lands of Uwharrie and its tributary, the Caraway, are of much larger extent than those of Deep River, and are very productive. The Uwharrie bottoms and adjacent uplands are naturally as fine for all agricultural purposes as any lands in the Piedmontane section of the South. The soil on Sandy Creek, in the northeastern part of the county, is kindly, producing fine returns for the labor bestowed.

The northern and western portions of the county are wooded principally with oak in its several varieties, interspersed on the Uwharrie lands with a sprinkle of black locust. The whole central and southeastern portion is thin land, (except narrow strips along the rivulets,) all covered with a growth of short-leaved pines. These pines within the last few years have come largely into use for building purposes.

The face of the country is gently undulating, with the exception of the bluffs along Deep River and the Caraway hills in the western part of the county. These last rise almost to the measure and dignity of mountains. The same may be said of the hills of Little River, immediately south, part of the same system, extending down through Montgomery. They are picturesque and striking to the eye of the beholder, and, from many points of view, really grand in outline. It looks as if a large lot of stuff left over in making the Alleghanies had been piled up in Randolph and Montgomery.

Mining was pursued to a considerable extent before the late political troubles stopped enterprise of all sorts. The spirit is reviving. The Hoover Hill Mine, under management of an English Company, is as yet, however, the only one efficiently wrought, and is represented to be rich in product.

There are six or seven large saw mills located in different portions of the pine woods, where lumber of all varieties is turned out in the rough for market. At Bush Hill, in the northwest corner of the county, there is an extensive sash and blind factory and planing mills, which have been in successful operation for several years. At the same place a tannery and shoe manufactory are doing good business. There is also a sash and blind factory at Randleman. The streams are everywhere dotted with grist and saw mills for neighborhood custom—many of them fitted up for "merchant work."

Trinity College, a seat of education known and valued for many years past throughout the Southern country, is situated in the northwestern corner of Randolph, within easy distance of the N. C. Railroad, at High Point. There are, besides, a few schools of academic grade in the county.

Ashboro is the Court House town, located at the centre of the county, a remarkably healthy and pleasant situation. There are but few other villages except along the river at the factories.

It is the cotton manufacturing interest on Deep River which gives to Randolph its chief distinction—a position which she is likely to maintain while water runs and cotton grows. The water power of this river is a power of nature, perpetual and exhaustless; never interrupted but in exceptional seasons of drought.

An intelligent gentleman, who is accurate in his observations and careful in his figures, remarks that there are eleven factories from Jamestown, in Guilford, to Enterprise, in Randolph. Of these nine are in Randolph. In order to give a view of this industry as a whole, beginning at Jamestown, the distance by road to Enterprise is about 36 miles. The distance by the river is of course much longer. From best information at hand the fall is over three hundred feet altogether. Something over one hundred feet have been utilized by the eleven factories already in operation. There are still nearly two hundred feet of fall that can and will be utilized. Most of the mills are provided with steam power to be used in the event of too high or too low water in the river. This water, as it flows down, now turns 28,000 spindles, and moves over 700 looms, besides various other machinery, such as corn mills, flour mills, saw mills, etc. The capital invested on the river in factories is now $786,000 ; and over 1,200 hands are worked in the factories, besides others who find concomitant work; so that some 4,000 or 5,000 are supported by these enterprises. The question is asked, Where does the capital come from ?—none of the citizens have large capital. The answer is easy. The people are forming joint stock companies, and co-operating to furnish work for those who need it and to build up the country.

The importance of this matter will justify a cursory view of these establishments in detail.

"Randleman," (formerly Union), stands at the head of the list, and first in order on the river in Randolph. It is situated on the main road leading from Greensboro, south. A considerable town has grown up around it, and is still growing. The site is what a landscape painter would call romantic. The statistics are not at hand at this writing for a detailed description. Suffice it, that it is the largest on the river.

"Naomi," just below, with over 200 hands, makes daily 2,300 pounds of warp. The pay rolls of Randleman and Naomi together count up over $8,000 per month.

"Worthville."—Building 50 by 240 feet, four stories. Runs at present 52 looms, 3,100 spindles, turning out 2,000 yards of sheeting and 600 seamless bags per day. Employs 175 hands and consumes 2,000 pounds cotton daily.

"Central Falls."—Building 50 by 200 feet, three stories.

Floor capacity for 150 looms and 5,000 spindles. A number up and more being placed in position.

"Cedar Falls."—The pioneer establishment, put up before 1840 by Col. B. Elliott and his son Henry B. Consumes 1,500 pounds cotton per day, made into sheetings, yarns, warps and twine. Sixty looms, 2,100 spindles, 90 operatives.

"Franklinsville."—Two miles below. 20 looms, 960 spindles, 18 cards, consumes 1,200 pounds cotton per day. The manufacture of seamless bags a specialty, the production inadequate to the large demand.

"Randolph," (late Island Ford.)—Capacity 50 looms, 2,000 spindles, 14 cards, producing 3,000 yards sheeting and consuming 1,200 pounds cotton per day.

"Columbia," (late Deep River), two and a half miles below. Much new machinery lately received. Only warps manufactured.

"Enterprise."—Last, but not to be the least, when everything is got in good working order.

It should be remembered that all these establishments are growing—new machinery coming in and being put in place. It is therefore difficult to give statistics which will last long.

Villages have grown up around these factories of from 200 or 300 to over 1,000. Churches and schools are encouraged and cherished by proprietors and operatives.

It is but just to say, here, that the people of Randolph are of a high average of intelligence ; steady-going, modest and moral ; in short, model North Carolinians.

L. S.

Guilford County.

Guilford County is situated in the north central part of North Carolina, measures 26 miles from north to south and 28 miles from east to west, containing 728 square miles. The surface is beautifully undulating, and well watered by the upper branches of Deep and Haw Rivers. The head springs of both these rivers are in the north-western part of the county. Over the whole central portion of the county, from the northern to the southern border, and covering perhaps two-thirds of the territory, the soil is a light sandy loam, interspersed in many places with more or less of clay soil, and in large sections on the southeastern and southwestern borders the clay predominates. The sandy loam produces well for the first three or four years after clearing; but then requires light manuring and judicious cultivation to keep it up. The clay lands last longer and produce better under hard usage, and are consequently considered the more valuable. But manure and wise forethought are required here, as elsewhere, to keep the lands in good condition. The alluvial strips along the numerous little streams are naturally productive and lasting.

In the old slavery days much of the finest farming land was worn out by careless and slovenly cultivation. Fresh fields were "cleared" every winter, and the worn lands "turned out," hence the thousands of acres of old fields now growing over with broom sedge and young pines, and some of them washed in ugly gullies. But it has been observed that where the land was originally good, nature is gradually, kindly, surely restoring under the genial influence of the growing pines, the fertility so recklessly exhausted.

Take it altogether, there is no territory of the same extent in the Piedmontane portion of Virginia and the Carolinas.

where the soil is more easily cultivated, or yields more satisfactory returns for the labor bestowed, and it only lacks the element of lime to make it equal to the best uplands in the section named.

Large bodies of original forests are interspersed over the county, where as fine oak and hickory grows as can be found anywhere. Valuable pine forests once grew in some sections, but the best trees have been used up for building purposes.

The usual grain crops are raised here; though not in quantities equal to the productions of the alluvial lands of the West, or of the highly cultivated farms of the North, yet in amount sufficient to be remunerative to the labor bestowed. One fact should be borne in mind, as a wise appointment of Providence, that if so great quantities of grain cannot be raised as in some other sections, the latitude and climate admit the successful production of a variety of the necessaries and comforts of life, such as no other latitude enjoys. Tobacco is raised here in highest perfection, within easy reach of four or five cash markets. Cotton can be successfully cultivated, and is growing in favor with the farmers as a profitable crop. Fruit is a specialty, and Guilford has some of the largest nurseries in the South. The grape grows nowhere better outside of Italy or California, but has hitherto received almost no attention. Sufficient trial of the white mulberry has been made to show that silk-making would be a productive industry, peculiarly suited to the geographical situation. Meadows, set with native grasses, are frequently set apart on the flat ravines along spring branches, requiring no care except regular mowing to get good crops of hay, and the cultivated grasses grow well on the uplands.

Gold and copper mines were, some years ago, extensively wrought in the western part of the county, and enterprise in this direction is again reviving.

The water power is valuable, some of the larger streams never failing except in excessively dry seasons. There are thirty grist mills in the county, so situated as to be convenient to every neighborhood. On Deep River there is a cotton factory producing over 1,300 lbs. daily of hosiery and coverlet yarns and plaid warps. A few miles below a woollen mill. And in the southeastern corner of the county a cotton factory has been recently erected.

The assessed value of the land for taxation in 1880, exclusive of town lots was $1,837,988, Guilford standing fifth in this respect among the counties of the State. It occupies about the same comparative stand in population. The average assessed value per acre for taxation is $4.58. The real average market value, at voluntary sale, may be put down at about $6 per acre. While there are some sections of the county where lands would command $15 or $20, in other parts not more than $2 to $5 could be obtained.

The white population of Guilford is chiefly made up of the descendants of emigrants coming from three principal sources in the old colonial days, to wit: Scotch-Irish, Presbyterians from Pennsylvania, Germans, (Lutheran and Reformed), from the Fatherland, and Quakers from Nantucket. There was besides a sprinkling of "all sorts," such as the restless pioneer days afforded. The elements have all combined, intermarried, mixed up, fused into a social fabric which, for natural intelligence and steadiness of character, prudence and economy, with a strong spice of shrewdness, will compare with any community on the continent. But, as it has been in other counties of the State, so it has been here: the sons of the *immigrants* soon began to be *emigrants*, and large numbers in the flower of youth and manhood have annually "gone West." All the consolation we have for their loss is the knowledge that they are as leaven to society, wherever they go, worthy of the fathers left behind them. Notwithstanding the continual loss by emigration, the census shows a steady and healthy increase in population.

As to the religious element: the Methodist Church was planted among the others at an early day; and in all the "faith of the fathers" still has healthy influence upon the sons.

In politics,—before the war the population was Whig by a very large majority. Now a considerable majority of the whites are conservative, acting with the Democratic party. Taking the whole body of the voting population, including the blacks, there is perhaps at present very little difference in numbers between the two political parties.

The whole rate of taxation last year for State, county and school purposes was 66 2-3 cents on each $100 valuation of real and personal property, and $2 on each poll.

The total population of the county, ascertained by the late census, was 23,585, of which number something over one-fourth was colored. An increase of 1,697 since 1870, the decade of war and reconstruction.

These remarks about Guilford will apply in a general way to many surrounding counties in middle North Carolina.

GREENSBORO.—Guilford Court House (Martinsville), where the Revolutionary battle of 1781 was fought, was situated five miles northwest of the present site of Greensboro. The old village has entirely disappeared.

Greensboro, the county seat of Guilford, was laid off and established in May, 1808. The population of the town and suburbs numbers something over three thousand. There has been a steady increase of population and business ever since the war. The North Carolina Railroad runs through the town, and is intersected here by the Piedmont, which is a continuation of the Richmond and Danville Railroad. The Cape Fear and Yadkin Valley Railroad, from Fayetteville to the upper valley of the Yadkin, is now in course of construction, crossing the North Carolina Railroad at this point. Thus there will soon be six railroad tracks concentrating in Greensboro : one east, one south-east, one south-west, one west, one north-west, one north-east,—furnishing direct communication with all desirable points of trade, and making Greensboro the chief railroad centre of the State.

A city charter was granted in 1870. The municipal government is in the hands of a Mayor and six Commissioners. The streets are of good width and symmetrically laid off, most of them handsomely shaded with elms, and those most used are substantially paved. The main business streets are lighted with gas. The county court house is an imposing edifice, built in the Roman-Corinthian style, with iron cornices and tower.

The Federal courts are held here twice a year—the District Judge, Attorney and Marshal having their offices here. An appropriation of $50,000 has been made for the erection of a government building to accommodate the Federal court and the post-office. The building will be finished this summer.

There are five churches for whites : Methodist, Presbyterian, Episcopal, Baptist, and Roman Catholic. Four for the colored people : Baptist, Presbyterian, African Methodist, and Northern Methodist.

Two graded schools are in successful operation, one for the whites, the other for the blacks, kept in comfortable brick buildings expressly erected for the purpose, and chiefly supported by city taxation.

On a commanding eminence at the western border of the town stands Greensboro Female College, established many years ago under Methodist auspices. The building is of brick, very spacious, and occupied by a large number of students.

Bennett Seminary, a brick building, 50x80, four stories high, established by the liberality of a Northern gentleman, is devoted to the education of colored youth of both sexes. The following general details will give an idea of the business of the town :

There are two spoke and handle factories, affording a market for large quantities of hickory and white oak timber ; one of them with an attachment for bending wheel rims. Handles for axes, picks, etc., are shipped from Greensboro to California and other States, and to Europe and Australia.

Two foundries, in which a variety of castings and agricultural implements are manufactured to order or kept in stock. Improved mill-gearing and turbine wheels are specialties in their work.

Two steam saw-mills, a sash and blind factory, two tobacco factories, and two large tobacco warehouses ; three extensive hardware stores, wholesale and retail, three silversmith shops, two saddle and harness shops, two marble yards, a bakery, two cabinet shops and two furniture stores with shops attached, several blacksmith and wagon shops, three or four shoemaker shops where custom work is done, a large tailoring and two millinery establishments, fourteen dry goods stores—three of them dealing largely by wholesale as well as retail, eight grocery stores—three of which do wholesale as well as retail business, three drug stores, one book and stationery store, two livery stables and numerous smaller business establishments difficult to classify.

A national bank with a capital of $100,000, a law school, a lodge of Freemasons, of Odd Fellows, of Knights of Honor, and of Good Templars, four hotels, two daily and three weekly newspapers.

It is remarkable that the region of Greensboro and the old court house has been a "strategic point" of momentous import in two wars. It was the centre of a series of complicated military manœuvres, for weeks, between Greene and Cornwallis in 1781, culminating in a battle which, in its results, turned the tide of war in favor of the patriots. And eighty-four years after, in 1865, the Confederate army under General Johnston, pursued from the east by General Sherman and cut off on the west by Federal troops, surrendered at Greensboro,—virtually ending the terrible war between the States. L. S.

Rockingham County.

Rockingham County was formed in 1785 from Guilford and was named in honor of Charles Watson Wentworth, Marquis of Rockingham. Wentworth, the County seat, is 116 miles north-west of Raleigh. The County is located in the Piedmont section of the State, on the line of the Piedmont Air Line Railway, which runs through the eastern portion of the County. There is also another railroad through the northern part of the County, connecting with the Piedmont Air Line at Danville. Its population in 1880 was 21,744. Its area is 552 square miles. About one-third of the land is in cultivation, probably a little over one-third in original forest and the balance in old field which is being rapidly improved by old field pine. The forests abound in all the trees known in the State, such as oaks, walnuts, pines, hickories, chestnuts, locusts, poplars, ashes, gums, sycamores, willows, cedars, etc. There are a great many saw mills in the County, which do a fine business in lumber. The general character of the surface is broken, though gently undulating, being of easy cultivation, and along the streams there is a great deal of bottom land of dark rich alluvial soil upon which fine crops are raised without any manures or fertilizers whatever. The soil of the uplands is mostly of the light gray sandy sort, so admirably adapted for the raising of fine yellow tobacco, for which the county is noted, though in some portions the land is heavy and dark, suitable for raising large crops of wheat. All the land produces wheat, oats, clover and all the grasses, and in portions there are fine meadows of natural grass.

Good farming land, (especially for fine tobacco) unimproved, sells at from $3 to $5 per acre; improved with houses, wells, barns, etc., sell at from $7 to $10, while river bottoms are held at from $20 to $50 per acre; land rents readily at one-fourth for uplands, and one-third for bottoms. The usual yield per acre of tobacco is from 500 to 1,000 pounds, according to whether the tobacco is fine or heavy and common; fine yellow tobacco sells at from $30 to $40 per hundred pounds around, (that is for lugs and all) while the heavy and common sells at from $3 to $10 per hundred. Farmers frequently realize as much as $150 to $250 for the tobacco from a single acre of land that they bought at $5. The bottom lands are usually devoted to corn, of which there is generally enough raised to supply the needs of the County and a good deal is exported to Danville, Va. Potatoes, cabbages and all vegetables are raised in great abundance, as are also all the fruits, apples, peaches, plums, cherries, etc., coming to great perfection.

The people find a most excellent market for the sale of all their products in the city of Danville, Va., which is only about 25 or 30 miles from Wentworth and is easily reached by the farmers of the eastern and southern portions of the County by way of the R. & D. R. R., while those of the northern and western portions find easy access through the D. M. & S. W. R. R. The Dan River, running through the County to Danville, is also navigable for large boats its entire length through the County.

The town of Reidsville, situated upon the R. & D. R. R., also affords a good market for all country produce and is fast becoming the leading tobacco market of the State; a few years since only a way station upon the railroad, with one house and a depot, now a town of over 2,000 inhabitants, with four of the largest warehouses for sale of leaf tobacco, numbers of tobacco factories, some doing the leading business in plug tobacco in the State, stores of all kinds, schools, churches, etc. Its business men are alive to the interests of their town and are destined to make it one of the cities of the State. Leaksville, Madison, Stoneville, Wentworth and Ruffin are all small towns with a population of from 200 to 500 inhabitants, that have good schools, stores, etc., and afford good markets for those immediately around them.

Rockingham is probably one of the best watered Counties in the State; the Dan running throuh the northern portion of the County, with its tributaries, the Smith and Mayo Rivers, with Wolf Island, Lickfork, Sauratown, Jacobs, Hogans, Buffalo, Matrimony and other numerous creeks, form a complete net-work of water courses. Each and all of these streams have most excellent water powers, suitable for the largest mills and factories. The Leaksville cotton mills, upon Smith River, has one of the finest water powers in the State. The southern part of the County is watered by the Haw River and its tributaries, Big and Little Troublesome Creeks.

Coal is found in a great many places along the line of Dan River, and iron near Troublesome Creek, in the southern part of the County and other places. Good building rock abounds in many places. J. D. G.

Person County.

Roxboro, the County Seat, contains about 400 inhabitants, 5 stores, 2 hotels, 2 tobacco factories and 1 warehouse, It is central to the County, is 50 miles north of Raleigh, 30 from Danville, 25 from Durham, 28 from Oxford, and is 20 miles from the Richmond and Danville Railroad.

The principal streams are Hyco, Flat and Tar Rivers and their tributaries, and the lands on the first named are famed for their fertility. The principal productions are tobacco, corn, wheat, oats, rye, clover, potatoes. sweet and Irish, apples, peaches, cherries, grapes, berries, etc. The chief money crops are tobacco, wheat and corn, and the bright yellow tobacco is raised here to great perfection, perhaps as fine as any produced any where in the world. Wheat and clover of a fine quality are raised and there are a number of very superior grist mills in the county. The soil and climate are well adapted to fruits of all kinds, and apples, peaches, pears, grapes, cherries and berries of the best qualities are produced in great abundance and variety.

The minerals of the County have not attracted the attention which they deserve, but their importance has lately awakened an interest among foreign capitalists. There are indications that very rich veins of copper and iron ores, of superior qualities, are found in a number of localities. Iron and copper will doubtless be yet mined to profit. Gold, graphite, kaolin and corundum are also found, good building stone abounds and also the best clays for brick and pottery.

Truck farming can be pursued to advantage and melons and all kinds of vegetables are procured in large quantities and of the finest varieties. There are no barren districts, very little land that it will not pay to cultivate, no malarial sections, and a comparatively small area that is subject to disastrous overflows.

The face of the country is rolling, but little broken by abrupt hills, never flat, but beautifully undulating, easy of culture and adapted to the highest improvements. The highest elevations are Haga's, about 1,000 feet, and Roxboro Mountains, so-called, with scenery picturesque and beautiful, and interesting alike to the pleasure-seeking tourist and to the botanist and geologist. The air is salubrious, the water pure, the average duration of human life is long. There is no more healthy region on the globe, chills and fever being scarcely known.

The price of the best lands is from $10 to $15, the average probably about $5; the farms are generally of moderate size, the County being remarkable for the comparative equality of its industrial population. It is well suited to farmers of small means. There are no great inequalities in society. The masses are thrifty, intelligent and moral.

The principal religious denominations are Methodists, Baptists, Primitive and Missionary, Christians, Presbyterians and Episcopalians; and there are a number of good high schools, while the common system has always had here a vigorous root.

Game and fish abound and more deer are found here than any where else in this region. There is no section better suited to fish culture, and the capabilities of the County for clover, for fruit, for fine tobacco, for a dense, thriving, healthy and happy agricultural population are not excelled any where in North Carolina.

Perhaps the most distinguishable characteristic of the County is the absence of extreme inequalities in soil, in society, in the distribution of wealth. The face of the country is every where diversified and pleasant. There is hardly a nook or corner in which a desirable building site may not be found. There is no want, no alternation of dense communities and of sparse and poor neighborhoods, and the population is eminently rural. The fine tobacco is of an extreme type, but its culture, like all other pursuits, does not require much capital, and the intelligent, industrious laborer can live and prosper by the work of his own hands.

J. W. C.

Orange County.

Climate: This county is at an elevation of about 600 ft. above the sea. The climate is remarkably healthy and free from malaria. The winters are very mild and the summers are not oppressive. The county is rolling and is well drained by natural streams.

Products: The products are corn, wheat, oats, cotton, rye, barley, grass, tobacco and potatoes. The soil is especially adapted to the raising of fine grade tobacco, of wheat, of hay and potatoes. Cattle, horses, hogs, sheep and goats are easily raised and thrive here.

Apples, pears, peaches, grapes, plums and figs grow in the greatest abundance and of fine quality. There is a large and growing industry in drying fruits, and in shipping them also fresh to the Northern markets.

The country is capable of the highest development in the direction of stock raising and fruit growing and dairy farming and tobacco raising. Some of the lands have yielded crops of tobacco worth $250 to the acre.

Soil: The soil is very strong and deep, mostly of decomposed granite. The lands lying along the many streams that form a network throughout the county are of inexhaustible fertility.

Minerals: Deposits of gold and iron are very abundant all through the county. The Iron Mountain near Chapel Hill contains inexhaustible ores of excellent quality.

Soapstone and whet-stone quarries of the finest grain exist in large deposits. Also unlimited supplies of granites.

Water-power: The county is well watered by scores of streams and rivers that furnish irrigation and drainage and a water power well nigh infinite. Neuse River, Eno, Flat and New Hope are especially valuable.

Timbers and Forests: By far the larger portion of the county is covered by the primeval forests, furnishing immense and valuable stores of timbers. Oak, elm, hickory, maple, ash, poplar, gum, dogwood, sassafras and walnut grow in profuse abundance.

Education: The county enjoys the best educational advantages in the State. It contains, besides a fine public school system, the University of North Carolina and the Agricultural and Mechanical College, the Bingham High School for boys, and the Nash and Kollock School for girls. At Chapel Hill is published the State Educational Journal. Here also is located the State Normal School, and here the State Association of teachers meets annually.

Population: The population is celebrated for its piety, industry and intelligence. All the religious denominations are represented. Only one-third of the population is negro. The population is rapidly increasing.

Railroad Facilities.—The county is traversed by two railroads that carry its products in a few hours to tidewater at Richmond, Fayetteville, Wilmington or Norfolk. The rapidly growing cities of Raleigh, Durham and Greensboro, are at its doors.

Chief Towns: The chief towns are Hillsborough, the County seat, one of the oldest in the State, and Chapel Hill, the seat of the University of the State. The University before 1861 had nearly five hundred students, and has now over two hundred, increasing constantly.   K. P. B.

Durham County

Adjoins Wake (in which is situated Raleigh, the capital of the State), Chatham, Orange, Person and Granville. Its county seat is Durham, twenty-six miles west of Raleigh, and 55 miles east of Greensboro, situated on the N. C. R. R.

The population of the county is 15,873, and of the county seat and its suburbs 4,500. Area of county 280 square miles. Assessed value of taxable property in 1882, $2,923,748.00 ; number of horses and mules 1882, 2,038 ; hogs, 7,546 ; sheep, 3,323 ; cattle, 2,161. Its waters are Flat, Eno, and Little Rivers, New Hope, Third Fork, Ellerby and several smaller creeks.

Durham is now the centre of the famous " *Golden Belt* " of North Carolina, the home of the fine, bright tobacco. The town of Durham is famed throughout the world for its great smoking tobacco manufactories, to which have now been added the manufacture of cigarettes, long cut smoking tobacco and fine cut chewing tobacco. In this town are located the factories of Blackwell's Durham Tobacco Company, who succeeded W. T. Blackwell & Co., the owners of the standard "*Bull*" brand ; W. Duke, Sons & Co., who are widely known by their "*Duke of Durham*" tobacco and cigarettes, besides many others. The United States Internal Revenue Tax paid by the various smoking tobacco factories in the year 1882, aggregated the sum of $733,817.80. In the town are five white and several colored churches, the spire of the Methodist being the highest in the State. There are many churches throughout the county. In the town is a graded school for whites with a membership of 400, besides several excellent private schools. There are 28 free public schools in the county for whites, and 21 for the colored.

The principal productions of the county are, in the order

named, tobacco of fine, bright color ; cotton, corn, wheat, oats, hay and rye. Fruits of all kinds usual in this latitude abound, cherries, apples, peaches, plums, grapes, pears, figs, and nuts growing in abundance. All kinds of garden vegetables and Irish and sweet potatoes, melons and turnips are produced in profusion. The usual yield of corn is from 15 to 25 bushels per acre ; wheat, 10 ; cotton, 500 to 1,000 pounds ; sweet potatoes 300 to 400 bushels ; Irish potatoes 100 bushels. The soil is varied, from gravelly and sandy through clay to the black waxy land. The lands around the town are poor, but in the southern portion of the county are magnificent bottom lands ; in the northern part are the finest tobacco lands. The land is worth from $3 to $25 per acre. The tobacco raised in this county brings from $3, for the lowest grades, to $150 for the highest grades, and is highly esteemed and eagerly sought after.

Our forests are filled with white, red, black, water, willow, post, spanish and chestnut oak, pine, willow, silver and sugar maple, gum, hickory, persimmon, dogwood, sassafras, sycamore, holly, poplar, elm, ash, walnut, chinquepin, locust, haw, mulberry, cherry, plum, apple, sweet gum, beech, cedar, ironwood, alder and birch.

In the town of Durham are two banks, and three leaf tobacco warehouses. The health of the county is excellent ; the water good, except around the town it is strongly impregnated with limestone. Winters mild, and summers temperate. W. W. F.

Chatham County

Was named in honor of William Pitt (Lord Chatham) and the county seat Pittsboro. This county from the Randolph line west to the Wake County line east, is about 40 miles, and from the Orange County line north to the Moore County south, is about 40 miles. It contains an immense amount of fine timber of oak and hickory, some walnut and dogwood, and in the southern portion of the county a vast forest of pine. The white and red oak, however, predominates ; so much so as to have attracted the attention of the first settlers. And so abundant was the hickory that they named the western portion of the county *Hickory Mountain.*

The chief streams passing through Chatham are the Saxapaha and Sapona, which form a junction at Haywood; from thence to salt water it is known as the Cape Fear.

Chatham County, situated in a high, healthy region, with a dark red clay soil, better adapted for raising wheat than any other, stands pre-eminent as a wheat country. The statistics show that she is the second largest wheat county in the State. It is within bounds to say that she contains 400 square miles of forest, principally oak, hickory and pine. Then she has the finest water power in the world; the Saxapaha and Sapona Rivers (Deep and Haw Rivers), forming the Cape Fear at their junction, pass through the entire county. Besides these streams there are Rocky River, Bear Creek, New Hope, Robeson's Creek and many others having only a local reputation, but upon all of which splendid mills have been erected and make the finest flour in our markets.

Chatham not only contains all the elements of wealth in these particulars, but she has some of the richest gas coal deposits on Deep River, as also hard coal or anthracite.

There are a good many shafts and slopes sunk. At one Wicker place there are 1800 acres of land and almost the entire property is underlaid with coal; 100 pits were dug by Mr. McLain for a Northern company and coal found at every place. It is now owned by persons in North Carolina and valued at $100 an acre. Then not far up the river is the celebrated Egypt property, owned by a Northern company. There they have sunk a shaft 400 feet and put up immense works for bringing the coal to the surface. The seam of coal measures $6\frac{1}{2}$ feet. The next coal property is on Deep River on the Taylor place, 1500 acres, owned by a company of Northern men and some North Carolinians. Here a slope was put in and disclosed a seam of coal 6 feet. The next place above the Taylor coal field is the Gulf, owned by the Haughtons and sold by them for $30,000. Here is a fine specimen of coal; there are several excavations and coal found in each place. Then comes the Evans place on the north side of the river above the Gulf. Here an immense deposit is found. Then the Wilcox place where both bituminous and anthracite coal is found. Then the Bingham property, 540 acres, above Evans. The coal on this property was found by deepening a well in the yard of the house, and a six foot vein of coal discovered. Then the Murchison property, adjoining the Bingham place, upon which I found a vein of 7 foot depth. Then the Chalmers' place, lying on the north side of Deep River, and adjoining the Murchison property, containing fine veins of coal. And directly across the river on the south side is the Fooshee place upon which a six foot vein of coal was discovered by a slope sunk.

Now let us look at the iron ore in Chatham. Two places alone contain the finest ore in the known world. One is below Lockville, known as the Heck and Lobdell Mine, and has produced an immense amount of the finest ore ever seen in market. Specimens of the native ore were as bright as steel, and when smelted made the finest car wheels ever seen, equal to the best Bessemer steel.

Then let me take you to the upper end of the county—Ore Hill, at the foot of which the Yadkin Valley Railroad passes from Fayetteville to Ore Knob, in Ashe County. On this Ore Hill immense deposits of the finest iron ore are found; indeed, it is one solid mass of iron ore, and has been worked successfully by a company for years; the railroad (Yadkin Valley) does not yet reach that point, but will in a short time. Chatham contains all the elements of wealth for many generations in the single articles of coal and iron.

The soil of Chatham is a deep red loam, and may be described as clayey. The population of Chatham is 24,000 : voters about 4,000. Agricultural pursuits have chiefly engaged the people of the county, but within a few years past their attention has been directed to branches of manufacture. The Bynum factory on Haw River is a splendid specimen of factory work, and the numerous mills for cutting lumber and grinding grain are unsurpassed by any county in the State. It is also one of the finest tobacco counties in all the South. M. Q. W.

Moore County

Was formed from Cumberland County in 1784, and was named after the Hon. Alfred Moore, one of the Justices of the Supreme Court of the United States. It is bounded on the north by Chatham, on the east by Harnett and Cumberland, on the west by Montgomery and Randolph, on the south by Richmond.

Its population in 1880 was : Whites, 11,485; blacks, 5,336; total, 16,821. Area 772 1-4 square miles. Valuation of real estate in 1883, $1,500,000. Personal estate, $150,000.

Carthage, the county seat, is 60 miles southwest from Raleigh, and has a population of 450. Two railroads traverse the county—the Raleigh & Augusta Air Line for 43 miles, and the C. F. & Y. V. R. R. for 12 miles. The water power in the county, Deep River, Little River, Drowning Creek, McLendon's Creek, and Richland Creek, is very fine indeed. Timber is of the greatest abundance and variety, consisting of pine, oak, hickory, walnut, dogwood, cypress, juniper. The amount of naval stores and lumber shipped from this county is in excess of that sent from any other county in the State. The pine forests are very extensive.

The face of the country is sandy and level in the south and east and clayey and hilly in the west and north. The principal products are cotton, corn, wheat, oats, rye and potatoes. Apples, peaches, pears and grapes grow in abundance.

The minerals are gold, copper, iron, coal, soapstone, and the best millstone grit in the world; all of which are in abundance.

There are also several mineral springs in the county, Jackson Springs in west and Lemon Springs in east, noted for their medicinal properties.

The agricultural interest of the county has very greatly improved within the past few years.

The county was settled by the Scotch chiefly, which descent still prevails.

Our county has perhaps improved as much or more in general intelligence and general appearance than any county in North Carolina. There are good academical schools, and the facilities for education and improvement good. There are three gold mines being worked in this county, and two carriage factories. Every thing in a prosperous condition. McI.& B.

Richmond County

Was laid off in 1779, of that part of Anson which was east of the Pee Dee River. It is situated southwest of Raleigh, about 90 miles, and bounded north by Montgomery, east by Moore, Cumberland and Robeson, south by South Carolina and west by Anson.

In the northern portion of the county it is undulating and even broken near Mountain Creek and other streams which flow through it. The soil is partly slate and partly red sandstone, in the section referred to, and the timber oak, hickory, short-leaf pine, maple, etc., with considerable long-leaf pine beyond Little River. It is not sandy, however, as in some other parts, the soil being such as is usually found overlying the red sandstone. In this part much cotton as well as small grain is raised, and the quality is equal to any upland cotton produced in the country. The productions and quality of articles are much the same all along the river, near which there is much clay and some decomposed granite—the formation being generally the same as that to be found near Raleigh and in Franklin County and west of Raleigh, nearly as far as Chapel Hill.

The central part of the county, except near the river and the creeks, is sandy, and was covered originally, and now is where the forests remain, with long leafed pine. It is naturally unproductive, but by heavy and judicious manuring, yields fair crops. It is well adapted to sweet potatoes. The staple of cotton is inferior. Indeed this is, I think, unusual in the sandy soils of the eastern part of the State. In the broken sand hills it is not so good as in the flat lands of the lower part of the county. Land is cheap in this section, and can be had in any quantities from 50 cents to $2 per acre, depending upon improvements. There is no healthier region in the world. This belt comprises half the territorial extent of the county—say 350 square miles. The other half is divided about equally between section 1, as described, and the lower, or level part of the county.

The lower part is generally quite level, and is sand formation, with a clay substratum a few inches below the surface. Farms in that section are worth from $8 to $25 per acre. Crops are cotton, corn and oats. By the use of fertilizers and good cultivation the yield of cotton per acre runs from 1000 to 1500 pounds in the seed. It is healthy and the water pure, having an average temperature of about 65° Fahr. The wells in the centre and northern belt afford cooler water, none of it, however, being less than 58°, and but little so low as that.

The Carolina Central Railroad passes through the county about 32 miles, and the Raleigh & Augusta, which connects at Hamlet, six miles below Rockingham, about 14 miles.

Many of the streams which have their sources in the sand hills, afford good water power, because of the constancy and equability of their flow. However heavy the rains, the water sinks in the soil, and keeps up the supply, instead of running off as in the up country and producing floods. We have neither "feasts" nor "famines" in these streams; and hence, when sufficient fall can be had, much power for machinery is within reach, and this has been and will be utilized.

There are now in operation in the county five mills engaged in making cotton goods. All of them spin and two of them weave also. Besides these another is in process of construction, three miles northeast of Rockingham on Hitchcock's Creek, a bold stream, and never failing. The dam is of stone 22½ feet high.

Malloy & Morgan's mill is in Gum Swamp (Little Pee Dee) two miles east of Laurel Hill station, C. C. Railway. It has about 1,000 spindles and makes warps only.

Leak, Wall & McRae's mill is on Hitchcock's Creek, one

mile southwest of Rockingham, and immediately on the line of the railroads. It has 1,000 spindles, and makes warps only.

Ledbetter's mill is five miles northeast of Rockingham on Hitchcock's Creek, has 1,000 spindles, and makes warps only.

The Great Falls mill is just on the western outskirts of Rockingham, on Falling Creek. The head of water is forty feet. It has 4,100 spindles and 140 looms. It makes plain sheetings, 7,000 yards daily.

The Pee Dee mill is on Hitchcock's Creek, just outside of the town. The head water is 18 feet. It has 4,000 spindles and 120 looms, with 18 more ordered and 12 more in contemplation. It makes plaids, 5,000 yards daily.

The new mill, before alluded to, will, when complete, have 6,000 spindles and 200 looms, and make sheetings. Its productive capacity will be about 10,000 yards daily. It will commence operations in November with 3,000 spindles and 100 looms.

On Hitchcock's Creek, three and a half miles west of Rockingham, and one and a half miles from the Pee Dee, Robert S. Ledbetter has a grist mill and cotton gin. This is a splendid site for a cotton mill, being on the line of the railroad. A head of water of 12 feet can be had, which will afford ample power for 5,000 spindles and 160 looms. Leak, Wall & McRae have water power sufficient for 3 to 4,000 spindles and 100 looms. The same is the case with the mill of T. B. and J. S. Ledbetter.

Besides these mills, sites for other small ones, from 1,000 to 4,000 spindles, can be had, on Naked and Mark's Creek, as well as Joe's Creek. And at the Grassy Islands, 12 miles northwest of Rockingham, power can be had for 20,000 spindles. These are on the Pee Dee. Other sites on the river can also be had. The only trouble would be that the locations might be unhealthy.

There are over 100,000 acres of land in the county well studded with long leafed pine, a large part of which, however, has been subjected to turpentine operations. Besides this timber there is a large quantity of persimmon, which would make the best of shuttles and bobbins. We have also quite a quantity of dogwood, which is unsurpassed for this purpose. Then our sandhill swamps contain excellent poplar, and quite a quantity of the trees familiarly called juniper.

A good deal of the water in the upper end of the county, where the formation is red sandstone, is somewhat brackish, as is usually the case in this formation. Farms are worth from $5 to $20 per acre.

The population of the county is now quite 20,000, of whom about 9,000 are whites. In religious views they are nearly all Baptists, Methodists and Presbyterians, and, in numbers, probably in the order named, though there is no great difference in the first two denominations.

Most fruits succeed well. Owing to climatic causes, apples of the later variety are not suited. We can raise as fine peaches, pears and grapes as any one need to want, and on a high range of hills between Mountain and Buffalo Creeks, in the northern part of the county, the peach crop does not fail one year in ten. The same can be said of a high range near the Grassy Islands. These locations are rather remote from the railroads for profit in fruit raising.

According to the census returns, the cotton crop of the county is about 12,000 bales. The cotton mills consume about 5,000 of them, and when the Roberdell is completed the consumption will be fully 7,500 bales.

The construction shops of the C. C. Railway are located at Laurinburg, 22½ miles southeast of Rockingham. This is a flourishing town of about 1200 inhabitants. Rockingham has about the same population. W. L. S.

Cumberland County.

This is the centre of the Southern Counties of the State, being equidistant from the ocean on the east and the State line on the west, and from Raleigh, the capital, on the north and the South Carolina line on the south. The 35° parallel of latitude passes through the County—average width from east to west is 40 miles—from north to south 25 miles, Total number of acres 640,000; acres of arable land 65,000; white population (census 1880,) 12,594; colored population (census 1880,) 11,242; total, 23,836.

Character of People.—The County was settled by Scotch Highlanders in 1746-7. Their descendants constitute probably about three-fourths of the white population. There is no more law-loving and law-abiding people on the face of the earth. They have been liberal friends of education and churches. Schools, public or private, and churches of different denominations are found in all parts of the County. The people are noted for their intelligence, thrift and generous hospitality.

Towns.—Fayetteville, the County Seat, has a population of 5,000 and is the only town of importance. It has an extensive trade in naval stores and cotton. It was once quite a manufacturing centre but the factories were burned by order of Gen. Sherman in 1865. Some of these cotton factories are now being rebuilt and the magnificent water powers here will probably soon be utilized. Fayetteville is at the head of navigation of Cape Fear River, 108 miles from Wilmington. There are daily lines of steamers. It has railroad communications north and south by the Cape Fear and Yadkin Valley Railroad. There are several villages in the County; among others, Rockfish, Beaver Creek and Manchester, the sites of large cotton factories.

Water Courses and Water Powers.—Cumberland is one

of the best watered Counties in the State. The Cape Fear River runs in a southerly direction for 40 miles through the County dividing it in territory, population and wealth into two-thirds on the west side and one-third on the east. This river is navigable to Fayetteville. During high water in winter and spring steamers make occasional trips to Averasboro, in Harnett County, 25 miles north of Fayetteville.

Black River, a considerable stream, forms the eastern boundary of the County for forty miles. Although it is not navigable for steamers it furnishes a cheap and convenient means for transporting timber and naval stores to Wilmington market. Rockfish and Lower Little River have their origin in the sand hills, 40 miles west of the Cape Fear, and flow eastward to their junctions with the same, 25 miles apart. These streams drain a large territory, carrying heavy volumes of water with an average fall of 12 feet per mile. They are fed by perpetual springs and in severe drought furnish an abundance of water—they are magnificent water powers. Into these streams many smaller creeks from 4 to 10 miles in length, flow both from north and south. As they have greater fall per mile, are less expensive to dam and furnish an unfailing supply of water, they are generally preferred for mill sites. Besides these water courses there are several creeks emptying into the Cape Fear from east and west, between Little River and Rock Fish, which furnish very valuable water powers. Grist and saw mills are abundant. I know of no farm in the County that is 5 miles from either. Good drinking water in natural springs or wells is found in all parts of the County—even in the ditches that drain the large swamps, many springs of delicious, cold, clear, free stone water are found. There are several springs of mineral water, chalybeates, which are much esteemed for their healing qualities.

Forests and Timbers.—Cumberland has an immense forest of very valuable timbers. All kinds of trees that are indigenous to this section are found in abundance and perfection, except walnut, of which little is left. The most valuable are the long straw or yellow pine, the short straw pine, oaks of many varieties, cypress, juniper, poplar, hickory, ash, gum, maple and many others of less value. Forestry Bulletin, No. 8, from U. S. Census Office gives amount of merchantable pine in the County as 806,000.000 feet.

Soils.—The surface of our lands is sufficiently undulating to admit of easy drainage, but not rolling enough to wash badly. Hill-side ditching is not practiced because there is little necessity for it. No County in North Carolina has greater diversity of soils. This causes it to be peculiarly adapted to small farms. It is very rare to find a farm of fifty acres without three or four varieties of soils, each adapted to some of the crops grown here. The kinds most esteemed are the black swamp, the clay loam, the clay lands on rivers and creeks and the sandy loams with clay sub-soil. The latter, though not as productive at first as the others, are growing in favor as they require no drainage and crops on them rarely suffer from the extremes of the weather. All crops grown in the temperate zone grow here in perfection. Those principally relied on are corn, cotton, all the small grains, peas, rice, sorghum, potatoes, chufas and grass. Agriculture is making rapid progress and the farming element is generally prosperous.

Fruits.—Fruits of all kinds grow in great perfection. Especially is this true of grapes and peaches. Orchards and vineyards are regarded as a necessary part of every well-regulated farm; few are without them. There are several extensive vineyards in the County; the largest of these is Tokay, with 125 acres in grapes, and an average yield of 25,000 gallons of wine, besides quantities of grapes shipped to northern cities, beginning generally first week in July.

Manufactories.—There are six cotton factories in the

County engaged in making yarns and cloth. The business is profitable.

Railroads.—The only railroad in operation is the Cape Fear and Yadkin Valley Railroad, which is completed to the Gulf in Chatham County. This road is graded to Greensboro and from Fayetteville to Shoe Heel, and the track is now being laid on both ends. It is under contract to be completed from Greensboro to Bennettsville, in South Carolina, in one year's time. There are several other roads now projected that will pass through the County, and there is every reason to believe that Fayetteville will be an important railroad centre at an early day.

Turpentine.—The principal production of the County is naval stores. It is probably the largest producer of turpentine of any one County in the United States. Great quantities of lumber and ton timber are annually shipped.

Value of Lands.—Farming lands are worth from $5 to $20 per acre, according to character and location. Turpentine lands from $2 to $5. Lands are rarely sold for cash—usually a small part is paid in cash and reasonable time given on balance.

Taken all in all, it is one of the best Counties in the State and the people will welcome any one who will come here to make an honest livelihood. J. E.

Harnett County

Lies in Middle North Carolina, and was formed from the Northern portion of Cumberland County.

It is bounded on the North by Wake and Chatham, on the East by Johnston and Sampson, on the South by Cumberland, and on the West by Moore.

Its county seat is Lillington, situated on the west bank of

the Cape Fear River. It embraces an area of 550 square miles, some 43,000 acres of which is under cultivation. Its population in 1880 was 10,862 ; though it can easily support double that population.

Its People.—The inhabitants are for the most part of Scottish origin, the names of McDonald, Stewart, Shaw, Campbell, McLean, McNeill, McLeod, McKay, &c., being still prominently associated with the history of the county. While there are few men of great prominence in any particular sphere in the county, still the people, as a class, are singularly intelligent, thriving and industrious, unassuming in their manners, yet markedly generous and hospitable in their dealings with each other and towards new comers.

Its Lands.—Within its bounds almost every variety of soil is found, ranging from the fertile bottom lands on the Cape Fear River to the sandy loams of the pine forests. The soil seems naturally to be divided into three great divisions, viz., those lands lying on either side of the Cape Fear, which, though watered by the same stream, are materially different, and that body of pine land in the western part of the county commonly known as the Sand Hills.

Commencing at Lower Little River, the dividing line between Cumberland and Harnett, and running thence from the confluence of the above stream with the Cape Fear along the western banks of the latter stream, there is a large tract of very fertile bottom-lands, varying from one to three miles in breadth, extending eight miles up this river to McNeill's Ferry. From this point up the river, the land corresponding to the above variety of soil is found lying on either side of the river. This body of land lying between the Upper and Lower Little Rivers is enclosed by one fence, established by the General Assembly of 1881 under the "Stock Law Act." This fence connects the two rivers alluded to above, the other boundaries to this section of country being Upper Little River on the North, Cape Fear River on the East, and Lower Little River on the South.

These lands are being thoroughly drained, and even now they are not excelled in productiveness by any in the State. The staple products are corn, cotton and small grain. From 750 to 2,800 lbs. of seed cotton are produced per acre according to the mode of cultivation employed.

The yield for corn is from 10 to 50 bushels per acre, and no better land can be found in the State for the production of wheat and oats. From recent experiments it has also been proved that tobacco of fine grade can be profitably grown here. About 7,000 acres of this section are opened for cultivation, the remainder being heavily timbered woodland, consisting principally of white oak, red oak, poplar, sweet gum, ash and hickory. The character of the soil is a gray-colored, sandy loam based upon a stiff red clay subsoil. These lands are susceptible of a very high state of cultivation, and some of them, after one hundred years of cultivation, seem not yet even to have lost their virgin fertility. They are now owned in large tracts, and can be bought in smaller lots at prices ranging from $6.00 to $12.00 per acre according to the state of improvement.

On the Eastern side of the Cape Fear the bottom lands are not so wide, and are principally under cultivation. These lands like those on the opposite side of the river are not subject to overflow even during the highest freshets. Adjoining these river bottoms are wider tracts of pine table lands, once considered not very productive, but now under skillful management and with improved methods of farming, have developed into fine farming lands, which extend as high as the Wake County boundary, where the lands become more undulating. Being level and well supplied with water courses, these lands have been found susceptible of easy cultivation, and, all things considered, equally productive and quite as varied in their products as the river lands.

A large portion of this section is still in its native state, but annually larger bodies are being brought under cultivation, and now some of the best and most prosperous farmers in the county are extensively cultivating these lands. They can be purchased in small tracts at from $2.00 to $5.00 per acre.

In the western portion of the county there is still another body of land known as the Sand Hills, which is rather sparsely settled, except those portions bordering on Upper Little River. These sand-hill lands, in my judgment, are not surpassed as a grazing country, especially for sheep grazing, by any in the State. This section is composed of rather undulating ground, with vast meadow-lands intervening, which are covered with a luxuriant growth of native grass, and which are watered by many small streams whose banks are studded with reeds and perennial grasses, making this one of the finest of ranges for cattle, sheep, &c., and rendering it especially adapted for stock raising of all kinds. From extensive travel in the Southern States, I may well say that I have never seen, in any of them, a section which would excel this for grazing purposes.

This land, though so bountifully endowed by nature for these purposes, can be bought, owing to the fact that it is now owned in such large tracts, at very moderate prices, varying from 50 cents to $2.00 per acre.

Principal Water Courses.—This county is unusually well drained and well watered. The Cape Fear is the largest river in the county, running through its centre from North-west to South-east. It is the largest water power in the State, and at Smiley's Falls, the base of which is at Averasboro Ferry in the lower part of the county, the natural situation is especially adapted for the purposes of machinery, the volume of water here being estimated as sufficient, if utilized, to run all the machinery of the Northern manufactories. Just below these falls there is a point, owing to the natural situation of an island in the river, at which a bridge could be built cheaper probably than at any other point on the river. A bridge thus constructed would bring into direct communication the most fertile farming lands of upper Cumberland and Harnett, and should the contemplated railroad from Wilson to Florence be built, the present location of which is about three miles distant from this point, this section of country, by means of this bridge, would contribute no less than 3,000 bales of cotton besides other products for exportation.

Lower Little River is the dividing line westward between Cumberland and Harnett. It is a never-failing stream, the water being perfectly pure, and having as its source the springs far up in the sand-hills. No stream of its size is superior to it as a water power, and for five miles of its course it runs through the famous cotton belt of lower Harnett. It has an average of 60 ft. in breadth with perpendicular banks 20 to 30 ft. in height, its fall averaging $12\frac{1}{2}$ ft. to the mile. Within the limits of this county there are, on this stream, three grist, one flouring and two saw mills and two cotton gins now in operation. A better site for a cotton manufactory could not well be found than this stream and the surrounding country offer.

About the centre of the county there is another stream but little inferior in water resources to the above, known as Upper Little River. The best locations for mills on this stream are probably near its confluence with the Cape Fear, though there are three other mills on it west of Lillington.

Black River, famous for its abundant supply of fresh water fish of all kinds, is about five miles from the Cape Fear, and runs parallel to it through the vast pine belt east of that river.

Besides these, there are numerous other smaller mill streams of varying volume in different parts of the county.

Products.—All the crops common to the South are produced in this county, cotton being, however, at present, the staple product. Vegetables, fruits of all kinds, etc., can be grown here as early and as well as in any section of the State short of the coast. Some portions of the county are especially adapted to grape culture, particularly the Scuppernong and the common varieties of bunch grapes. It has been proved by successful experiments that silk culture can be carried on profitably and at small cost.

Its Capacities.—This county, as a whole, is not yet fully developed, though in certain sections, such as those lying along the Lower Little River and Cape Fear, and in the Eastern part of the county, the farming interests have been very materially advanced, and the lands now show a high grade of cultivation and improvement. Those lands, which have not as yet received a like amount of attention as these, could very easily, on account of the diversified character of the soil, be brought to a state of cultivation which would well repay the small outlay of money needed to bring about this desirable end. In the Eastern and Western portions of this county there are still large bodies of pine forests untouched, besides other varieties and species of trees that are valuable in any market in the world. The timber interest is one of the greatest of the county's resources, and is rapidly growing in magnitude. Those who do not desire to purchase lands at once can rent them, either wild or improved, on very favorable and advantageous terms.

The most probable cause of this county's delay in the onward march of progress is perhaps its poor means of transportation for its abundant products, as well as its very limited railway system. The only railroad which runs through the county is the Cape Fear and Yadkin Valley, which runs along its Western border through the grazing section of which I spoke above. Should some of the projected roads, the Wilson and Florence, for instance, either run through the county or build a branch road, crossing the Cape Fear at Smiley's Falls, it would develop beyond measure the resources of the county and bring into market some of the most valuble land in middle Carolina. The geographical situation of the county is such that at no distant day there must and will be direct railroad communication between this and her sister counties. The principal markets now for the produce raised are Fayetteville, Raleigh and Smithfield, all being about equally distant from Lillington, the county seat. From the above topographical description of the county, the salubrity of the climate can well be judged. Except in a very few of the bottom lands, the healthfulness of this section is not surpassed in our State.

The school advantages are good, there being numerous first-class schools now in successful operation in different parts of the county. The Christian denominations are all represented, and all have commodious houses of worship in different localities. Stores and small villages dot every part of our land, while the social privileges and advantages are of the very highest order.

The system of county government is good; taxes are lower than in many of the adjoining counties, and property has advanced at least 50 per cent. in the last several years; in short, the capacities of this county are unbounded, and as yet but very inadequately developed, awaiting only greater railroad facilities and larger capital to make it rank equal with any other county in our State. J. P. H.

Johnston County

Was formed from Craven in the year 1746, and was named in honor of Gabriel Johnston, at that time and for twenty years Royal Governor of the province and who died in 1752.

It is situated in a central part of the state, from north to south, and is about on the dividing line between the flat lands of the coast and the more elevated rocky lands of middle and western North Carolina. It is bounded on the north by Wake and Nash, on the east by Wilson and Wayne, on the south by Sampson, and on the west by Harnett and Wake, and is divided into twelve townships, with thirteen voting precincts.

It has an area of 670 square miles or 428,800 acres, a large proportion of which is uncleared ; it has a diversity of soils, but principally three kinds, located about as follows : southwestern portion, a light sandy loam ; in the western and northern, red and gravelly ; and in the centre and eastern stiff, dark gray soil, with a red clay subsoil. It will be seen by this that taken as a whole, the county is capable of producing almost any crop necessary for the sustenance and comfort of man and beast. Large yields of wheat, oats, rye, peas, corn, millet, chufas and sweet potatoes are reported every year ; apples, peaches, plums, and grapes, especially the scuppernong grow luxuriantly. Experience has shown also that clover, timothy and other grasses may be cultivated profitably in our soil ; and hence, that sheep husbandry can be made and no doubt will be a paying business in the county. Some experiments have been made in this branch of industry, and with satisfactory results.

The soil in the southwestern portions of the county is well adapted to truck gardening. Cabbages, turnips, garden peas, beans, Irish potatoes, and melons of all kinds do well in any part of the county. The culture of cotton is a profitable business which is shown by the increase of area devoted to that crop every year. Twenty years ago there were only about *one thousand bales* of cotton 400 pounds each, produced in the county, while the crop of 1881 and 1882 is estimated at *twenty thousand bales.* Johnston is set down as the fifth largest cotton producing county in the State, and there is no doubt it has some of the finest cotton lands to be found any where between the coast and the mountains.

Neuse River about equally divides the county, passing through it from northwest to southeast, the bottom lands of which produce astonishing quantities of corn and oats. The channel of the river under the supervision of General Robert Ransom, by an appropriation of Congress is being cleaned out and deepened and the work is completed to within about 10 miles of Smithfield, the capital of the county. There is in this river about eight miles above Smithfield, and some two miles from the North Carolina Railroad, a very fine water power, awaiting capital and energy to develop and utilize. Along the banks of the Neuse are large forests of the different species of oak, measuring many of them, several feet in diameter, with long straight trunks, which are not only valuable for the fine quality of the timber, but which are prized for the fabulous quantities of acorns they bear upon which hogs thrive well, with no other kind of food; and large quantities of pork are slaughtered every year from the marshes, with little or no cost to the producers; hickory, elm and ash are also abundant. There are also large forests of pine.

Johnston is well opened up with public roads, usually kept in good order. Our territory is well watered and our streams are well bridged. We have also excellent mail service. The North Carolina Railroad passes through the centre of the county, on the line of which are Clayton,

Wilson Mills, Selma, Pine Level and Princeton, all thriving towns. We have also the Midland Railroad from Goldsboro to Smithfield, the terminus of which is within 30 steps of the finest Court House in the State, and within 4 miles of the North Carolina Railroad. This Midland road is connected at Goldsboro with the Atlantic road leading to Kinston, Newbern and Morehead City, and also the Wilmington and Weldon Road. We have also every prospect of a railroad from Wilson, North Carolina, through this county, *via* Smithfield to Fayetteville, thence to Florence; when this road is completed the county will be bisected both ways with railroads, and will be well supplied with the means of traffic and pleasure.

About four miles west of Smithfield there is an iron mine containing ore said to be rich in quality and which was discovered about one hundred years ago, and which, with modern apparatus for mining and smelting, might be worked with profit. Copperas was made too at Bentonville during the late war in quantities sufficient to be remunerative.

Smithfield, the county seat of Johnston, is eligibly situated on the north bank of the Neuse, four miles from the N. C. railroad, equidistant from Raleigh and Goldsboro, twenty-five miles from each, and is about the centre of the county. It is beautifully laid out, well shaded, healthy, and contains a population of about six hundred.

The population of the county by the last census was over twenty-three thousand, about one-third of whom are colored. In the county poorhouse are only eleven paupers and only one person in jail, and he a crazy man. Our people are industrious, provident and peaceable. The county has a very small debt. The cause of education here is also looking up. School houses are being erected with an eye to comfort and convenience, the grade of teachers is being improved, and a spirit of education is taking hold of the people, and very soon we shall see our territory thickly dotted with beautiful academies, occupied by earnest students and competent teachers. Several religious denominations are represented in the county, having comfortable church buildings, regular preaching and large audiences : and everything considered Johnston County, for its healthful climate, good water, variety of soils, fine timber, unfailing streams, railroad facilities and peaceable, industrious, independent citizens, is in advance of a majority of the counties of the State and will compare favorably with the best. M. Q. W.

Wake County.

Wake, one of the old colonial counties, was established in 1770, and chartered by the King in 1771. It was named in honor of the Wake family, of which the Archbishop of Canterbury, Dr. Wake, was the head, and with which family the Royal Governor Tryon had intermarried. It is situated on both sides of the Neuse, and was erected out of parts of Orange, Johnston and Cumberland. It has an area of 787 square miles, and contains 47,000 inhabitants. (1883). Raleigh, the capital, and suburbs has a population of 14,000, and is situated in lat. 35° 47 min.

Soils are of all grades, from light gray to dark brown ; both easily tilled and quite productive. The upper part of the county is rocky and broken, while quartz and soapstone predominate. Gold and garnet are found in all the branches of the upper Neuse, but not in sufficient quantities to work profitably. Soapstone in large beds is to be found in Oak Grove and Barton's Creek Townships ; plumbago in inexhaustible quantities in House's Creek Township; sandstone in White Oak, and granite in St. Mary's and Raleigh

Townships. All parts of the county are well adapted to the cultivation of peaches, apples, pears and other fruits, corn, wheat, oats, cotton, tobacco and potatoes. Oak, hickory, pine and walnut prevail as timber trees. The valuable long leaf pine forests cover nearly one-third of the area of the county, principally in the south and southwestern portions. R. B. H.

WAKE COUNTY is centrally located between the mountains and the sea, and is traversed by numerous bold and living streams, shedding their waters to the southeast. Chief among these are Neuse and Little Rivers, Crabtree, Swift, Middle, White Oak, Buckhorn, Walnut, Marsh, Buffalo, Big Lick, Moccasin and Mark's Creeks, on which are situated upwards of seventy (70) mills and manufactories. The surface is rolling and hilly, descending to the southeast to meet and blend with the prehistoric seacoast of the adjoining counties.

The soil is composed largely of clay, red brown and yellow, interspersed and underlaid with calcareous stone, sand and mica. The principal crops are cotton, corn, wheat, oats, tobacco, peas, hay, sweet and Irish potatoes, peanuts, millet, etc. Apples, pears, peaches, figs, grapes, and smaller fruits and vegetables are grown. Nothing can excel the luscious beauty and flavor of the grape and its vinous product as grown upon the calcareous soil of Thomasberg vineyards, two miles east of Raleigh. No disease or insect affects vine or fruit, and a failure of crop is unknown.

The soil of the bottom lands varies from pipe clay to rich loam and sands, easy of cultivation and more productive than that of the hills. These are, pre-eminently, the corn lands of the county.

Wake County has thirty-six (36) post offices, three (3) colleges, two seminaries for boys and two for girls, eight private schools, and one hundred and twenty-four public free schools, the latter including the public free *graded* schools of Raleigh.

Raleigh, the county seat, was chartered and declared the seat of State Government in 1791. The city stands upon a group of hills, shedding naturally in all directions from the centre, at an elevation of 365 feet above tide water, and is one of the most healthful cities of the State. It is increasing rapidly in wealth and numbers. 75,000 bales of cotton were handled here in 1881-2. Her broad streets, beautiful residences, imposing public buildings and overarching elms constitute, for at least three-fourths of the year, one of the finest cities of the South.

Other prosperous towns are Morrisville, Carey, Forestville, Rolesville, Wake Forest and Holly Springs.

Railroads traverse the county at right angles, and new roads are projected and building. Farm lands range in value from $5 to $20 per acre, according to soil, improvement and location. Labor is plentiful at $8 to $10 per month and board. Thoroughbred Jersey cattle have been largely introduced during the last ten years with great benefit and satisfaction. Sheep are self-supporting, free from disease, productive and—evanescent. A pack of stray curs can lay out a hundred an hour without expense to the owner, and generally manage to do it once a year. A. W. S.

Granville County.

Was formed in 1746 and was so called from the name of the owner of the soil. In 1663 Charles II. granted to Sir Geo. Carteret and seven other noblemen a charter for this region with much more, and it was called Carolina for the king. In 1729 these proprietors, except Sir

Geo. Carteret, who was afterwards created Earl of Granville, surrendered their franchises to the English Crown.

This county lies north of the centre of the State adjoining Virginia. Oxford, its county seat, is the terminus of the Oxford and Henderson Railroad, and is remarkable for its intelligent population.

The soil is of two kinds (1) red heavy soil, (2) light sandy land. The former lies mostly in the northern and northwestern parts of the county, the latter is in the southern portion. The former is productive of wheat, oats, rye, the grasses, corn, red heavy tobacco, and cotton; often producing without stimulus 20 bushels of wheat to the acre. Upon the latter soil is grown the celebrated Granville bright yellow or gold-leaf tobacco, that sometimes sells for one dollar a pound, and, after analysis by the great chemist Bunsen and others, is pronounced devoid of nicotine. Lands in this section have advanced 100 per cent. in the past ten years. A farmer raises 600 to 800 pounds of this fine tobacco to the acre and hauls to market in one wagon drawn by two horses enough of the weed to net him six hundred dollars.

The county is undulating, in some parts hilly; and in these regions, which are mostly northern, are found splendid lands for pasturage. To the superior combination of grasses in northern Granville is attributed the inimitably fine flavor of the mutton, said to be the finest in the world.

Here also are found mines of gold, iron, whetstone, copper and granite in great quantities. These mines are not yet developed, except the Gillis copper mine, which is pronounced by Prof. Emmons, formerly the State geologist, to be of great extent and excellent quality. Before the war the Lewis gold mine was worked with profit.

The cost of living in Granville is very little. Board from

$8 to $12 a month ; chickens, 12 to 25 cents ; fresh pork, $7 to $10 ; meal, 60 cents to $1.00 per bushel.

The air is fresh and invigorating, the drinking water pure and healthful, the climate salubrious. No standing water except in a few mill ponds, and hence no malaria. The Tar River flows through the county, but is not navigable. Many streams and brooks fertilize the soil and empty into the Tar and Roanoke Rivers,

Oxford rivals Durham in the sale of leaf tobacco, has one of the best male academies in the United States, an excellent female college, a capital high grade female boarding school, and also boasts of the Oxford Orphan Asylum, a noble institution. Commodious churches of all denominations dot the county.

In the county are three iron foundries, one sash and blind factory, two dog wood factories, four very large tobacco warehouses and many tobacco factories. The people, raised among the hills, are large in size, of a Saxon hue, and are strong and healthy.

· The county debt has been funded and is now about $12,000, and is being rapidly liquidated. Lands sell for $5 to $8 an acre in the red lands, and for $15 to $25 an acre in the sandy lands, and the tendency of the price of land in both sections is upward.

The county is rapidly growing and the county script brings dollar for dollar. The population as a whole is one of unusual energy, thrift and intelligence.   A. H. A. W.

Vance County

Is in N latitude 36° 15', and W. longitude 78° 25', and is known as one of the northern tier of counties in North Carolina. The county was organized in 1881 by the Legislature as a pressing need of the territory composing it on account of its rapid growth and business necessities, and was formed out of the most desirable and prosperous portions of Granville, Franklin and Warren Counties. The county has an area of 420 square miles and extends from the Roanoke River on the Virginia State line (its Northern boundary) to the Tar River on the South, a distance of about 30 miles, and has a width of from 14 miles to 18 miles. It is most advantageously situated as to railroads, waterpower, character of soil, diversity of crops and healthfulness. Being a new county it has no floating or bonded debt, and the assessment of taxes heretofore levied by the old counties, out of which it is formed, raises funds more than sufficient to meet its annual current expenses.

The county seat and chief shipping and trading point of the county is Henderson, situate on the Raleigh and Gaston Railroad, 44 miles north of Raleigh, and 53 miles south of Weldon, and is the highest point on the line of the road, being 203 feet higher than Raleigh. This town has grown very rapidly in the last few years and now has over 2,000 people, while more building is being done this year than any year before, and its prospects were never so bright. It is most advantageously situated. The tobacco and cotton crops here over-lap each other. Until within the past few years very little or no tobacco was raised east of Henderson, and very little or no cotton west. Now the bright, yellow tobacco, for which this section is so famous, is raised in large quantities east, as well as west, of Henderson ; and cotton is planted successfully west, as well as east, of this town.

The business of the place is large and growing, cotton and tobacco being sold here from an area of 40 to 50 miles, and merchandise is sold to farmers from same sections in large quantities at close figures. Besides Henderson, the county has two railroad towns, Kittrell and Middleburg, and three county villages—Williamsboro, Townesville and Brookston—all of which are thrifty and growing. The principal railroad facility is offered by the Raleigh and Gaston Railroad, which passes through the county from its southern to its northeast border and is in first-class condition and attentive to the needs of its patrons. This road is under the same management as the Seaboard and Roanoke Railroad, the Raleigh and Augusta Air-Line Railroad and the Carolina Central Railroad, and also connects at Weldon with the railroad going North, via Richmond and Washington, and at Raleigh with the Richmond and Danville Railroad system going South. The Oxford and Henderson Railroad connects Henderson with Oxford, the county seat of Granville County, and has a charter to Clarksville, Virginia, to which point it is proposed to extend the road. This road has a charter to Raleigh, via Louisburg, the county seat of Franklin, and is now actively making preparations to build to Louisburg. The new air-line road from Richmond South, much of which is now under contract, will strike the Raleigh and Gaston Railroad in this county. A road has also been chartered and surveyed from Keysville, on the Richmond and Danville Railroad, via Clarksville, to this point. Thus we see that Henderson promises in the near future to be a great railroad centre.

The county is traversed by many streams, along whose banks are a large quantity of lowlands, rich and luxuriant. They furnish, in addition to a never failing water supply for stock and vegetation, water power in abundance. No county in the State is better supplied with water-power than this. Most of it is never failing. The county has 17 manufacturing mills many of which are very large and fine.

For diversity of crops Vance County yields the palm to none. The principal market crops are tobacco and cotton, which are marketed within the county at fair and remunerative prices. The cotton is of an unusually fine staple and the tobacco is mostly the fine yellow, six millions of pounds of tobacco being sold at Henderson each year and from five thousand to six thousand bales of cotton. In addition to tobacco and cotton, wheat, corn and oats are raised in abundance, while the usual yield of rye, potatoes, millet, peas, beans, peanuts and melons is large and somewhat above the general average of the State. Apples, peaches, pears, plums, cherries, strawberries and grapes have done well and are raised in large quantities in many parts of the county. Along the railroad these fruits are raised for shipment to Northern markets and when properly cared for yield large profits. There are several large vineyards where the different varieties of wine of superior quality are manufactured in quantities and profitably.

The county is well timbered, having the following trees in abundance: Pine, oak, hickory, ash, maple, sweetgum, walnut, dogwood, cedar, locust, beech and elm, which furnish lumber in abundance for all purposes.

About three-fourths of the area of the county is adapted to grazing purposes, and in addition to the native grasses, clover and the cultivated grasses grow luxuriantly and find the soil well suited to them. The hay crop of native and cultivated grasses is profitable wherever any attention is paid to it. Sheep are unusually healthy and increase rapidly. Cattle, for both beef and dairy purposes are raised to advantage and prove remunerative. Horses and mules are raised to some extent and advantage. Domestic fowls are raised in large numbers. There are a few deer, while turkeys, quail, wild ducks and squirrels are found in large quantities and the ordinary varieties of fresh water fish are abundant in most of the streams.

The county is noted for its healthfulness—a necessary consequence of its fine climate, pure air, and excellent water. Many visitors annually seek its borders on this account. During the summer months many come from Virginia and Eastern North Carolina, and stay until frost, while during the winter the towns along the railroad, especially Kittrell, is eagerly sought by Northern visitors seeking a milder climate, mostly for health, while many come for sport and spend their time hunting turkeys, quail and other game.

The religious and educational advantages are deserving of especial mention. Good churches of the various Protestant denominations are scattered throughout the county, and are regularly open for worship and well attended. In addition to numerous and good private schools in the towns, villages and neighborhoods, the public schools are regularly conducted and under the school system of the State are yearly improving. The Church and school buildings are good. The population is generally intelligent and law-abiding. The surface of the country is undulating and well-drained and averages about 473 feet above the level of the sea. J. R. Y.

Franklin County.

In 1779, the county of Bute was divided into two distinct counties, and the name of Bute, distasteful to the Whigs of the Revolutionary period, gave place to the patriotic names of Franklin and Warren. It was said then: "There are no Tories in Bute," and the liberty-loving, law-abiding and orderly character of the people of this section for more than a century, has shown that they were worthy of their ancestors.

Franklin County is situated just above the level region of the long-leaf pine, and in the edge of the rolling lands. In the lower or southeastern part of the county there are considerable forests of long-leaf pine, with oak, of many kinds, hickory, ash, maple, gum, elm, etc., while in the western and northern portion of the county, yellow pine, oaks, hickory, maple, dogwood, and a great variety of other trees grow. Upon exhausted land (and bad cultivation has exhausted many tracts) the old field pine grows in great luxuriance and very soon restores fertility.

The climate is that of Raleigh, and is healthy and invigorating. Throughout the county abundant springs are found of pure water of the best quality, and the entire county is well watered. Tar River runs diagonally through the county and upon this stream there is valuable water power, especially at Louisburg. On Cedar Creek, Sandy Creek, Lynch's Creek and a number of other never failing streams, are excellent mill sites and a number of fine mills. At Laurel, on Sandy Creek, there is a cotton factory, which has been in successful operation for several years. There is ample water power in the county for large and extensive factories.

The population of the county is intelligent, industrious, hospitable, law-abiding, generous and tolerant. It is nearly equally divided between the white and colored races, and a better class of colored people can not be found. It is not a wealthy county, there are no very large estates, and property is, perhaps, more evenly distributed than in any section of the Union. There are no overgrown fortunes and no suffering paupers. It has the general school system of the State and the moral, intellectual, religious and industrial character of its people is good.

Agriculture is the chief employment, and there is a steady

improvement in the farms. Prior to the late war, corn, wheat, oats, peas, etc., were produced in great quantities, and hogs were raised for market. Cotton and tobacco were cultivated with success and constituted thus the chief market crops, but, as a general rule there was an abundant supply of all food crops for home consumption. Since the war the cotton mania has prevailed here, as elsewhere in the south, and supply crops have been neglected, to the great detriment of the material welfare of the county. No one product of the soil, however well it may be produced, can be relied upon to enrich an Agricultural State. It is not an unusual thing to produce two bales of cotton to the acre in Franklin and the capabilities of its soil are very great. One farmer in the county (Mr. Henry Pearce, near Franklinton) has, for many years, averaged more than one bag and a-half to the acre, and in 1880, on 42 acres of land he produced 73 bags of cotton, averaging 475 pounds ; on 28 acres he made 59 bags. Mr. Pearce did not confine himself to cotton, but has raised abundant supply crops and illustrates the capabilities of the land of the county. Every section of the county could be made to produce as well.

All the fruits of this latitude and climate can be produced in Franklin. Apples, pears, peaches, grapes, melons, strawberries and many other varieties of fruit flourish.

In the northeastern portion of the county are valuable gold mines ; from one of them (the Portis mine) gold, to the value of more than $1,000,000, has been taken. These mines present an inviting field for enterprise.

The Raleigh and Gaston Railroad passes through the western part of the county and the town of Franklinton, on that road, 28 miles from Raleigh, is the principal depot for the county. The contemplated road from Raleigh to the Albemarle section will pass through the southeastern part of the county and a road is chartered from the town of Louisburg (the county seat) to Henderson, on the Raleigh and

Gaston Road, and there is little doubt it will soon be built. These roads will greatly enhance the value of the land in the county. Land along the Raleigh and Gaston Railroad can be purchased at from $10 to $20 per acre. Lands off from the Railroad, of equal or greater fertility, can be purchased at from $4 to $8 per acre. The lands in the western and northern portions of the county are undulating, well watered with many streams and these are usually skirted with fertile bottoms, and corn, wheat, tobacco, and cotton, grow well, and also clover and other grasses.

The southern and eastern portions of the county are level, with a gray, sandy soil, and admirably adapted to cotton, corn, and peas. In many sections of the county, granite, of an excellent quality can be found in inexhaustible quantities.

The population of the county in 1870, was 14,134, in 1880, it was 20,829. The Baptist and Methodist are the leading religious denominations. Louisburg, the county seat, is situated on Tar River, 28 miles northeast from Raleigh, and has a population of about 800, with two Baptist, two Presbyterian, one Methodist and one Episcopal church.

As already stated the chief occupation of the people of the county is agriculture. Manufactures and other pursuits have been neglected, but the water power of the county will admit of extensive factories, especially of cotton, with the raw material at hand, and her forests of wood will admit of great enterprise in the manufacture of wood.

To people desiring homes among agriculturists, moral, kind, hospitable and tolerant, where lands can be purchased cheap in good neighborhood, and where, with moderate labor and ease, fortunes may be accumulated, Franklin presents an inviting field. To men desiring to engage in the undeveloped field of manufactures and to make available the resources of the water powers of the county and the woods of the forests, there is ample scope for untold wealth.　　　　　　　　　　　　　　　　　　J. J. D.

Halifax County.

As to the geographical characteristics of this County, it may be stated that when in remote ages the sea covered so large a part of the eastern United States it extended to the Falls of the Tar River and to the Falls of the Roanoke, and a line drawn between these points divides the County in nearly equal parts. The western half is a rolling hill country and the eastern is level, though certainly not a flat country, and contains much marl and other fossil remains. The Roanoke River is the northern boundary and gives to the County a beautiful and fertile valley sixty miles long and about one-and-a-half miles wide. Quite a large stream, Fishing Creek, is the southern boundary for about 25 miles and many fine farms are located upon it. Into these two streams a great number of brooks and branches flow; indeed there is scarcely a road in the County upon which one can travel six miles without crossing some perennial stream.

There are a great many churches in the County, all Protestant. Schools are numerous and good. Halifax has always stood high for its social advantages. At almost every cross road we have a little village, and there are four in the County which will range from two hundred to one thousand inhabitants. Health is good everywhere except immediately on the river and creeks.

There is a constitutional limit to taxation, which is $66\frac{2}{3}$ cents per $\$100$, of which last year 31 cents was for State and residue for County taxes.

As to the population, the whites, who constitute about one-third, are nearly all of British descent. Owing to the large negro population labor is cheap and abundant; wages last year for No. 1 hands was from $8 to $10 per month, with rations of $4\frac{1}{2}$ pounds of meat and one peck of meal per week. We have a plenty of cotton gins, corn, wheat and saw mills; but manufactures are at a low ebb. Merchants as a rule do a safe business and prosper. As to transportation, our river is navigable about nine months in the year. We also have two trunk lines and one branch railroad running through the County.

Greatest heat in a well built house is 97° Fahrenheit, and greatest cold 22°. Rainfall is 37 inches per annum.

Every variety of fruit suitable to latitude 36° 10' to 30' flourishes here. I have seen this spring strawberries as large as a pullet's egg. In the western part of the County is one of the largest vineyards in the south, where thousands of gallons of excellent wine are made yearly.

As to cotton, I know one man, who, with one horse, has made, besides the necessary corn, 25 bales. One of my neighbors last year on 125 acres made 124 bales, averaging 450 pounds, and several others did nearly as well and it goes without saying that land which will make such crops will make any thing else.   W. R. B.

Nash County.

Nash County is situated in the western part of the Eastern Division of the State and is bounded on the north by Halifax County, east by Edgecombe, south by Wilson and Johnston, and west by Franklin. Its capital is Nashville, 44 miles east of Raleigh.

Its population in 1880 was: white, 9,417; colored, 8,314. An increase of 33 1/3 per cent in 10 years.

Value of Real Estate in 1882, $1,415,270; value of personal property in 1882, $612,933. Assessed value of land, $4.08 per acre.

Number of children of school age: white, 3,003; colored,

2,886. Of these one half attended the public school. Length of public school term, 2¾ months.

Tar River, one of the most notable streams in the Western Hemisphere, waters this county, together with several large tributary creeks, and hence we have a large proportion of swamp and heavily-timbered land. In southern and western portions of the County it is broken and the soil red and stiff with some rock, well adapted to the growth of grain and tobacco. It grows fine cotton also. In other parts the soil is generally gray and the face of the country level.

In the Western, Northwestern and Northern portions there is some lack of timber except in the swamps. All the other portions are well timbered. The long leaved pine, red and white and spanish oak, hickory and blackjack are the leading varieties on the upland, and all of these and the water oak, cypress and gum on the low land.

The improved farms produce from ¾ to 1¼ bales of cotton of 450 lbs. and from 30 to 40 bushels of corn and 20 bushels of wheat to the acre. The unimproved from ¼ to ¾ bale cotton and from 10 to 20 bushels corn. No wheat is grown on the unimproved land worthy of mention. On the red land the grasses and clover do well. Large yields of peas and potatoes are grown on the gray land. If the swamp lands in this County were reclaimed it would be one of the wealthiest in the State. It is estimated that if this were done enough corn could be raised in this County alone to supply one half the entire State.

The Baptist and Methodist are the leading denominations of Christians, and a church of one of these sects may be found in almost every community, and a good moral and religious tone pervades our society.

The Wilmington & Weldon Railroad is the boundary line on the east and Fishing Creek on the north.

The famous Falls of Tar River are in this County, one

mile from the town of Rocky Mount. The large and valuable Cotton Factory known as the Rocky Mt. Mills is located here. There are several excellent localities in this County where the water power is sufficient for large manufacturing establishments.

The water is good and the climate mild. Our laws are rigidly enforced and there is no lack of protection to life, liberty or property. A. W. B.

Wilson County.

Was formed in 1855 from portions of Edgecombe, Johnston, Nash and Wayne Counties.

Population in 1870 was 12,258; in 1880, 16,064. Assessed value of taxable property in 1882, $3,003,700; that of live stock was $211,859.

In 1880 there were 66,027 acres of improved land in the county out of 196,146 acres listed for taxation.

The surface is slightly undulating, with sandy and clayey soils varied. The price of the improved land ranges from $10 to $25 per acre.

The products of the soil are corn, cotton, wheat, oats, rye, peas, potatoes, rice, grasses, and a variety of vegetables, all of which are successfully and profitably grown here, though more attention is given to the cultivation of cotton and corn than to any other crops.

Of the fruits, apples, peaches, pears, grapes, cherries, melons and berries are produced in great abundance, and the Westbrook Nurseries, perhaps the largest and most successful in the State, are located near the town of Wilson.

The forests are well timbered with pine, oak, hickory, ash, birch, maple, cypress and gum.

Iron ore has been found in several places in the county, and there are several iron and magnesia springs.

The farms are cultivated by tenants and by hired labor. When the landlord furnishes the tenant a house, team and agricultural implements, and the tenant all the labor necessary to cultivate and harvest the crop, the customary rental is one-half of the products of the farm.

The average price paid for hired labor is about $10 per month and board, with a house, garden, potato patch and fire wood furnished to those laborers who contract for twelve months.

The railway stations of the county are Wilson, Black Creek and Toisnot. Wilson, the county seat and principal shipping point, is 108 miles north of Wilmington on the Wilmington and Weldon Railroad, about 50 miles east of Raleigh. It has now a population of about 2,000 inhabitants, and is a beautiful, thrifty and progressive town.

The Wilson Cotton Mills, equipped with entirely new and the most improved machinery, have recently been completed, and are daily turning out an excellent quality of warps and yarns.

In the town of Wilson there are five churches of different denominations for the whites and four for the colored people, and the number of churches conveniently located in different parts of the county affords every facility for religious worship.

Besides the excellent graded schools at Wilson and Toisnot, there are in the county 31 public schools for whites and 24 for colored children, and the Wilson Collegiate Institute for white females, Prof. S. Hassell, A. M., Principal, is a school of deservedly high reputation throughout the State.

Moccasin River, a beautiful stream, well stocked with white shad, runs through the southern part of the county, affording a fine water power for the several wheat, grist and saw mills on its banks, and affording eligible sites for the erection of manufactories.

The county is entirely out of debt, and a tax of only 15 cents on the $100 worth of property was levied in 1882 for county purposes.

There are few or no local causes of sickness, and the climate of the county is generally mild and healthful.

J. E. W.

The Census Figures.

[Compendium 10th United States Census.]

The area of North Carolina, land surface, 48,580 square miles ; 31,091,200 acres.

The population, 1,399,750 ; to the square mile, 28.81; 270,-994 families, inhabiting 264,305 dwellings ; male, 687,908 ; female, 711,842 ; native, 1,396,008 ; foreign, 3,742 ; white, 867,242 ; colored (including 1 Japanese and 1,230 Indians) 532,508 ; voters, 294,750 ; white, 189,732 ; colored, 105,018 ; of the natives, 1,344,553 born in North Carolina, and 51,455 in 48 other States and Territories.

The farms, 157,609 ; 22,363,558 acres ; 6,481,191 improved ; 15,882,367 unimproved ; average size of farms, 142 acres ; value of farms, $135,793,602 ; of farming implements, $6,078,476; live stock, $22,414,659; cost of building and repairing fences for census year, $1,869,654; cost of fertilizers per year, $2,111,767; products, $51,729,611.

The principal vegetable productions : Barley, 2,421 bushels; buckwheat, 44,668 bushels; corn, 28,019,839 bushels; oats 3,838,068 bushels; rye, 285,160 bushels; wheat, 3,397,-393 bushels; orchard products, $903,513 ; hay, 93,711 tons; rice, 5,609,191 lbs. ; cotton, 389,598 bales; potatoes, Irish, 722,773; sweet, 4,576, 148 bushels; tobacco, 26,986,213 lbs.

The live stock: Horses, 133,686; mules and asses, 81,871; working oxen, 50,188; milch cows, 232,133; other cattle, 375,105; sheep, 461,638; hogs, 1,453,541. Products: Wool, 917,756 lbs; milk, 446,798 gallons; butter, 7,212,507 lbs. ; cheese, 57,380 lbs.

Assessed valuation, $156,100,202, viz.: real property, $101,709,326; personal property, $54,390,876.

Taxation, $1,916,132, viz. : State, $706,903; county, $986,-956; city, town and village, $222,273. Debt, $8,194,606, viz.: State, $5,706,616; county, $1,524.654; city and town. $963,336.

Manufacturing establishments, 3,802; capital, $13,045,639; employes, 18,109; wages $2,740,768; materials used, $13,090,937; product, $20,095,037.

Public schools: White, 4,015; colored, 2,146; teachers, white, 4,291; colored, 1,975; average daily attendance of pupils, white, 102,254; colored, 62,316; value of school property, $248,015; revenue, $553,464.

Newspapers and periodicals, 142; daily, 13; weekly, 113; semi-weekly, 3; tri-weekly, 2; monthly, 7; semi-monthly, 4.

IN THE COAL AND IRON COUNTIES.

ALEXANDER COUNTY.—The population is 8,355: white, 7,458; colored, 897; male, 4,025; female. 4,330; native, 8,350; foreign, 5; voting, 1,652; white, 1,494; colored, 158.

Property and Taxation.—The real and personal property was assessed at $713.000; State, County and Town taxation, property and poll, $6,038; no debt.

Farm Areas and Values.—There were 1,355 farms of 48,985 acres improved land; value, $697,665; farming implements, $33,602; live stock, $146,600; products, $212,292.

Principal Vegetable Productions.—Corn 212,382 bushels; 51,752 of oats; 2,445 of rye; 35,338 of wheat; hay, 167 tons; cotton, 182 bales; potatoes—Irish, 5,493; sweet, 9,237 bushels; tobacco, 11,799 lbs.; orchard products, $17,473.

Live Stock and Products.—Horses, 976; mules, 794; working oxen, 182; milch cows, 1,836; other cattle, 2,431; sheep, 4,403; hogs, 9,509; wool, 6,779 lbs.; milk, 3 gallons; butter, 70,510 lbs.; cheese 1,052 lbs.

Manufactures.—Manufacturing establishments, 32; capital, $69,972; employes, 49; wages, $5,371; materials used, $62,130; products, $81,715.

ALAMANCE.—Population, 14.613: white, 9,997; colored,

4,613; male, 6,992; female, 7,621; native, 14,576; foreign, 37; voters, 3,066; white, 2,193; colored, 873.

Property and Taxation.—Assessment, $2,272,248; taxes, $18,284; debt, $7,664.

Farm Areas and Values.—1,615 farms; 77,799 acres; value, $1,500,876; implements, $72,556; live stock, $250,823; products, $470,758.

Vegetable Productions.—Corn, 305,874 bushels; oats, 48,869; rye, 619; wheat, 82,163; orchard products, $35,487; hay, 2,590 tons; cotton, 91 bales; potatoes (Irish), 7,087; sweet, 13,252; tobacco, 695,013 lbs.

Live Stock and Products.—Horses, 2,422; mules, 693; oxen, 73; cows, 2,891; other cattle, 3,869; sheep, 5,000; hogs, 11,796; wool, 11,018 lbs.; milk 3,586 gallons; butter, 103,356 lbs.; cheese, 385 lbs.

Manufactures.—Establishments, 58; capital, $724,766; employes, 693; wages, $93,622; materials, $422,489; products, $709,196.

ALLEGHANY.—Population, 5,486: white, 4,967; colored, 519; male, 2,760; female, 2,726; native, 5,484; foreign, 2; voters, 1,181—white, 1,080, colored, 101.

Property and Taxation.—Real and personal property, $602,601; taxes, $5,999; debt, $5,462.

Farm Areas and Values.—914 farms; acres, 74,747; value, $827,828; implements, $27,345; live stock, $165,791; product, $146,182.

Vegetable Productions.—Buckwheat, 6,254 bushels; corn, 122,587; oats, 19,365; rye, 17,638; wheat, 10,291; hay, 3,603 tons; potatoes—Irish, 5,009, sweet, 285 bushels; tobacco, 2,049 lbs.; orchard products, $5,114.

Live-stock and Products.—Horses, 1,432; mules, 110; oxen, 410; cows, 2,287; other cattle, 3,049; sheep, 6,738;

hogs, 7,522; wool, 19,159 lbs.; butter, 81,605 lbs.; cheese, 3,205 lbs.

Manufactures.—Establishments, 6; capital, $7,000; employes, 7; wages, $750; material, $8,950; product, $11,243.

ANSON.—Population, 17,994: white, 8,790, colored, 9,204; male, 8,712, female, 9,282; native, 17,966, foreign, 28; voters, 3,568—white, 1,914, colored, 1,654.

Property and Taxation.—Assessment, $1,556,731; taxes, $27,409; debt, $35,000.

Farm Areas and Values.—2,083 farms; 90,061 acres; value, $1,816,037; implements, $83,234; live-stock, $302,135; products, $966,456.

Vegetable Productions.—Corn, 305,139 bushels; oats, 72,454; rye, 574; wheat, 25,846; orchard products, $3,193; hay, 217 tons; cotton, 11,857 bales; potatoes—Irish, 4,908, sweet, 39,645 bushels; tobacco, 4,880 lbs.

Live Stock and Products.—Horses, 1,182; mules, 1,546; oxen, 725; cows, 2,885; other cattle, 4,682; sheep, 4,085; hogs, 14,229; wool, 8,817 pounds; milk, 110 gallons; butter, 98,907 pounds.

Manufactures.—Establishments, 51; capital, $82,160; employes, 137; wages, $17,750; materials, $126,095; products, $169,353.

ASHE.—Population, 14,437: white, 13,471, colored, 966; male, 7,249, female, 7,188; native, 14,404, foreign, 33; voters, 2,904—white, 2,658, colored, 246.

Property and Taxation.—Assessment, $1,059,934; taxes, $11,249; debt, $4,000.

Farm Areas and Values.—1,942 farms, 117,174 acres; value, $1,747,351; implements, $62,269; live stock, $354,048; products, $469,669.

Vegetable Productions.—Buckwheat, 6,131 bushels; corn,

277,027; oats, 37,955; rye. 33,809; wheat, 39,407; orchard products, $15,265; hay, 7,349 tons; potatoes—Irish. 12,688, sweet, 411 bushels; tobacco, 11,064 pounds.

Live Stock and Products.—Horses, 2,396; mules, 208; oxen, 709; cows, 4,455; other cattle, 6,320; sheep, 12,292; hogs, 18,170; wool, 37,483 lbs.; milk, 6,740 gallons; butter, 176,478 lbs.; cheese, 10,596 lbs.

Manufactures.—Establishments, 57; capital, $49,810; employes, 67; wages, $9,801; material, $82,576; product, $109,231.

BUNCOMBE.—Population, 21,909: white, 18,422; colored, 3,487; male, 10,938; female, 10,971; native, 21,781; foreign, 128; voters, 4,613: white. 3,842; colored, 771.

Property and Taxation.—Assessment, $2,636,721; taxes, $35,789; debt, $97,900.

Farm Areas and Values.—2,560 farms; 99,602 acres; value, $2,589,897; implements, $90,064; live stock, $467,991; products, $521,625.

Vegetable Productions.—Buckwheat, 3,981 bushels; corn, 490,544; oats, 62,699; rye, 12,707; wheat, 84,974; orchard products, $22,270; hay, 2,281 tons; potatoes, Irish, 19,211; sweet, 5,872 bushels; tobacco, 475,428 lbs.

Live Stock and Products.—Horses, 2,352; mules, 1,247; oxen, 291; cows, 4,350; other cattle, 6,746; sheep, 10,897; hogs, 18,516; wool, 18,425 lbs.; milk, 46,273 gallons; butter, 248,455 lbs.; cheese, 1,270 lbs.

Manufactures.—Establishments, 58; capital, $156,035; employes, 145; wages, $24,615; material, $127,897; products, $198,886.

BURKE.—Population, 12,809: white, 10,088; colored, 2,721; male, 6,157; female, 6,652; native, 12,792; foreign, 17; voters, 2,503; white, 2,055; colored, 448.

Property and Taxation.—Assessment, $888,497; taxes, $14,689; debt, $25,000.

Farm Areas and Values.—1,648 farms; 44,496 acres; value, $812,157; implements, $29,786; live stock, $151,758; products, $261,005.

Vegetable Productions.—Buckwheat, 46 bushels; corn, 325,656; oats, 21,762; rye, 4,009; wheat, 49,338; orchard products, $6,772; hay, 632 tons; rice, 4,508 lbs.; cotton, 361 bales; potatoes, Irish, 6,782; sweet, 11,358 bushels; tobacco, 20,079 lbs.

Live Stock and Products.—Horses, 1,091; mules, 917; oxen, 347; cows, 2,123; other cattle, 3,032; sheep, 4,418; hogs, 9,426; wool, 6,856 lbs.; milk, 428 gallons; butter, 80,107 lbs.; cheese, 1,232 lbs.

Manufactures.—Establishments, 35; capital, $61,485; employes, 113; wages, $14,232; material, $84,214; product, $112,376.

CABARRUS.—Population: 14,964: white, 9,849; colored, 5,115; male, 7,358; female, 7,606; native, 14,933; foreign, 31; voters, 3,172; white, 2,141; colored, 1,031.

Property and Taxation.—Assessment, $2,253,988; taxes, $23,186; debt, $3,340.

Farm Areas and Values.—1,729 farms; 90,514 acres; value, $2,205,643; implements, $90,364; live stock, $296,697; product, $764,084.

Vegetable Productions.—Corn, 381,321 bushels; oats, 54,519; rye, 355; wheat, 84,656; orchard products, $8,772; hay, 3,496 tons; cotton, 7,467 bales; potatoes, Irish, 7,062; sweet, 11,241 bushels; tobacco, 3,239 lbs.

Live Stock and Products.—Horses, 2,167; mules, 1,583; oxen, 37; cows, 2,547; other cattle, 3,575; sheep, 3,551; hogs, 12,284; wool, 7,663 lbs.; milk, 25 gallons; butter, 127,927 lbs.; cheese, 325 lbs.

Manufactures.—Establishments, 74; capital, $155,579; employes, 278; wages, $44,009; materials, $213,561; products, $313,624.

CALDWELL.—Population, 10,291: white, 8,91; colored, 1,600; male, 4,977; female, 5,314; native, 10,279; foreign, 12; voters, 2,001: white, 1,738; colored, 263.

Property and Taxation.—Assessment, $963,114; taxes, $11,886; debt, $1,400.

Farm Areas and Values.—1,442 farms; 47,405 acres; value, $1,183,428; implements, $78,497; live stock, $170,225; products, $278,529.

Vegetable Productions.—Buckwheat, 304 bushels; corn, 274,495; oats, 30,592; rye, 2,855; wheat, 42,513; orchard products, $15,418; hay, 695 tons; rice 1,649 lbs.; cotton, 12 bales; potatoes, Irish, 14,487; sweet, 21,071 bushels; tobacco, 25,384 lbs.

Live Stock and Products.—Horses, 1,065; mules, 731; oxen, 290; cows, 2,045; other cattle, 2,808; sheep, 4,915; hogs, 11,424; wool, 9,714 lbs.; milk, 51,051 gallons; butter, 87,064 lbs.; cheese, 1,002 lbs.

Manufactures.—Establishments, 49; capital, $98,025; employes, 132; wages, $16,072; materials, $89,055; products, $126,190.

CATAWBA.—Population, 14,946; white, 12,469; colored, 2,477; male, 7,153; female, 7,793; native, 14,905; foreign, 41; voters, 3,037; white, 2,588; colored, 449.

Property and Taxation.—Assessment, $2,052,931; taxes, $13,572; debt, $4,700.

Farm Areas and Values.—1,725 farms; 78,080 acres; value, $1,723,438; implements, $86,140; live stock, $241,219; products, $458,257.

Vegetable Productions.—Corn, 358,210 bushels; oats,

64,236 ; rye, 783 ; wheat, 104,770 ; orchard products, $14,-857 ; hay, 1,137 tons; cotton, 2,012 bales ; potatoes—Irish, 12,687 ; sweet, 19,325 bushels ; tobacco, 26,380 lbs.

Live Stock and Products.—Horses, 1,698 ; mules, 1,243 ; oxen, 66 ; cows, 2,871 ; other cattle, 3,769 ; sheep, 6,299 ; hogs, 10,594 ; wool, 10,862 lbs. ; milk, 352 gallons ; butter, 120,784 lbs. ; cheese, 1,338 lbs.

Manufactures.—Establishments, 77 ; capital, $168,865 ; employes, 318 ; wages, $34,510 ; material, $193,251, products, $282,604.

CHATHAM.—Population 23,453 : white, 15,500 ; colored, 7,953 ; male, 11,416 ; female 12,037 ; native 23,414 ; foreign, 39 ; voters, 4,862—white, 3,404 ; colored, 1,458.

Property and Taxation.—Assessment, $2,496,248 ; taxes, $26,451 ; debt, $5,000.

Farm Areas and Values.—3,554 farms ; 126,940 acres ; value, $2,098,668 ; implements, $143,672 ; live stock, $476,788 ; products, $995,369.

Vegetable Productions.—Corn, 558,281 bushels ; oats, 120,341 ; rye, 328 ; wheat, 122,760 ; orchard products, $22,-165 ; hay, 77 tons ; cotton, 5,858 bales ; potatoes—Irish 18,-957 ; sweet, 53,334 bushels; tobacco, 49,837 lbs.

Live Stock and Products.—Horses, 3,040 ; mules, 2,164; oxen, 464 ; cows, 5,736 ; other cattle, 9,124 ; sheep; 15,089 ; hogs, 30,150 ; wool, 31,595 lbs. ; milk, 356 gallons ; butter, 226,078 lbs. ; cheese, 1,926 lbs.

Manufactures.—Establishments, 93 ; capital, $576,885 ; employes, 180 ; wages, $22,853 ; material, $227,993 ; products, $286,709.

CHEROKEE.—Population, 8,182 ; white, 7,796 ; colored, 288 ; male, 3,991 ; female, 4,191 ; native, 8,177 ; foreign, 5 ; voters, 1,570—white, 1,494 ; colored, 76.

Property and Taxation.—Assessment, $607,527; taxes. $5,595; debt, $8,111.

Farm Areas and Values.—964 farms, 30,668 acres; value, $566,734; implements, $24,753; live stock, $133,668; products, $182,913.

Vegetable Productions.—Buckwheat, 77 bushels; corn, 227,650; oats, 11,657; rye, 4,781; wheat, 17,898; orchard products, $7,021; hay, 997 tons; potatoes—Irish, 12,379; sweet, 11,789 bushels; tobacco, 8,411 lbs.

Live Stock and Products.—Horses, 888; mules, 307; oxen, 598; cows, 1,821; other cattle, 3,374; sheep, 6,861; hogs, 11,533; wool, 8,878 lbs.; milk, 3 gallons; butter, 95,680 lbs.; cheese, 66 lbs.

Manufactures.—Establishments, 21; capital, $29,420; employes, 46; wages, $4,705; material, $23,722; products, $37,971.

CLAY.—Population, 3,316; white, 3,175; colored, 141; male, 1,679; female, 1,637; native, 3,316; voters, 675—white, 655; colored, 20.

Property and Taxation.—Assessment, $254,261; taxes, $3,075; debt, $1,500.

Farm Areas and Values.—544 farms; 17,691 acres; value. $403,348; implements, $17,582; live stock, $90,423; products, $95,402.

Vegetable Productions.—Buckwheat, 157 bushels; corn, 113,462; oats, 7,607; rye, 3,562; wheat, 13,093; orchard products, $1,246; hay, 475 tons; potatoes—Irish, 3,512; sweet, 7,058 bushels; tobacco, 5,771 lbs.

Live Stock and Products.—Horses, 642; mules, 318; oxen, 162; cows, 989; other cattle, 1,899; sheep, 3,238; hogs, 1,113; wool, 8,333 lbs.; butter, 49,581 lbs.; cheese, 98 lbs.

Manufactures.—Establishments, 4; capital, $4,500; employes, 4; wages, $625; material, $15,297; products, $16,732.

CLEVELAND.—Population, 16,571: white, 13,700; colored, 2,871; male, 8,022; female, 8,549; native, 16,559; foreign, 12; voters, 3,365—white, 2,843; colored, 522.

Property and Taxation.—Assessment, $1,609,361; taxes, $26,078; debt, $30,000.

Farm Areas and Values,—2,247 farms, 87,691 acres; value, $2,444,056; implements, $80,576; live stock, $248,707; products, $702,578.

Vegetable Productions.—Corn, 390,281 bushels; oats, 62,211; rye, 875: wheat, 55,983; orchard products, $5,642; hay, 119 tons; rice, 835 lbs.; cotton, 6,126 bales; potatoes—Irish, 3,221, sweet, 35,834 bushels; tobacco, 5,122 lbs.

Live Stock and Products.—Horses, 1,403; mules, 1,846; oxen, 172; cows, 3,556; other cattle, 4,397; sheep, 8,342; hogs, 11,327; wool, 9,879 lbs.; milk, 1,858 gallons; butter, 176,411 lbs.; cheese, 387 lbs.

Manufactures.—Establishments, 52; capital, $133,200; employes, 195; wages, $25,700; material, $172,575; products, $262,128.

CUMBERLAND.—Population, 23,836: white, 12,594; colored, 11,241; male, 11,493; female, 12,343; native, 23,717; foreign, 119; voters, 4,861—white, 2,726; colored, 2,135.

Property and Taxation.—Assessment, $2,380,402; taxes, $41,118; debt, $310,000.

Farm Areas and Values.—1,987 farms; 59,639 acres; value, $1,284,067; implements, $55,121; live stock, $220,936; products, $570,533.

Vegetable Productions.—Corn, 282,423 bushels; oats, 13,791; rye, 4,343; wheat, 7,494; orchard products, $8,560;

hay, 1,195 tons; rice, 19,963 lbs.; cotton, 3,905 bales; potatoes—Irish, 2,104, sweet, 91,355 bushels.

Live Stock and Products.—Horses, 1,089; mules, 914; oxen, 495; cows, 2,457; other cattle, 5,379; sheep, 5,801; hogs, 23,179; wool, 11,666 lbs.; milk, 616 gallons; butter, 39,453, lbs.; cheese, 215 lbs.

Manufactures.—Establishments, 81; capital, $460,750; employes, 754; wages, $120,348; material, $353,701; products, $612,461.

DAVIDSON.—Population, 20,333: white, 16,341; colored, 3,992; male, 9,934; female, 10,399; native, 20,308; foreign, 25; voters, 4,375—white, 3,574; colored, 801.

Property and Taxation.—Assessment, $2,305,859; taxes, $23,654; debt, none.

Farm Areas and Values.—3,087 farms; 129,664 acres, value, $2,666,746; implements, $159,609; live stock, $476,352; products, $777,659.

Vegetable Productions.—Barley, 364 bushels; corn, 549,906; oats, 122,063; rye, 1,414; wheat, 174,671; orchard products, $40,076; hay, 8,667 tons; cotton, 1,553 bales; potatoes—Irish, 26,108, sweet, 30,665 bushels; tobacco, 260,538 lbs.

Live Stock and Products.—Horses, 3,386; mules, 1,366; oxen, 220; cows, 4,334; other cattle, 5,745; sheep, 11,051; hogs, 23,682; wool, 20,926 lbs.; milk, 740 gallons; butter, 157,757 lbs.; cheese, 276 lbs.

Manufactures.—Establishments, 92; capital, $161,230; employes, 245; wages, $42,937; material, $336,878; products, $452,668.

DAVIE.—Population, 11,096: white, 7,770; colored, 3,326; male, 5,396; female, 5,700; native, 11,091; foreign, 5; voters, 2,359—white, 1,718; colored, 641.

OF NORTH CAROLINA.

Property and Taxation.—Assessment, $1,224,206; taxes, $14,358 ; debt, none.

Farm Areas and Values.—1,492 farms; 66,810 acres; value, $1,298,178; implements, $56,420; live stock, $401,425; product, $467,979.

Vegetable Productions.—Corn, 438,595 bushels; oats, 139,126; rye, 1,986; wheat, 71,127; orchard products, $8,210; hay, 2,041 tons; cotton, 302 bales; potatoes—Irish, 8,233; sweet, 6,231 bushels; tobacco, 633,339 lbs.

Live Stock and Products.—Horses, 1,563; mules, 826; oxen, 105; cows, 1,866; other cattle, 2,409; sheep, 3,415, hogs, 12,695; wool, 7,031 lbs. ; milk, 175 gallons; butter, 74,944 lbs. ; cheese, 8 lbs.

Manufactures.—Establishments, 60; capital, $80,552; employes, 144; wages, $14,937; material, $108,188; products, $150,965.

FORSYTH.—Population, 18,070: white, 13,441; colored, 4,629; male, 8,832; female, 9,238; native, 18,003; foreign, 67; voters, 4,164—white, 3,130; colored, 1,034.

Property and Taxation.—Assessment, $2,893,252; taxes, $27,995; debt, $26,400.

Farm Areas and Values.—1,871 farms; 79,350 acres. value, $1,361,975; implements, $81,006; live stock, $203,661; products, $496,759.

Vegetable Productions.—Corn, 335,164 bushels; oats, 95,304; rye, 1,968; wheat, 77,082; orchard products, $38,605; hay, 4,312 tons; cotton, 10 bales; potatoes—Irish, 17,629; sweet, 18,447 bushels; tobacco, 822,788 lbs.

Live Stock and Products.—Horses, 1,820; mules, 703; oxen, 84; cows, 2,658; other cattle, 2,594; sheep, 4,258; hogs, 10,658; wool, 8,977 lbs.; milk, 17,205 gallons; butter, 122,715 lbs. ; cheese, 737 lbs.

Manufactures.—Establishments, 96; capital, $708,850;

employes, 1,434; wages, $199,509; material, $734,840; products, $1,104,749.

FRANKLIN.—Population, 20,829: white, 9,476, colored, 11,353; male, 10,294, female, 10,535; native, 20,820, foreign, 9; voters, 4,257—white, 2,145, colored, 2,112.

Property and Taxation.—Assessment, $2,444,807; taxes, $43,652; debt, $5,000.

Farm Areas and Values.—2,415 farms; 90,118 acres; value, $2,224,478; implements, $125,151; live-stock, $289,617; products, $1,020,331.

Vegetable Productions.—Corn, 338,239 bushels; oats, 45,812; rye, 961; wheat, 45,504; orchard products, $7,690; hay, 156 tons; cotton, 12,938 bales; potatoes—Irish, 4,265, sweet, 48,684 bushels; tobacco, 58,932 lbs.

Live Stock and Products.—Horses, 1,901; mules, 990; oxen, 1,306; cows, 2,866; other cattle, 5,054; sheep, 4,544; hogs, 16,428; wool, 989 lbs.; milk, 10 gallons; butter, 66,611 lbs.; cheese, 220 lbs.

Manufactures.—Establishments, 46; capital, $111,825; employes, 139; wages, $18,895; materials, $90,689; products, $134,112.

GASTON.—Population, 14,254: white, 10,188, colored, 4,066; male, 6,916, female, 7,338; native, 14,200, foreign, 54; voters, 2,918—white, 2,098, colored, 820.

Property and Taxation.—Assessment, $2,018,005; taxes, $15,012; debt, none.

Farm Areas and Values.—1,547 farms; 70,672 acres; value, $1,836,591; implements, $68,906; live stock, $246,926; products, $625,459.

Vegetable Productions.—Corn. 373,472 bushels; oats, 50,244; rye, 265; wheat, 62,860; orchard products, $2,766 hay, 821 tons; cotton, 4,588 bales; potatoes—Irish, 5,439, sweet, 19,290 bushels; tobacco, 2,180 lbs.

Live Stock and Products.—Horses, 978; mules, 1,505; oxen, 34; cows, 2,303; other cattle, 3,608; sheep, 4,636; hogs, 10,310; wool, 6,317 lbs.; milk, 126,000 gallons; butter, 125,505 lbs.; cheese, 120 lbs.

Manufactures.—Establishments, 87; capital, $635,965; employes, 453; wages, $72,245; material, $570,014; products, $844,308.

GRAHAM.—Population, 2,335: white, 2,123; colored, 212; male, 1,155; female, 1,180; native, 2,332; foreign, 3; voters, 459—white, 413, colored, 46.

Property and Taxation.—Assessment, $160,026; taxes, $3,846; debt, $3,000.

Farm Areas and Values.—312 farms; 8,551 acres; value, $160,772; implements, $7,197; live stock, $44,972; products, $57,420.

Vegetable Productions.—Buckwheat, 25 bushels; corn, 66,092; oats, 3,914; rye, 2,126; wheat, 2,919; orchard products, $3,883; hay, 115 tons; potatoes—Irish, 5,963; sweet, 5,460 bushels; tobacco, 1,095 lbs.

Live Stock and Products.—Horses, 330; mules, 74; oxen, 168; cows, 628; other cattle, 1,160; sheep, 2,253; hogs, 5,263; wool, 3,921 lbs.; butter, 31,265 lbs.

GRANVILLE.—Population, 31,286: white, 13,603; colored, 17,679; male, 15,558; female, 15,728; native, 31,163; foreign, 123; voters, 6,574—white, 3,201, colored, 3,373.

Property and Taxation.—Assessment, $3,443,785; taxes, $40,165; debt, $45,000.

Farm Areas and Values.—2,864 farms; 150,127 acres; value, $3,203,404; implements, $125,676; live stock, $372,991; products, $1,463,887.

Vegetable Productions.—Corn, 515,159 bushels; oats, 110,690; rye, 360; wheat, 90,764, orchard products, $13,871;

hay, 95 tons; cotton, 2,535 bales; potatoes—Irish, 14,622; sweet, 52,307 bushels; tobacco, 4,606,358 lbs.

Live Stock and Products.—Horses, 3,633; mules, 1,009; oxen, 1,067; cows, 4,765; other cattle, 6,209; sheep, 6,599; hogs, 21,124; wool, 15,046 lbs.; milk, 135 gallons; butter, 181,129 lbs.; cheese, 150 lbs.

Manufactures.—Establishments, 97; capital, $147,800; employes, 293; wages, $35,240; material, $246,761; products, $354,172.

GUILFORD.—Population, 23,585: white, 16,885; colored, 6,700; male, 11,322; female, 12,263; native, 23,388; foreign, 197; voters, 5,305—white, 3,962; colored, 1,343.

Property and Taxation.—Assessment, $3,839,946; taxes, $34,772; debt, $3,050.

Farm Areas and Values.—2,810 farms; 148,392 acres; value, $2,234,735; implements, $106,029; live stock, $353,726; products, $797,184.

Vegetable Productions.—Barley, 1,068 bushels; buckwheat, 62; corn, 519,185; oats, 129,723; rye, 1,725; wheat, 127,214; orchard products, $49,223; hay, 7,017 tons; cotton, 114 bales; potatoes—Irish, 13,777; sweet, 20,302 bushels; tobacco, 422,716 lbs.

Live Stock and Products.—Horses, 3,313; mules, 1,186; oxen, 416; cows, 5,081; other cattle, 7,559; sheep, 10,148; hogs, 17,404; wool, 21,218 lbs.; milk, 12,472 gallons; butter, 185,990 lbs.; cheese, 50 lbs.

Manufactures.—Establishments, 98; capital, $438,800; employes, 374; wages, $72,305; material, $350,383; products, $498,526.

HALIFAX.—Population, 30,300: white, 9,137; colored, 21,163; male, 15,212; female, 15,088; native, 30,239; foreign, 61; voters, 6,730—white, 2,236; colored, 4,494.

Property and Taxation.—Assessment, $3,111,799; taxes, $27,236; debt, $8,000.

Farm Areas and Values.—2,683 farms; 137,245 acres; value, $2,172,467; implements, $100,398; live stock, $349,-105; products, $1,141,365.

Vegetable Productions.—Barley, 76 bushels; corn, 437,-321; oats, 41,771; rye, 520; wheat, 9,235; orchard products, $13,117; hay, 357 tons; cotton, 16,661 bales; potatoes—Irish, 6,128; sweet, 52,709 bushels; tobacco, 8,487 lbs.

Live Stock and Products.—Horses, 2,026; mules, 1,581; oxen, 2,472; cows, 3,065; other cattle, 5,127; sheep, 1,771; hogs, 20,034; wool, 5,213 lbs.; milk, 33 gallons; butter, 35,-683 lbs.; cheese, 295 lbs.

Manufactures.—Establishments, 22; capital, $58,725; employes, 87; wages, $12,270; material, $71,660; products, $99,020.

HARNETT.—Population, 10,862: white, 7,092; colored, 3,770; male, 5,362; female, 5,500; native, 10,836; foreign, 26; voters, 2,214—white, 1,564, colored, 650.

Property and Taxation.—Assessment, $842,347; taxes, 9,209; debt, $18,750.

Farm Areas and Values.—1,450 farms; 42,927 acres; value, $809,073; implements, $44,640; live stock, $170,071; products, 443,197.

Vegetable Productions.—Corn, 180,458 bushels; oats, 7,640; rye, 1,257; wheat, 10,957; orchard products, $7,048; hay, 38 tons; rice, 830 lbs.; cotton, 3,627 bales; potatoes—Irish, 1,286, sweet, 96,118 bushels; tobacco, 9,510 lbs.

Live Stock and Products.—Horses, 763; mules, 645; oxen, 725; cows, 1,974; other cattle, 4,057; sheep, 4,213; hogs, 15,404; wool, 8,464 lbs.; milk, 174 gallons; butter, 30,238 lbs.; cheese, 80 lbs.

COAL AND IRON COUNTIES

Manufactures.—Establishments, 23 ; capital, $42,950; employes, 42; wages, $4,765; materials, $32,075; products, $52,202.

HAYWOOD.—Population, 10,271: white, 9,787; colored, 484; male, 5,097; female, 5,174; native. 10,267; foreign, 4; voters, 1,963—white, 1,874; colored, 89.

Property and Taxation.—Assessment, $918,792; taxes, $11,553; debt, $4,000.

Farm Areas and Values.—1,355 farms; 52,132 acres; value, $1,089,033; implements, $41,866; live stock, $211,093; products, $256,161.

Vegetable Productions.—Buckwheat, 4,684 bushels; corn, 314,446; oats, 35,834; rye, 4,383; wheat, 56,587; orchard products, $8,112; hay, 1,016 tons; potatoes—Irish, 8,072, sweet, 2,405 bushels; tobacco, 39,516 lbs.

Live Stock and Products.—Horses, 1,534; mules, 423; oxen, 197; cows, 2,570; other cattle, 5,353; sheep, 8,830; hogs, 16,126; wool, 13,999 lbs.; butter, 127,157 lbs.; cheese, 980 lbs.

Manufactures.—Establishments, 20 ; capital, $30,160; employes, 24; wages, $3,540; materials, $43,759; products, $52,868.

HENDERSON.—Population, 10,281: white, 8,893; colored, 1,388; male, 5,019; female, 5,262; native, 10,223; foreign, 58; voters, 2,041—white, 1,794; colored, 247.

Property and Taxation.—Assessment, $1,026,266; taxes, $22,131; debt, $105,050.

Farm Areas and Values.—1,327 farms; 45,445 acres; value, $958,738; implements, $34,836; live stock, $187,921; products, $179,604.

Vegetable Productions.—Buckwheat, 637 bushels; corn, 227,411; oats, 23.087; rye, 16,351; wheat, 12,295; orchard products, $9,089; hay, 892 tons; cotton, 4 bales; potatoes—Irish, 9,675, sweet, 2,627 bushels; tobacco, 4,087 lbs.

Live Stock and Products.—Horses, 932; mules, 434: oxen, 600; cows, 2,176; other cattle, 3,282; sheep, 6,514; hogs, 8,419; wool, 10,476 lbs.; milk, 210 gallons; butter, 81,335 lbs.; cheese, 360 lbs.

Manufactures. — Establishments, 30; capital, $18,925; employes, 43; wages, $4,689; material, $29,685; products, $48,074.

IREDELL.—Population, 22,675: white, 16,752; colored, 5,913; male, 10,876; female, 11,799; native, 22,634; foreign, 41; voters, 4,636—white, 3,530; colored, 1,106.

Property and Taxation.—Assessment, $2,656,050; taxes, $30,715; debt, $56,000.

Farm Areas and Values.—2,476 farms; 112,365 acres; value, $2,506,368; implements, $104,493; live stock, $344,706; products, $834,862.

Vegetable Productions.—Buckwheat, 85 bushels; corn, 588,220; oats, 126,429; rye, 1,581; wheat, 88,056; orchard products, $18,811; hay, 2,252 tons; cotton, 4,657 bales; potatoes—Irish, 9,667; sweet, 11,601 bushels; tobacco, 242,714 lbs.

Live Stock and Products.—Horses, 2,494; mules, 1,862; oxen, 202; cows, 3,789; other cattle, 5,218; sheep, 8,179; hogs, 17,696; wool, 14,233 lbs.; milk, 1,780 gallons; butter, 177,206 lbs.; cheese, 1,885 lbs.

Manufactures.— Establishments, 78; capital, $157,920; employes, 137; wages, $17,698; material, $200,004; products, $256,429.

JACKSON.—Population, 7,343: white, 6,591; colored, 752; male, 3,643; female, 3,700; native, 7,331; foreign, 12; voters, 1,409—white, 1,258; colored, 151.

Property and Taxation.—Assessment, $471,478; taxes, $6,341; debt, $1,500.

Farm Areas and Values.—1,087 farms; 32,853 acres; value, $2,118,971; implements, $101,594; live stock, $1,485,667; products, $191,002.

Vegetable Productions.—Buckwheat, 1,100 bushels; corn, 188,521; oats, 9,440; rye, 7,878; wheat, 21,801; orchard products, $8,496; hay, 477 tons; cotton, 6 bales; potatoes—Irish, 11,169; sweet, 10,278 bushels; tobacco, 4,801 lbs.

Live Stock and Products.—Horses, 1,162; mules, 341; oxen, 317; cows, 1,943; other cattle, 3,327; sheep, 5,828; hogs, 15,071; wool, 9,990 lbs.; butter, 92,459 lbs.; cheese, 1,131 lbs.

Manufactures.—Establishments, 11; capital, $14,900; employes, 19; wages, $1,918; materials, $25,597; products, $31,677.

JOHNSTON.—Population, 23,461: white, 15,996; colored, 7,465; male, 11,581; female, 11,880; native, 23,428; foreign, 33; voters, 4,879—white, 3,404; colored, 1,475.

Property and Taxation.—Assessment, $2,872,820; taxes, $26,210; debt, none.

Farm Areas and Values.—3,231 farms; 107,585 acres; value, $2,853,246; implements, $127,373; live stock, $433,960; products, $1,269,610.

Vegetable Productions.—Corn, 428,996 bushels; oats, 29,958; rye, 1,032; wheat, 25,111; orchard products, $12,409; hay, 48 tons; rice, 19,672 lbs.; cotton, 15,151 bales; potatoes—Irish, 1,951; sweet, 210,456 bushels; tobacco, 12,881 lbs.

Live Stock and Products.—Horses, 1,873; mules, 1,629; oxen, 1,780; cows, 3,718; other cattle, 6,676; sheep, 7,263; hogs, 39,328; wool, 13,308 lbs.; milk, 835 gallons; butter, 46,310 lbs.; cheese, 71 lbs.

Manufactures.—Establishments, 48 ; capital, $109,550 ; employes, 132 ; wages, $20,044 ; material, $105,011; products, $156,264.

LINCOLN.—Population 11,061 : white, 8,180 ; colored, 2,881 ; male, 5,341 ; female 5,720 ; native 11,049 ; foreign, 12 ; voters, 2,286—white, 1,728 ; colored, 558.

Property and Taxation.—Assessment, $1,670,731 ; taxes, $15,547 ; debt, $1,500.

Farm Areas and Values.—1,350 farms; 57,523 acres; value, $1,423,637; implements, $72,419; live stock, $206,532; products, $500,945.

Vegetable Productions.—Corn, 313,907 bushels; oats, 44,939; rye, 155; wheat, 65,949; orchard products, $7,312; hay, 1,316 tons; rice, 1,230 lbs. ; cotton, 2,945 bales; potatoes—Irish, 7,966; sweet, 19,179 bushels; tobacco, 6,085 lbs.

Live Stock and Products.—Horses, 1,210 ; mules, 1,234; oxen, 52 ; cows, 2,170 ; other cattle, 3,035 ; sheep, 3,851 ; hogs, 8,102 ; wool, 5,305 lbs. ; milk, 943 gallons ; butter, 115,682 lbs. ; cheese, 228 lbs.

Manufactures.—Establishments, 61 ; capital, $286,355 ; employes, 192 ; wages, $36,783 ; material, $240,589 ; products, $339,726.

MCDOWELL.—Population, 9,836 : white, 7,939 ; colored, 1897 ; male, 4,847 ; female, 4,989 ; native, 9,813 ; foreign, 23 ; voters, 2,002—white, 1,574 ; colored, 428.

Property and Taxation.—Assessment, $577,977; taxes, $7,888; debt, $55,000.

Farm Areas and Values.—1,363 farms ; 38,795 acres ; value, $864,933 ; implements, $23,910 ; live stock, $120,149; products, $196,154.

Vegetable Productions.—Buckwheat, 202 bushels ; corn, 265,934; oats, 13,111 ; rye, 5,016; wheat, 32,903 ; orchard products, $6,500; hay, 103 tons ; rice, 545 lbs.; cotton, 9 bales ; potatoes—Irish, 10,635 ; sweet, 12,707 bushels ; tobacco, 30,541 lbs.

Live Stock and Products.—Horses, 841; mules, 715; oxen, 267; cows, 1,937; other cattle, 2,863; sheep, 4,428; hogs, 8,727; wool, 6,466 lbs.; milk, 927 gallons; butter, 74,162 lbs.; cheese, 845 lbs.

Manufactures.—Establishments, 22 ; capital, $41,300; employes, 54; wages, $8,208; materials, $40,204; products, $58,036.

MACON.—Population, 8,064 : white, 7,395; colored, 656; male, 3,932; female, 4,132; native, 8,043; foreign, 21; voters, 1,612—white, 1,488; colored, 124.

Property and Taxation.—Assessment, $715,782; taxes, $9,447; debt, $1,000.

Farm Areas and Values.—1,182 farms; 39,370 acres; value, $707,864; implements, $38,940; live stock, $179,144; products, $199,580.

Vegetable Productions.—Barley, 50 bushels; buckwheat, 761; corn, 222,855; oats, 12,209; rye, 8,734; wheat, 27,038; orchard products, $4,101; hay, 1,719 tons; potatoes—Irish, 11,315; sweet, 11,214 bushels; tobacco, 9,154 lbs.

Live Stock and Products.—Horses, 1,532; mules, 504; oxen, 382; cows, 2,288; other cattle, 3,945; sheep, 7,318; hogs, 15,058; wool, 9,930 lbs.; butter, 94,094 lbs.; cheese, 1,031 lbs.

Manufactures.—Establishments, 11 ; capital, $15,240; employes, 11; wages, $1,675; materials, $26,458; products, $32,990.

MADISON.—Population, 12,810: white, 12,351; colored, 459; male, 6,468; female, 6,342; native, 12,797; foreign, 13; voters, 2,524—white, 2,410; colored, 114.

COAL AND IRON COUNTIES 413

Property and Taxation.—Assessment, $677,727; taxes, $11,041; debt, none.

Farm Areas and Values.—1,702 farms; 69,087 acres; value, $1,083,057; implements, $39,508; live stock, $239,841; products, $400,081.

Vegetable Productions.—Barley, 70 bushels; buckwheat, 2,809; corn, 348,858; oats, 38,816; rye, 4,641; wheat, 40,192; orchard products, $13,623; hay, 679 tons; cotton, 4 bales; potatoes—Irish, 11,822, sweet, 1,764 bushels; tobacco, 807,911 lbs.

Live Stock and Products.—Horses, 1,455; mules, 786; oxen, 283; cows, 2,927; other cattle, 3,834; sheep, 10,269; hogs, 17,489; wool, 17,027 lbs.; milk, 405 gallons; butter, 139,872 lbs.; cheese, 616 lbs.

Manufactures.—Establishments, 7; capital, $17,500; employes, 13; wages, $1,692; material, $19,045; products, $24,392.

MECKLENBURG. — Population, 34,175; white, 17,922; colored, 16,253; male, 17,027; female, 17,148; native, 33,869; foreign, 306; voters, 7,698—white, 4,179; colored, 3,519.

Property and Taxation.—Assessment, $5,577,852; taxes, $103,261; debt, $316,750.

Farm Areas and Values.—2,645 farms; 146,243 acres; value, $3,382,544; implements, $143,314; live stock, $439,740; products, $1,451,470.

Vegetable Productions. — Barley, 138 bushels; corn, 539,385; oats, 94,356; rye, 403; wheat, 66,767; orchard products, $7,985; hay, 135 tons; cotton, 19,129 bales; potatoes.—Irish, 9,459, sweet, 26,393 bushels; tobacco, 2,291 lbs.

Live Stock and Products.—Horses, 2,205; mules, 3,041; oxen, 60; cows, 3,299; other cattle, 3,380; sheep, 3,478; hogs, 10,963; wool, 7,709; lbs.; milk 1,025 gallons; butter, 240,208 lbs.

Manufactures.—Establishments, 75; capital, $218,925; employes, 296; wages, $66,608; material, $202,791; product, $349,846.

MITCHELL.—Population, 9,435: white, 8,932; colored, 503; male, 4,666; female, 4,769; native, 9,427, foreign, 8; voters 1,799,—white, 1,701; colored, 98.

Property and Taxation.—Assessment, $283,856; taxes, $7,316; debt, $700.

Farm Areas and Values.—1,451 farms; 42,572 acres; value, $728,928; implements, $20,727; live stock, $171,099; product, $187,013.

Vegetable Productions.—Buckwheat, 3,468 bushels; corn, 209,131; oats, 40,845; rye, 9,021; wheat, 19,725; orchard products, $12,491; hay, 1,960 tons; cotton, 6 bales; potatoes—Irish, 20,988, sweet, 2,661 bushels; tobacco, 29,647 lbs.

Live Stock and Products.—Horses, 1,311; mules, 354; oxen, 1,631; cows, 2,544; other cattle, 3,349; sheep, 7,057; hogs, 14,125; wool, 14,297 lbs.; milk, 170 gallons; butter, 114,458 lbs.; cheese, 2,345 lbs.

Manufactures.—Establishments, 21; capital, $169,200; employes, 57; wages, $6,393; material, $43,785; products, $67,850.

MONTGOMERY.—Population, 9,374: white, 6,857; colored, 2,517; male, 4,616; female, 4,758; native, 9,362; foreign, 12; voters, 1,916—white, 1,476; colored, 440.

Property and Taxation.—Assessment, $858,040; taxes, $10,918; debt, $15,000.

Farm Areas and Values.—1,290 farms; 48,117 acres; value, $811,550; implements, $54,541; live stock, $176,100; products, $407,249.

Vegetable Productions.—Corn, 210,521 bushels; oats, 50,248; rye, 425; wheat, 39,702; orchard products, $781; hay,

296 tons; cotton, 2,989 bales; potatoes—Irish, 11,260, sweet, 21,849 bushels; tobacco, 14,370 lbs.

Live Stock and Productions.—Horses, 1,055; mules, 703; oxen, 301; cows, 2,201; other cattle, 3,480; sheep, 6,713; hogs, 10,375; wool, 12,748 lbs.; milk, 127 gallons; butter, 80,076 lbs.; cheese, 25 lbs.

Manufactures.—Establishments, 51; capital, $95,025; employes, 105; wages, $11,323; material, $95,295; products, $129,724.

MOORE.—Population, 16,821: white, 11,485, colored, 5,332; male, 8,395; female, 8,426; native, 16,768; foreign, 53; voters, 3,689—white, 2,553; colored, 1,136.

Property and Taxation.—Assessment, $1,565,733; taxes, $18,898; debt, $60.

Farm Areas and Values.—2,098 farms; 70,922 acres; value, $1,310,615; implements, $94,910; live-stock, $291,577; products, $617,710.

Vegetable Productions.—Corn, 302,196 bushels; oats, 48,744; rye, 3,954; wheat, 45,413; orchard products, $13,585; hay, 366 tons; cotton, 3,988 bales; potatoes—Irish, 6,257, sweet, 65,018 bushels; tobacco, 15,724 lbs.

Live Stock and Products.—Horses, 1,727; mules, 1,123; oxen, 460; cows, 3,765; other cattle, 7,036; sheep, 9,531; hogs, 19,865; wool, 18,814 lbs.; milk, 780 gallons; butter, 107,604 lbs.

Manufactures.—Establishments, 123; capital, $225,110; employes, 672; wages, $115,459; material, $278,463; products, $522,862.

NASH.—Population, 17,731: white, 9,417, colored, 8,314; male, 8,777, female, 8,954; native, 17,718, foreign, 13; voters, 3,701—white, 2,076, colored, 1,625.

Property and Taxation.—Assessment, $2,145,371; taxes, $15,241; debt, none.

Farm Areas and Values.—2,130 farms; 85,685 acres, value, $2,193,732; implements, $90,191; live stock, $279,270; products, $957,376.

Vegetable Productions.—Corn, 295,619 bushels; oats, 30,135; rye, 336; wheat, 27,560; orchard products, $8,882; hay, 66 tons; cotton, 12,567 bales; potatoes—Irish, 4,460; sweet, 93,997 bushels; tobacco, 7,562 lbs.

Live Stock and Products.—Horses, 1,404; mules, 1,171; oxen, 1,626; cows, 2,120; other cattle, 4,028; sheep, 4,063; hogs, 21,475; wool, 7,640 lbs.; milk, 20,123 gallons; butter, 36,040 lbs.; cheese, 25 lbs.

Manufactures.—Establishments, 31; capital, $263,875; employes, 214; wages, $25,933; materials, $119,950; products, $178,038.

ORANGE.—Population, 23,698: white, 14,555; colored, 9,143; male, 11,780; female, 11,918; native, 23,658; foreign, 40; voters, 5,283—white, 3,365; colored, 1,918.

Property and Taxation.—Assessment, $3,013,002; taxes, $29,377; debt, $1,200.

Farm Areas and Values.—2,395 farms; 86,401 acres, value, $1,844,319; implements, $94,855; live stock, $299,802; products, $693,512.

Vegetable Productions.—Corn, 366,640 bushels; oats, 86,268; rye, 208; wheat, 96,006; orchard products, $16,087; hay, 1,214 tons; cotton, 1,919 bales; potatoes—Irish, 7,627, sweet, 22,360 bushels; tobacco, 1,178,732 lbs.

Live Stock and Products.—Horses, 2,769; mules, 1,273; oxen, 392; cows, 4,056; other cattle, 4,769; sheep, 7,055; hogs, 16,359; wool, 14,954 lbs.; milk, 4,140 gallons; butter, 169,735 lbs.; cheese, 1,074 lbs.

Manufactures.—Establishments, 96; capital, $823,000;

employes, 1,131; wages, $129,560; materials, $725,972; products, $1,236,984.

PERSON.—Population, 13,719: white, 7,206; colored, 6,513; male, 6,692; female, 7,027; native, 13,715; foreign, 4; voters, 2,918—white, 1,643; colored, 1,275.

Property and Taxation.—Assessment, $1,489,224; taxes, $15,839; debt, $8,000.

Farm Areas and Values.—1,299 farms. 76,797 acres; value, $1,402,200; implements, $60,623; live stock, $212,646; products, $634,579.

Vegetable Productions.—Corn, 241,523 bushels; oats, 56,926; rye, 86; wheat, 51,935; orchard products. $15.691; hay, 118 tons; cotton, 1 bale; potatoes—Irish. 7,522; sweet, 12,843 bushels; tobacco, 3,012,387 lbs.

Live Stock and Products.—Horses, 1,814; mules, 726; oxen, 475; cows, 2,530; other cattle, 3,333; sheep, 4,414; hogs, 10,281; wool, 7,499 lbs.; milk, 2 gallons; butter, 106,096 lbs.

Manufactures.—Establishments, 42; capital, $138,400; employes, 202; wages, $16,367; material, $116,821; products, $160,895.

RANDOLPH.—Population, 20,836: white, 17,758; colored, 3,078; male, 10,050; female, 10,786; native, 20,828; foreign, 8; voters, 4,440—white, 3,858; colored, 582.

Property and Taxation.—Assessment, $2,412,914; taxes, $25,471; debt, $5,000.

Farm Areas and Values.—2,923 farms; 100,888 acres; value, $1,707,892; implements, $123,932; live stock, $365,692; products, $633,167.

Vegetable Productions.—Barley, 407 bushels; corn, 477,168; oats, 88,380; rye, 729; wheat, 137,104; orchard products, $16,019; hay, 4,951 tons; cotton, 295 bales; potatoes—Irish, 15,790, sweet, 19,809 bushels; tobacco, 11,-101 lbs.

Live Stock and Products.—Horses, 3,254; mules, 1,336; oxen, 560; cows, 4,670; other cattle, 7,771; sheep, 15,742; hogs, 21,146; wool, 29,868 lbs.; milk, 5,741 gallons; butter, 152,041 lbs.; cheese, 1,578 lbs.

Manufactures.—Establishments, 98; capital, $487,665; employes, 828; wages, $111,009; material, $617,053; products, $894,462.

RICHMOND.—Population, 18,245: white, 8,141; colored, 10,104; male, 8,963; female, 9,282; native, 18,185; foreign, 60; voters, 3,715—white, 1,871; colored, 1,844.

Property and Taxation.—Assessment, $1,885,868; taxes, $30,021; debt, $45,000.

Farm Areas and Values.—1,698 farms; 76,067 acres; value, $1,612,457; implements, $85,091; live stock, $244,-409; products, $971,293.

Vegetable Productions.—Corn, 277,974 bushels; oats, 32,279; rye, 2,338; wheat, 19,994; orchard products, $3,958; hay, 10 tons; rice, 17,460 lbs.; cotton, 12,754 bales; potatoes—Irish, 2,701, sweet, 65,374 bushels; tobacco, 1,305 lbs.

Live Stock and Products.—Horses, 1,171; mules, 1,297; oxen, 390; cows, 2,759; other cattle, 4,748; sheep, 1,504; hogs, 16,501; wool, 33,430 lbs.; milk, 275 gallons; butter, 56,679 lbs.; cheese, 20 lbs.

Manufactures.—Establishments, 31; capital, $208,000; employes, 230; wages, $36,594; materials, $143,707; products, $232,854.

ROCKINGHAM.—Population, 21,744: white, 12,431; colored, 9,313; male, 10,770; female, 10,974; native, 21,673; foreign, 71; voters, 4,679—white, 2,826: colored, 1,853.

Property and Taxation.—Assessment, $2,393,622; taxes, $25,569; debt, $6,011.

Farm Areas and Values.—2,105 farms; 84,188 acres; value, $1,912,548; implements, $104,988; live stock, $327,890; products, $866,706.

Vegetable Productions.—Barley, 60 bushels; buckwheat, 126; corn, 392,767; oats, 139,266; rye, 1,383; wheat, 71,187; orchard products, 28,701; hay, 412 tons; cotton, 3 bales; potatoes—Irish, 19,561, sweet, 27,911 bushels; tobacco, 4,341,259 lbs.

Live Stock and Products.—Horses, 1,660; mules, 1,212; oxen, 372; cows, 3,393; other cattle, 3,599; sheep, 3,870, hogs, 12,822; wool, 8,411 lbs.; milk, 1,375 gallons; butter, 172,080 lbs.

Manufactures.—Establishments, 67; capital, $404,905; employes, 743; wages, $81,099; material, $325,103; products, $503,596.

ROWAN.—Population. 19,965: white, 13,621; colored, 6,344; male, 9,633; female, 10,332; native, 19,923; foreign 42; voters, 4,369—white, 3,040; colored, 1,329.

Property and Taxation.—Assessment, $3,058,170; taxes, $28,700; debt, $2,400.

Farm Areas and Values.—2,467 farms; 110,178 acres; value, $2,337,516; implements, $136,936; live stock, $299,763; products, $789,306.

Vegetable Productions.—Buckwheat, 43 bushels; corn, 597,519; oats, 142,121; rye, 1,134; wheat, 138,278; orchard products, $32,482; hay, 5,348 tons; cotton, 4,381 bales; potatoes—Irish, 22,858; sweet, 25,452 bushels; tobacco, 115,251 lbs,

Live Stock and Products.—Horses, 3,076; mules, 1,564; oxen, 44; cows, 3,807; other cattle, 5,408; sheep, 6,506;

hogs, 20,907; wool, 13,659 lbs.; milk, 4,192 gallons; butter, 152,433 lbs.

Manufactures.—Establishments, 71; capital, $148,165; employes, 257; wages, $32,077; material, $214,384; products, $293,949.

STOKES.—Population, 15,353: white, 11,730; colored, 3,623; male, 7,554; female, 7,799; native, 15,349; foreign, 4; voters, 3,077—white, 2,446, colored, 631.

Property and Taxation.—Assessment, $1,148,174; taxes, $16,961; debt, $2,000.

Farm Areas and Values.—1,765 farms; 57,393 acres; value, $1,207,505; implements, $52,561; live stock, $220,457; products, $549,481.

Vegetable Productions.—Buckwheat, 40 bushels; corn, 338,781; oats, 72,391; rye, 5,023; wheat, 55,284; orchard products, $19,859; hay, 813 tons; cotton, 7 bales; potatoes—Irish, 17,816; sweet, 19,860 bushels; tobacco, 2,131,161 lbs.

Live Stock and Products.—Horses, 1,359; mules, 1,096; oxen, 278; cows, 2,507; other cattle, 2,855; sheep, 4,073; hogs, 11,772; wool, 8,055 lbs.; butter, 123,321 lbs.; cheese, 134 lbs.

Manufactures.—Establishments, 69; capital, $95,102; employes, 228; wages, $16,506; material, $165,875; products, $213,804.

SURRY.—Population, 15,302: white, 13,227; colored, 2,075; male, 7,504; female, 7,798; native, 15,294; foreign, 8; voters, 3,181—white, 2,782, colored, 399.

Property and Taxation.—Assessment, $1,421,662; taxes, $12,998; debt, $10,000.

Farm Areas and Values.—2,164 farms; 81,690 acres; value, $1,345,547; implements, $57,156; live stock, $209,046; products, $434,168.

Vegetable Productions.—Buckwheat, 505 bushels; corn, 397,143; oats, 70,737; rye, 10,482; wheat, 42,046; orchard products, $10,831; hay, 924 tons; cotton, 1 bale; potatoes—Irish, 18,139; sweet, 24,669 bushels; tobacco, 905,250 lbs.

Live Stock and Products.—Horses, 1,495; mules, 761; oxen, 594; cows, 2,621; other cattle, 2,524; sheep, 6,191; hogs, 14,015; wool, 12,708 lbs.; milk, 13,055 gallons; butter, 119,150 lbs.; cheese, 2,481 lbs.

Manufactures.—Establishments, 65; capital, $218,050; employes, 338; wages, $33,084; material, $183,419; products, $262,705.

SWAIN.—Population, 3,784: white, 3,234; colored, 550; male, 1,912; female, 1,872; native, 3,784; voters, 764—white, 648; colored, 116.

Property and Taxation.—Assessment, $286,745; taxes, $3,114; debt, $991.

Farm Areas and Values.—654 farms; 14,275 acres; value, $295,480; implements, $10,106; live stock, $68,294; products, $73,527.

Vegetable Productions.—Buckwheat, 146 bushels; corn, 100,542; oats, 4,301; rye, 2,259; wheat, 6,578; orchard products, $1,082; hay, 83 tons; potatoes—Irish, 2,558, sweet, 2,154 bushels; tobacco, 1,166 lbs.

Live Stock and Products.—Horses, 493; mules, 157; oxen, 250; cows, 959; other cattle, 1,777; sheep, 3,329; hogs, 7,089; wool, 4,412 lbs.; butter, 27,313 lbs.; cheese, 100 lbs.

TRANSYLVANIA.—Population, 5,340: white, 4,823; colored, 517; male, 2,682; female, 2,658; native, 5,319; foreign, 21; voters, 1,041—white, 946, colored, 95.

Property and Taxation.—Assessment, $540,256; taxes, 9,014; debt, none.

Farm Areas and Values.—734 farms; 20,369 acres;

value, $431,605; implements, $21,540; live stock, $102,713; products, $139,938.

Vegetable Productions.—Buckwheat, 395 bushels; corn, 154,769; oats, 2,870; rye, 16,043; wheat, 3,760; orchard products, $531; hay, 493 tons; potatoes—Irish, 8,226; sweet, 3,444 bushels; tobacco, 3,853 lbs.

Live Stock and Products—Horses, 691; mules, 279; oxen, 233; cows, 1,410; other cattle, 2,859; sheep, 5,063; hogs, 7,345; wool, 7,485 lbs.; milk, 15 gallons; butter, 45,365 lbs.; cheese, 30 lbs.

Manufactures.—Establishments, 10; capital, $10,000; employes, 10; wages, $2,170; material, $22,469; products, $28,529.

WAKE.—Population, 47,939: white, 24,289; colored, 23,650; male, 23,835; female, 24,104; native, 47,675; foreign, 264; voters, 10,968—white, 5,840; colored, 5,128.

Property and Taxation.—Assessment, $9,072,884; taxes, $109,387; debt, $158,357.

Farm Areas and Values.—4,381 farms; 161,272 acres; value, $4,378,331; implements, $200,371; live stock, $581,646; products, $2,044,397.

Vegetable Productions.—Corn, 612,869 bushels; oats, 98,962; rye, 1,109; wheat, 72,341; orchard products, $20,386; hay, 390 tons; cotton, 30,115 bales; potatoes—Irish, 8,138; sweet, 155,260 bushels; tobacco, 94,354 lbs.

Live Stock and Products.—Horses, 2,731; mules, 3,052; oxen, 1,296; cows, 5,315; other cattle, 7,888; sheep, 7,069; hogs, 34,666; wool, 13,706 lbs.; milk, 20,589 gallons; butter, 178,246 lbs.; cheese, 450 lbs.

Manufactures.—Establishments, 137; capital, $364,198; employes, 861; wages, $174,894; material, $352,960; products, $712,735.

WATAUGA—Population, 8,160: white, 7,746; colored, 414; male, 4,022, female, 4,138; native, 8,160; voters, 1,600—white, 1,522; colored, 78.

Property and Taxation.—Assessment, $705,655 ; taxes, $7,536 ; debt, $2,845.

Farm Areas and Values.—1,348 farms; 691,999 acres; value, $794,749; implements, $34,130; live stock, $185,432; products, $205,283.

Vegetable Productions.—Buckwheat, 7,937 bushels; corn, 148,204; oats, 23,205; rye, 18,850; wheat, 22,247; orchard products, $10,091; hay, 3,980 tons; cotton, 3 bales; potatoes—Irish, 14,470; sweet, 769 bushels; tobacco, 7,210 lbs.

Live Stock and Productions.—Horses, 1,414; mules, 230; oxen, 343; cows, 2,785; other cattle, 3,755; sheep, 8,902; hogs, 12,405; wool, 24,023 lbs.; milk, 150 gallons; butter, 119,623 lbs.; cheese, 9,102 lbs.

Manufactures—Establishments, 25; capital, $23,550; employes. 21; wages, $2,807; material, $28,545; products, $38,-346.

WILKES.—Population, 19,181: white, 17,257; colored, 1,924; male, 9,089; female, 10,092 ; native, 19,175; foreign, 6; voters, 3,684—white, 3,377, colored, 367.

Property and Taxation.—Assessment, $1,050,956; taxes, $15,525; debt, $11,000.

Farm Areas and Values.—2,984 farms, 100,151 acres; value, $1,486,820; implements, $62,152; live stock, $269,-318; products, $402,845.

Vegetable Productions.—Buckwheat, 1,530 bushels; corn, 480,089; oats, 55,360; rye, 17,569; wheat, 37,696; orchard products, $25,269; hay, 657 tons; cotton, 29 bales; potatoes—Irish, 25,991, sweet, 22,255 bushels; tobacco, 33,211 lbs.

Live Stock and Products.—Horses, 2,097; mules, 760; oxen, 1,169; cows, 4,493; other cattle, 5,422; sheep, 10,036; hogs, 23,431; wool, 19,776 lbs.; butter, 142,951 lbs.; cheese, 2,201 lbs.

Manufactures. — Establishments, 32; capital, $35,500; employes, 29; wages, $3,462; material, $48,922; products, $58,926.

WILSON. — Population, 16,064: white, 8,655; colored, 7,409; male, 7,958; female, 8,106; native, 16,047; foreign, 17; voters, 3,437—white, 1,958; colored, 1,479.

Property and Taxation.—Assessment, $2,587,974; taxes, $19,821; debt, $500.

Farm Areas and Values.—1,672 farms; 66,027 acres; value, $1,740,070; implements, $60,551; live stock, $224,513; products, $895,771.

Vegetable Productions.—Corn, 299,957 bushels; oats, 13,682; rye, 522; wheat, 21,115; orchard products, $3,913; hay, 35 tons; rice, 1,800 lbs.; cotton, 13,049 bales; potatoes—Irish, 2,033; sweet, 58,336 bushels; tobacco, 8,745 lbs.

Live Stock and Products.—Horses, 1,143; mules, 1,220; oxen, 816; cows, 1,131; other cattle, 2,466; sheep, 1,779; hogs, 20,255; wool, 3,326 lbs.; butter 7,442 lbs.; cheese, 130 lbs.

Manufactures. — Establishments, 30; capital, $77,100; employes, 126; wages, $22,450; material, $70,429; products, $120,039.

YADKIN.—Population, 12,420: white, 10,876; colored, 1,544; male, 5,954; female, 6,466; native, 12,419; foreign, 1; voters, 2,461—white, 2,198; colored, 263.

Property and Taxation.—Assessment, $1,141,001; taxes, $15,683; debt, $8,000.

Farm Areas and Values.—1,641 farms; 60,170 acres;

value, $1,159,640; implements, $50,974; live stock, $188,441; products, $303,269.

Vegetable Productions.—Buckwheat, 188 bushels; corn, 343,070; oats, 79,443; rye, 3,723; wheat, 48,762; orchard products, $19,906; hay, 1,091 tons; cotton, 26 bales; potatoes—Irish, 7,635; sweet, 8,266 bushels; tobacco, 177,595 lbs.

Live Stock and Products.—Horses, 1,448; mules, 813; oxen, 194; cows, 2,327; other cattle, 2,841; sheep, 5,412; hogs, 12,447; wool, 10,095 lbs.; milk, 2 gallons; butter, 87,294 lbs.; cheese, 1,253 lbs.

Manufactures.—Establishments, 50; capital, $51,640; employes, 50; wages, $5,674; materials, $55,727; products, $77,262.

YANCEY.—Population, 7,694: white, 7,369; colored, 325; male, 3,793; female, 3,901; native, 7,693; foreign, 1; voters, 1,474—white, 1,417; colored, 57.

Property and Taxation.—Assessment, $325,146; taxes, $7,844; debt, $2,000.

Farm Areas and Values.—1,183 farms; 45,689 acres; value, $618,881; implements, $24,192; live stock, $162,032; products, $186,203.

Vegetable Productions.—Barley, 64 bushels; buckwheat, 2,915; corn, 205,659; oats, 43,631; rye, 7,647; wheat, 21,452; orchard products, $12,785; hay, 1,359 tons; potatoes—Irish, 6,934; sweet, 2,113 bushels; tobacco, 33,898 lbs.

Live Stock and Products.—Horses, 1,146; mules, 404; oxen, 115; cows, 1,926; other cattle, 2,791; sheep, 6,041; hogs, 10,659; wool, 9,344 lbs.; butter, 104,312 lbs.; cheese, 76 lbs.

Manufactures.—Establishments, 19; capital, $18,940; employes, 19; wages, $2,176; materials, $27,155; products, $35,642.

www.ingramcontent.com/pod-product-compliance
Lightning Source LLC
Chambersburg PA
CBHW030543300426
44111CB00009B/837